The State of
Social Safety Nets 2018

The State of
Social Safety Nets *2018*

ISBN (print): 978-1-4648-1254-5
ISBN (electronic): 978-1-4648-1255-2
DOI: 10.1596/978-1-4648-1254-5

Cover photo: Third grader from Niger, Mariama. © Stephan Gladieu/World Bank. Further permission required for reuse.

Part 1 opener photo: Children in the village of Ambohimahatsinjo, Madagaskar. © Mohammad Al-Arief/World Bank. Further permission required for reuse.

Part 2 opener photo: A young girl in an evacuation center, Philippines. © Jerome Ascano/World Bank. Further permission required for reuse.

Cover design: Bill Pragluski, Critical Stages, LLC.

Library of Congress Cataloging-in-Publication Data has been requested.

Contents

Figures

Foreword

The need for social safety net/social assistance (SSN/SA) is a critical concern for governments across the globe. Which SSN/SA programs to choose, how to best structure and deliver them, and how to make them fiscally sustainable over the long term are important questions because the answers to these questions affect the well-being of millions of poor and vulnerable people around the world. As the interest in and the use of SSN/SA programs continue to grow, countries are also exploring how to better integrate SSN/SA programs into their overall social protection and jobs agenda.

The global focus on social protection and jobs in general and on the role of SSN in particular has intensified. For the first time, social protection is part of a comprehensive agenda of the Sustainable Development Goals (SDGs). SDG 1 calls to end (extreme) poverty in all its manifestations by 2030, ensure social protection for the poor and vulnerable, increase access to basic services, and support people harmed by climate-related extreme events and other economic, social, and environmental shocks and disasters. Target 1.3 (Goal 1) seeks to implement nationally appropriate social protection systems and measures for all, including floors, and by 2030 achieve substantial coverage of the poor and the vulnerable. Naturally, many questions arise in implementing this agenda; for example, what is deemed "nationally appropriate" in a given country or context? What is a mix of SSN/SA programs and interventions that makes sense in a specific context or a given set of policy objectives? How much of the SSN spending is too little versus too much?

A robust evidence base is needed to answer these questions. The main objective of this book is to benchmark where individual countries, regions, and the world stand in terms of SSN/SA spending and key performance indicators, such as program coverage, beneficiary incidence, benefit level, and impacts on reducing poverty and inequality. To evaluate and benchmark these indicators consistently across space (countries/programs) and time, a major data collection and processing effort is required. This has been the goal of a World Bank initiative called Atlas of Social Protection: Indicators of Resilience and Equity (ASPIRE), a compilation of comprehensive social protection indicators derived from administrative and household survey data (http://datatopics.worldbank.org/aspire/). The empirical analysis presented in this edition of the book uses administrative (program-level) data for 142 countries and household survey data for 96 countries.

The evidence presented unequivocally indicates that SSN/SA programs matter. The book shows that SSN investments in coverage and adequacy reduce the poverty gap/headcount and lower income inequality, and coverage of the poor tends to be larger in those places where coverage of the general population is also substantial. It is not surprising that coverage and adequacy of SSN/SA programs come at a fiscal cost; globally, developing and transition economies spend an average of 1.5 percent of gross domestic product (GDP) on these programs. Whereas many countries still do not spend enough on SSN/SA programs to affect poverty, others have dedicated spending that has helped millions escape extreme poverty and millions more to become less poor.

For the poor and vulnerable around the world, much more needs to be done, and much more can be done regarding SSN/SA programs. Significant gaps in coverage and benefit levels remain. Even more disconcerting is that the gaps are more pronounced in low-income countries. The data suggest that in low-income countries, SSN/SA programs cover only 18 percent of the poorest quintile, and the average transfer accounts for only 13 percent of the lowest quintile's consumption. The international development community needs to stand ready to work further with countries in addressing the gaps.

Beyond presenting the key numbers on spending and performance around the world, this book also dives deeper into two thematic areas pertinent to managing risk and vulnerability. The first is *social assistance and aging*, which looks specifically into the role of old-age social pensions. The second is *adaptive social protection*, which discusses shocks and how SSN/SA programs can be adapted to better respond to them. It is clear that the risk of old age is more predictable, but the risk of natural disasters is much less so; hence, different approaches and instruments are needed to help people manage those risks.

We are excited to offer you the full range of data and analysis that inform this book, and we hope that you will keep coming back to this book as a reference guide and a compass to chart your thinking on the issues presented here. In the meantime, we look forward to producing, sharing, and disseminating the latest global, regional, and country-level data and developments in this crucial field of social safety nets, through this 2018 edition and the ones to come. The reader is encouraged to further explore the rich dataset that the ASPIRE online platform offers.

I hope you enjoy reading this book.

Michal Rutkowski
Senior Director
Social Protection and Jobs Global Practice
World Bank Group

Acknowledgments

This book was prepared by the Atlas of Social Protection: Indicators of Resilience and Equity (ASPIRE) team led by Alex (Oleksiy) Ivaschenko and composed of Marina Novikova (lead author for chapter 2), Claudia P. Rodríguez Alas (lead author for chapter 3), Carolina Romero (lead author for chapter 4), Thomas Bowen (lead author for chapter 5), and Linghui (Jude) Zhu (lead author for the cross-chapter data analysis).

Overall guidance was provided by Michal Rutkowski (senior director), Steen Jorgensen (director), Margaret Grosh (senior advisor), Anush Bezhanyan (practice manager), and Ruslan Yemtsov (lead economist and social safety nets [SSNs] global lead), of the Social Protection and Jobs Global Practice of the World Bank.

Many thanks go to the reviewers for the ASPIRE database and the *State of Social Safety Nets* report, whose views helped shape the direction of this work, including Francesca Bastagli, Margaret Grosh, Aline Coudouel, Philip O'Keefe, Phillippe Leite, Cem Mete, Emma Monsalve, Carlo Del Ninno, Aleksandra Posarac, and Ramya Sundaram.

The authors thank the regional focal points and teams for ongoing efforts with data sharing and verification: Aline Coudoue and Emma Monsalve of the Africa region; Pablo Acosta, Jesse Doyle, and Puja Dutta of the East Asia and Pacific region; Renata Gukovas, Aylin Isik-Dikmelik, Mattia Makovec, and Frieda Vandeninden of the Europe and Central Asia region; Ursula Milagros Martinez Angulo, Lucia Solbes Castro, and Junko Onishi of the Latin America and Caribbean region; Amr Moubarak and Wouter Takkenberg of the Middle East and North Africa region; and Cem Mete of the South Asia/Europe and Central Asia regions.

Special thanks go to Maddalena Honorati (former task team leader for the ASPIRE work) for the generous advice and guidance provided to the team in the early stages of this work. The team is also grateful to Robert Palacios, who provided invaluable guidance on chapter 4 of the book. The authors also acknowledge valuable support from Jewel McFadden (acquisitions editor), Rumit Pancholi (production editor), and Deb Appel-Barker (print coordinator) on design, layout, management, and printing of this book.

The authors give special thanks to the country teams for collecting, sharing, and validating detailed program-level data on SSN programs. The team members include Pablo Acosta, Ihsan Ajwad, Mahamane Amadou, Diego Angel-Urdinola, Ignacio R. Apella, Philippe Auffret, Clemente Avila Parra, Joao Pedro de Azevedo, Juan M. Berridi, Shrayana Bhattacharya, Gaston M. Blanco, John D. Blomquist, Gbetoho J. Boko, Bénédicte de la Brière, Stefanie Brodmann, Hugo Brousset, Tomas Damerau, Christabel E. Dadzie, Ivan Drabek, Puja Dutta, John van Dyck, Heba Elgazzar, Adrian Nicholas Gachet Racines, Jordi Jose Gallego-Ayala, Sara Giannozzi, Endashaw T. Gossa, Rebekka E. Grun, Nelson Gutierrez, Carlos S. Iguarán, Fatima El-Kadiri El-Yamani, Alex Kamurase, Toni Koleva, Matthieu Lefebvre, Raquel T. Lehmann, Victoria Levin, Ana Veronica Lopez, Zaineb Majoka, Dimitris Mavridis, Emma S. Mistiaen, Muderis Mohammed, Vanessa Moreira, Matteo Morgandi, Ingrid Mujica, Iene Muliati, Rose Mungai, Michael Mutemi Munavu, Edmundo Murrugarra, Bojana Naceva, Suleiman Namara, Minh Cong Nguyen, Ana Ocampo, Foluso Okunmadewa, Katerina Petrina, Marina Petrovic, Juul Pinxten, Serene Praveena Philip, Lucian Pop, Avantika Prabhakar, Ali N. Qureshi, Aneeka Rahman, Laura Ralston, Randa el-Rashidi, Laura B. Rawlings, Gonzalo Reyesy, Nina Rosas Raffo, Solène Rougeaux, Manuel Salazar, Nadia Selim, Veronica Silva Villalobos, Julia Smolyar, Victor Sulla, Hadyiat El-Tayeb Alyn, Cornelia M. Tesliuc, Fanta Toure, Maurizia Tovo, Andrea Vermehren, Asha M. Williams, Sulaiman A. Yusuf, Giuseppe Zampaglione, and Eric Zapatero.

The authors apologize to anyone who has been unintentionally not mentioned here.

About the Authors

Oleksiy Ivaschenko is a senior economist in the World Bank's Social Protection and Jobs Global Practice. He is a versatile empirical economist with extensive experience in operations and analytical work in social protection and labor, poverty analysis, migration, and impact evaluations. His work has been published in many development journals including the *Journal of Comparative Economics, Journal of Development and Migration, Journal of Policy Modeling, Migration Letters,* and *Economic Development and Cultural Change.* Oleksiy holds a Ph.D. in development economics from the Gothenburg School of Economics in Sweden.

Claudia P. Rodríguez Alas is a social protection specialist in the World Bank's Social Protection and Jobs Global Practice. Her work at the World Bank focuses on generating global knowledge products on social protection, including development of the Atlas of Social Protection: Indicators of Resilience and Equity (ASPIRE) database. She has also worked with nonprofit organizations on community outreach and immigrants' rights. She received her bachelor's degree in economics from Montana State University, where she was a Fulbright Scholar. Claudia also holds a master's degree in international development from American University in Washington, DC.

Marina Novikova is a consultant in the World Bank's Social Protection and Jobs Global Practice. She is a global focal point for administrative data for the ASPIRE database; her other projects comprise operational and analytical work in social protection and labor, public expenditure reviews, and labor market analysis. Marina holds a bachelor's degree in economics and a master's degree in labor economics from the National Research University Higher School of Economics in Moscow, Russia.

Carolina Romero is a research analyst in the World Bank's Social Protection and Jobs Global Practice. She has more than a decade of experience reforming publicly and privately managed pension systems worldwide. She is also a coauthor of multiple books and articles on pension systems, labor markets, and youth and female empowerment. She holds an M.B.A. from The Wharton School of the University of Pennsylvania and a master's degree in economics from the Universidad de Los Andes in Colombia.

Thomas Bowen is a social protection specialist in the World Bank's Social Protection and Jobs Global Practice. In this capacity, Thomas has worked extensively on issues related to social safety nets, cash transfer programs and their role in building household resilience to disasters, and climate change, with a particular focus on the East Asia Pacific region. He holds an MA in economics and international relations from the School of Advanced International Studies at The Johns Hopkins University in Washington, DC.

Linghui (Jude) Zhu is a consultant in the World Bank's Social Protection and Jobs Global Practice with extensive experience in research, analysis, and technical assistance. He specializes in applied labor economics and has worked widely on social protection, labor market, education, and migration. His current research is on the labor mobility in China, exploring the link between migration and welfare distribution. Jude is a Ph.D. candidate in economics at Kobe University in Japan and holds a master's degree from the University of Pittsburgh in Pennsylvania.

Structure of the Book

This book is the third edition of a publications that monitors the state of social safety nets around the world by presenting key global social safety net statistics on spending, coverage, benefit level, and poverty/inequality impact.

This 2018 edition of *The State of Social Safety Nets* presents a richer and more comprehensive set of SSN/SA data compared with the 2015 edition. The main empirical analysis is presented in Part I, "Analytics." This book also takes a deeper conceptual dive into selected topics, which are discussed in Part II, "Special Topics." The book consists of five chapters:

- Chapter 1 sets the stage for the discussion of the social safety nets/social assistance by presenting the context of risks, rationale for the social safety net instruments, and key definitions used throughout the book.
- Chapter 2 presents levels, trends, and patterns in countries' social safety nets spending.
- Chapter 3 discusses what happens with social safety nets around the world through the lens of performance indicators.
- Chapter 4 looks at social assistance and aging.
- Chapter 5 explores adaptive social safety nets.

The book also includes two highlights:

- Highlight 1 looks at the evidence from impact evaluations in Sub-Saharan Africa on the role of social safety nets in enhancing productive inclusion.
- Highlight 2 discusses policy considerations for introducing old-age social pensions and the special considerations that inform their design.

Abbreviations

AOV	Algemene Oudedags Voorzieningsfonds
ASP	adaptive social protection
ASPIRE	Atlas of Social Protection: Indicators of Resilience and Equity
BEAM	Basic Education Assistance Module
BRP	basic retirement pension
CCT	conditional cash transfer
CGH	Coady-Grosh-Hoddinott
CGP	Child Grant Program
CPI	consumer price index
EECF	enhanced elemental chlorine-free
ESSPROS	European System of Integrated Social Protection Statistics
GDP	gross domestic product
GNI	gross national income
HH	household
HSCT	harmonized social cash transfer
HSNP	Hunger Safety Net Program
JSLU	Jaminan Sosial Lanjut Usia
LEAP	Livelihood Empowerment against Poverty
LEWIE	Local Economy-Wide Impact Evaluation
LIPW	Labour-Intensive Public Works
MASAF	Malawi Social Action Fund
MGNREG	Mahatma Gandhi National Rural Employment Guarantee
MOP	Materijalno Obezbedenje Porodice (Family Material Support)
MOPMED	Ministry of Primary and Mass Education Department
NCIP	National Commission of Indigenous Peoples
NHIS	National Health Insurance Scheme
OECD	Organisation for Economic Co-operation and Development
PASD	Program Apoio Social Directo (Direct Social Support Program)
PBS	Pensión Básica Solidaria
PCF	processed chlorine-free
PET	Programa de Empleo Temporal
PPP	purchasing power parity
PRAF	Programa de Asignación Familiar (Family Allowance Program)
PRODEP	Projet National de Développement Communautaire Participatif (National Project of Community Participation Development)
PRRO	Protracted Relief and Recovery Operations
PSNP	Productive Safety Net Program
PSSB	Programa de Subsido Social Basico
PSSN	Productive Social Safety Net
PtoP	Protection to Production
PW	public works
RCIW	Rural Community Infrastructure Works
S.V.	Securite Vieillesse
SA	social assistance
SCT	social cash transfer
SCTPP	Social Cash Transfer Pilot Program

SDG	Sustainable Development Goal
SIUBEN	Sistema Único de Beneficiarios (Unique Registry of Beneficiaries)
SOCX	Social Expenditure Database (OECD)
SPL	social protection and labor
SSN	social safety net
SUF	Subsidio Familiar
TCF	totally chlorine-free
TSA	Targeted Social Assistance
UCT	unconditional cash transfer
UNICEF	United Nations Children's Fund
USP	Universal social protection
VUP	Vision 2020 Umurenge Programme
WEF	World Economic Forum
WFP	World Food Progamme

Executive Summary

The *State of Social Safety Nets 2018* aims to compile, analyze, and disseminate data and developments at the forefront of the social safety net (SSN)/social assistance (SA) agenda.[1] This series of periodic reports is part of broader efforts to monitor implementation progress of the World Bank 2012–2022 Social Protection and Labor Strategy against the strategic goals of increasing coverage—especially among the poor—and enhancing the poverty impact of the programs.[2]

This third edition of *The State of Social Safety Nets* examines trends in coverage, spending, and program performance using the World Bank Atlas of Social Protection Indicators of Resilience and Equity (ASPIRE) updated database.[3] The book documents the main safety net programs that exist around the world and their use to alleviate poverty and build shared prosperity. The 2018 edition expands on the 2015 version in its coverage of administrative and household survey data. This edition is distinctive, in that for the first time it describes what happens with SSN/SA program spending and coverage over time, when the data allow such analysis.

The State of Social Safety Nets 2018 also features two special themes—*social assistance and aging*, focusing on the role of old-age social pensions; and *adaptive social protection*, focusing on what makes SSN systems and programs adaptive to various shocks.

This book provides much-needed empirical evidence in the context of an increasing global focus on social protection, as is evident in the Sustainable Development Goals (SDGs).[4] For the first time, social protection is part of a comprehensive SDG agenda. SDG 1 calls to end (extreme) poverty in all its manifestations by 2030, ensure social protection for the poor and vulnerable, increase access to basic services, and support people harmed by climate-related extreme events and other shocks and disasters. Target 1.3 (Goal 1) seeks to implement nationally appropriate social protection systems and measures for all, including floors, and by 2030

achieve substantial coverage of the poor and the vulnerable. Target 1.5 (Goal 1), which relates to adaptive social protection, aims to build the resilience of the poor and those in vulnerable situations and to reduce their exposure and vulnerability to climate-related extreme events and other economic, social, and environmental shocks and disasters. Measuring performance on those targets requires reliable data.

As chapter 1 shows, most countries have a diverse set of SSN/SA instruments. Of 142 countries in the ASPIRE administrative database, 70 percent have unconditional cash transfers, and 43 percent have conditional cash transfers. More than 80 percent of countries provide school feeding programs. Also, 67 percent of countries have public works, and 56 percent have various fee waivers. The number of countries with old-age social pensions has also grown rapidly in the past two decades.

A growing commitment to SSN/SA is also evident; many countries tend to spend more on these programs over time. From the analysis of the subset of countries with comparable data over time, chapter 2 shows that in the Latin America and the Caribbean region, for example, average spending on SSN/SA programs as a percentage of gross domestic product (GDP) increased from 0.4 percent of GDP in 2000 to 1.26 percent of GDP in 2015. This happened while regional GDP grew, which means that SSN spending has increased in relative and absolute terms. Many countries in other regions, including Europe and Central Asia and Sub-Saharan Africa, have also substantially increased their spending on flagship SSN programs.

Globally, developing and transition countries spend an average of 1.5 percent of GDP on SSN programs. However, as chapter 2 highlights, spending varies across countries and regions. The Europe and Central Asia region currently spends the most on SSN programs, with average spending of 2.2 percent of GDP; the Sub-Saharan Africa and Latin America and the Caribbean regions are in the middle of the spending range; and the Middle East and North Africa and South Asia regions spend the least, at 1.0 percent and 0.9 percent, respectively.

The increase in spending has translated into a substantial increase in program coverage around the world. For example, several countries are introducing flagship SSN programs and are rapidly expanding their coverage. In Tanzania, the Productive Safety Net Program expanded from covering 2 percent to 10 percent of the population between 2014 and 2016. In Senegal, the National Cash Transfer Program expanded from 3 percent to 16 percent of the population in four years. In the Philippines, the Pantawid conditional cash transfer program has expanded from 5 percent to 20 percent of the population since 2010. These examples are only a few of the rapidly expanding programs.

Chapter 3 shows that SSN programs are making a substantial contribution to the fight against poverty. From the available household survey data, it is estimated that 36 percent of people escape absolute poverty because of receiving SSN transfers.[5] In other words, in the absence of transfers, many more people would be living in absolute poverty. Even if the SSN transfers do not lift the beneficiaries above the poverty line, they reduce the poverty gap by about 45 percent.[6] SSN programs also reduce consumption/income inequality by 2 percent, on average. These positive effects of SSN transfers on the poverty headcount, poverty gap, and inequality are observed for all country income groups.

Despite the progress that has been made, the social protection community needs to do more. Significant gaps in program coverage persist around the globe. These gaps are especially pronounced in low-income countries, where only 18 percent of the poorest quintile are covered by SSN programs. Even in lower-middle-income countries, less than 50 percent of the poor have access to SSN programs. Moreover, very few of the poor are included in social insurance programs. As the book suggests (see chapter 3), coverage is much better in upper-middle-income countries and high-income countries, but even there the gaps remain.[7]

Benefit levels also need to be increased. As chapter 3 shows, SSN benefits as a share of the poor's income/consumption are lowest in low-income countries, at only 13 percent. The situation is not much better in lower-middle-income countries, where the ratio stands at 18 percent. The book also shows that countries differ substantially in absolute average per capita SSN spending (in terms of U.S. dollars, in purchasing power parity terms). For example, Sub-Saharan African countries spend an average of US$16 per citizen annually on SSN programs, whereas countries in the Latin America and the Caribbean region spend an average of US$158 per citizen annually.

It is important to close these gaps because countries with low coverage and benefit levels achieve only a very small reduction in poverty. Analysis of the ASPIRE database indicates that only countries with substantial coverage and benefit levels make important gains in poverty reduction. Countries with the highest levels of coverage combined with high benefit levels achieve up to a 43 percent reduction in the poverty headcount (the share of the population in the poorest quintile). Similar strong effects are found with respect to reduction in the poverty gap and decline in income/consumption inequality.

This book also goes beyond data analytics and considers two specific areas of social protection policy that require further understanding and exploration: *social assistance and aging* and *adaptive social protection*. Under the first special topic, chapter 4 looks through the numerical lens on the growing role of old-age social pensions around the world. This is a global trend largely reflecting the limited coverage and adequacy of contributory pension schemes. The important contribution of the chapter on old-age social pensions is its attempt to quantify the poverty impact of this policy instrument using household surveys with reliable data.

Chapter 5 discusses the key features that make SSNs adaptive to various types of shocks, both natural (such as cyclones and droughts) and human-made (such as conflicts and forced displacement). Adaptive social protection instruments are important for people, irrespective of where they are in the life cycle. The chapter on adaptive social protection aims to shed light on what adaptability is about and how to achieve it. It also highlights examples of what countries are already doing to make their social protection schemes more flexible and efficient.

NOTES

1. The terms "social safety nets" and "social assistance" are used interchangeably in this book. They are non-contributory measures designed to provide regular and predictable support to poor and vulnerable people. They are also referred to as "safety nets," "social assistance," or "social transfers" and are a component of larger social protection systems.

2. The World Bank 2012–2022 Social Protection and Labor Strategy (www.worldbank.org/spstrategy) states that the "overarching goals of the strategy are to help improve resilience, equity, and opportunity for people in both low- and middle-income countries through integrated social protection and labor systems, increasing coverage of social safety nets programs, especially in lower-income countries, and improved evidence."

3. The ASPIRE database can be found at www.worldbank.org/aspire.

4. The ASPIRE database and the analysis for this book consider social protection to consist of social safety nets social assistance, social insurance, and labor market programs.

5. Extreme poverty is measured with a poverty line of US$1.90 per day in purchasing power parity terms.

6. The poverty gap is the distance between the poverty line and the average income of the poor. It is typically expressed as the percentage shortfall in income of the poor with respect to the poverty line.

7. In this book, the high-income countries category includes only a few high-income countries that are members of the Word Bank Group and for which household survey data are available. For a list of these countries, see table 1.3 in chapter 1.

PART I
Analytics

CHAPTER 1

Explaining the Social Safety Net's Data Landscape

INTRODUCTION

What are social protection and social safety net (SSN) interventions? How does this book classify SSN programs? What is the Atlas of Social Protection: Indicators of Resilience and Equity (ASPIRE) database? How does the ASPIRE team collect data and ensure data quality? What are the limitations of the administrative and household survey data used in this book? How is the performance of SSN programs measured? This chapter aims to answer these questions, and, by doing so, lays out the landscape for understanding the book in its entirety.

WHAT ARE SOCIAL PROTECTION AND SOCIAL SAFETY NET INTERVENTIONS? WHAT IS THE ASPIRE CLASSIFICATION OF SOCIAL SAFETY NET PROGRAMS?

Social protection and labor (SPL) interventions are well recognized for promoting resilience, equity, and opportunity. The *World Bank 2012–2022 Social Protection and Labor Strategy: Resilience, Equity, and Opportunity* argues that SPL systems, policies, and instruments help individuals and societies manage risk and volatility and protect them from poverty and destitution (World Bank 2012). Equity is enhanced through instruments that help protect against destitution and promote equality of opportunity. Resilience is promoted through programs that minimize the negative effect of economic shocks and natural disasters on individuals and families. Opportunity is enhanced through

policies and instruments that contribute to building human capital and facilitate access to jobs and investments in livelihoods.

SPL instruments generally fall into the following three categories:

1. *Social safety net (SSN)/social assistance (SA) programs* are noncontributory interventions designed to help individuals and households cope with chronic poverty, destitution, and vulnerability. SSN/SA programs target the poor and vulnerable. Examples include unconditional and conditional cash transfers, noncontributory social pensions, food and in-kind transfers, school feeding programs, public works, and fee waivers (see table 1.1).

2. *Social insurance programs* are contributory interventions that are designed to help individuals manage sudden changes in income because of old age, sickness, disability, or natural disaster. Individuals pay insurance premiums to be eligible for coverage or contribute a percentage of their earnings to a mandatory insurance scheme. Examples include contributory old-age, survivor, and disability pensions; sick leave and maternity/paternity benefits; and health insurance coverage.

3. *Labor market programs* can be contributory or noncontributory programs and are designed to help protect individuals against loss of income from unemployment (passive labor market

TABLE 1.1 Social Protection and Labor Market Intervention Areas

Social protection and labor programs	Objectives	Types of programs
Social safety nets/social assistance (noncontributory)	Reduce poverty and inequality	• Unconditional cash transfers • Conditional cash transfers • Social pensions • Food and in-kind transfers • School feeding programs • Public works • Fee waivers and targeted subsidies • Other interventions (social services)
Social insurance (contributory)	Ensure adequate living standards in the face of shocks and life changes	• Contributory old-age, survivor, and disability pensions • Sick leave • Maternity/paternity benefits • Health insurance coverage • Other types of insurance
Labor market programs (contributory and noncontributory)	Improve chances of employment and earnings; smooth income during unemployment	• Active labor market programs (training, employment intermediation services, wage subsidies) • Passive labor market programs (unemployment insurance, early retirement incentives)

Source: World Bank 2012.
Note: ASPIRE = Atlas of Social Protection: Indicators of Resilience and Equity.

policies) or help individuals acquire skills and connect them to labor markets (active labor market policies). Unemployment insurance and early retirement incentives are examples of passive labor market policies, whereas training, employment intermediation services, and wage subsidies are examples of active policies.

This book, in its empirical analysis, focuses on the state of SSN/SA programs. This focus reflects an increased use of social safety net instruments as well as the need to capture up-to-date data and to assess the status of SSN programs globally. The advance of available data resources positions the ASPIRE team well to analyze SSN/SA programs. In addition, by focusing on the SSN/SA programs (as a subset of SPL programs), this book provides continuity with the two previous books on the state of social safety nets (2014 and 2015).

This book also extends to the broader SPL agenda. The "Special Topics" section considers *old-age social pensions*, which are linked to the social insurance agenda, and *adaptive social protection*, which can be achieved through both safety nets and contributory/insurance programs. Ultimately, the policy issues related to social safety nets, social insurance, and labor market agendas are closely connected.

There is clear demand for a tool that helps monitor the scope, performance, and effect of SPL programs in countries worldwide. The Social Protection and Jobs Global Practice of the World Bank Group is committed to developing and continuously updating a comprehensive set of comparable and accessible indicators to help measure the performance of SSN/SA (as well as broader SPL) programs.

The Social Protection and Jobs Global Practice has created a user-friendly benchmarking tool that continuously updates key SSN/SPL indicators: ASPIRE. This portal serves as a one-stop shop for SPL indicators for both World Bank staff and external practitioners. ASPIRE links directly to the World Bank Group Databank to provide users with tools to search the database and to generate customized tables and charts. In addition, the portal includes related survey information from the World Bank Microdata Library.

For cross-country comparability, this book follows the ASPIRE harmonized classification of SSN/SA programs. ASPIRE groups SSN/SA programs into eight harmonized categories on the basis of program objectives (see table 1.2 and appendix A). This classification is applied to each country in the database to generate comparable program

TABLE 1.2 ASPIRE Classification of Social Safety Net Programs

Program category	Program subcategory
Unconditional cash transfers[a]	Poverty-targeted cash transfers, last-resort programs
	Family, children, orphan allowance, including orphans and vulnerable children benefits
	Noncontributory funeral grants, burial allowances
	Emergency cash support, including support to refugees and returning migrants
	Public charity, including *zakāt*
Conditional cash transfers[b]	Conditional cash transfers
Social pensions (noncontributory)[c]	Old-age social pensions
	Disability benefits
	War veteran benefits
	Survivorship benefits
Food and in-kind transfers	Food stamps, rations, vouchers
	Nutrition programs (therapeutic, supplementary feeding)
	School supplies (free textbooks, uniforms)
	In-kind/nonfood emergency support
	Other in-kind transfers
School feeding	School feeding programs
Public works, workfare, and direct job creation	Cash-for-work
	Food-for-work, including food-for-training, food-for-assets
Fee waivers and targeted subsidies	Health insurance exemptions, reduced medical fees
	Education fee waivers
	Food subsidies
	Housing subsidies and allowances
	Utility and electricity subsidies and allowances
	Agricultural-inputs subsidies
	Transportation benefits
Other social assistance	Scholarships, education benefits
	Social services, transfers for caregivers (care for children, youth, family, working-age, disabled, and older persons)
	Tax exemptions

Source: ASPIRE database.
Note:
a. Conditional cash transfer programs aim to reduce poverty by making welfare programs conditional upon actions by the beneficiary. The government (or an implementing agency) transfers the money only to those households or persons (beneficiaries) that meet certain criteria in the form of actions, such as enrolling children in public schools, getting regular check-ups at the doctor's office, receiving vaccinations, or the like. Conditional cash transfer programs seek to help the current generation in poverty and to break the cycle of poverty for the next generation by developing human capital.
b. Unconditional cash transfer programs do not require beneficiaries to perform any specific actions to be eligible for the benefit. However, these programs may require benficiaries to meet certain criteria or have a certain status to be eligible; for example, for a poverty-targeted benefit, a household must be below a poverty threshold.
c. Social pensions here encompass various types of social pensions, such as old-age pensions, disability benefits, and survivorship benefits, whereas chapter 4 focuses exclusively on old-age social pensions.
ASPIRE = Atlas of Social Protection: Indicators of Resilience and Equity.

expenditure and performance indicators. Whereas table 1.2 reflects various types of social pensions as captured by the ASPIRE database, this book's Special Topics section focuses exclusively on old-age social pensions, which facilitates a clean comparison of this instrument across countries.

WHAT IS THE ASPIRE DATABASE? HOW DOES THE ASPIRE TEAM COLLECT AND ENSURE QUALITY OF THE DATA? WHAT ARE THE LIMITATIONS OF THE DATA?

The ASPIRE database has achieved significant scale and has become the World Bank's premier compilation of performance indicators for social protection and labor programs. ASPIRE has two main sources of data: administrative data, from which program expenditures and number of beneficiaries are derived; and household survey data, which are used to estimate the coverage, benefit incidence, benefit levels, and poverty/inequality impact of SPL programs. The two data sources complement each other, and thus provide a more comprehensive view of SPL program performance around the world.

The ASPIRE work program supports continuous improvement in the quality, comparability, and availability of SPL/SSN data to facilitate SPL benchmarking and inform policies. As of November of 2017, the ASPIRE database included administrative spending data for 124 developing and transition countries and economies (see appendix D) and administrative data on the number of beneficiaries of the largest programs for 142 countries (see appendix C).[1] This book uses only the most recent subset of the ASPIRE data—specifically, the most recent year of data available per country. These data constitute the basis for the analysis in chapter 2. For the performance analysis presented in chapter 3, the book uses the most recent household survey data from 96 countries (see appendix B).[2] The examples of monthly benefit levels per household for selected programs are presented in appendix E. Appendix F presents key performance indicators. Appendix G takes stock of old-age social pensions around the world (which are discussed in chapter 4). The full list of countries found in the household and administrative data used in this book is presented, by country income group, in table 1.3. Basic characteristics of these countries, such as the total country population and gross national income GDP per capita, can be found in appendix H.

World Bank staff and in-country consultants collect and harmonize the administrative data using standardized terms of reference, data templates, and classifications. Publicly available government statistics, such as annual program budget expenditures, are the primary source of administrative data. In the case of donor-funded programs, the program budget provided by the donor is also considered a primary source of data. Other information and data received from program and sector officials, as well as existing analysis such as public expenditure reviews, constitute the secondary source of administrative data.

Although the SSN classification of programs facilitates cross-country comparison, it does not necessarily imply an easy and clean-cut differentiation of programs. As mentioned, ASPIRE classifies and aggregates individual SSN/SA programs into eight categories, largely on the basis of the objective and nature of each program. However, in practice, program objectives often tend to overlap, blurring the line between classifications. For example, although a cash transfer program may not have explicit eligibility conditions (making it an unconditional cash transfer), it may have strong uptake incentive mechanisms or soft conditions that influence decisions on how households spend the transfer, making it in principle a conditional cash transfer (Daidone and others 2015).

Available program-level administrative spending data currently covers 124 countries representing 80 percent of the world's population. Updates are available for 28 countries through 2016; for 42 countries through 2015; and for 41 countries through either 2013 or 2014. The year of reference for the remaining countries in the database ranges from 2010 to 2013, except for Bhutan, Jordan, Marshall Islands, and Vanuatu. For these four countries, only total SSN spending is available from secondary sources, and the reference year is 2009. Countries with data points before 2009 are considered outdated and are not included in the analysis. A complete summary of spending indicators disaggregated by program categories can be found in appendix D.[3] The program-level administrative data facilitates a granular look at country-level spending on social safety nets/social assistance. Furthermore, by comparing global spending trends and patterns, the spending profiles and program portfolios of countries and regions can be benchmarked.

The presence on the ground of the larger ASPIRE and Social Protection and Jobs Global Practice teams, including consultants, facilitates information flows that help improve the quality of administrative data. The engagement in the country helps establish a dialogue with government counterparts and assists in

TABLE 1.3 Countries with the Household and Administrative Data Used in This Book, by Country Income Group

Income group	No. of countries		Country/economy/region name	
	Administrative data	Household data	Administrative data	Household data
Low-income countries	26	22	Benin; Burkina Faso; Burundi; Central African Republic; Chad; Comoros; Congo, Dem. Rep., Ethiopia; Guinea; Guinea-Bissau; Liberia; Madagascar; Malawi; Mali; Mozambique; Nepal; Niger; Rwanda; Senegal; Sierra Leone; Somalia; South Sudan; Tanzania; Togo; Uganda; Zimbabwe	Afghanistan; Burkina Faso; Central African Republic; Chad; Congo, Dem. Rep.; Ethiopia; The Gambia; Guinea; Haiti; Liberia; Madagascar; Malawi; Mozambique; Nepal; Niger; Rwanda; Senegal; Sierra Leone; South Sudan; Tanzania; Uganda; Zimbabwe
Lower-middle-income countries	48	37	Angola; Armenia; Bangladesh; Bhutan; Bolivia; Cabo Verde; Cambodia; Cameroon; Congo, Rep.; Côte d'Ivoire; Djibouti; Egypt, Arab Rep.; El Salvador; Georgia; Ghana; Guatemala; Honduras; India; Indonesia; Jordan; Kenya; Kiribati; Kosovo; Kyrgyz Republic; Lao PDR; Lesotho; Mauritania; Moldova; Mongolia; Morocco; Myanmar; Nicaragua; Nigeria; Pakistan; Papua New Guinea; Philippines; São Tomé and Príncipe; Sri Lanka; Sudan; Swaziland; Tajikistan; Timor-Leste; Tunisia; Ukraine; Vanuatu; Vietnam; West Bank and Gaza; Zambia	Armenia; Bangladesh; Bhutan; Bolivia; Cameroon; Côte d'Ivoire; Djibouti; Egypt, Arab Rep.; El Salvador; Georgia; Ghana; Guatemala; Honduras; India; Indonesia; Jordan; Kosovo; Kyrgyz Republic; Mauritania; Moldova; Mongolia; Morocco; Nicaragua; Nigeria; Pakistan; Papua New Guinea; Philippines; Sri Lanka; Sudan; Swaziland; Tajikistan; Timor-Leste; Tunisia; Ukraine; Vietnam; West Bank and Gaza; Zambia
Upper-middle-income countries	38	31	Albania; Azerbaijan; Belarus; Bosnia and Herzegovina; Botswana; Brazil; Bulgaria; Argentina; China; Colombia; Costa Rica; Croatia; Dominican Republic; Ecuador; Fiji; Gabon; Grenada; Iraq; Kazakhstan; Lebanon; Macedonia, FYR; Malaysia; Maldives; Marshall Islands; Mauritius; Mexico; Montenegro; Namibia; Panama; Peru; Romania; Russian Federation; Samoa; Serbia; South Africa; St. Lucia; Thailand; Turkey	Albania; Argentina; Belarus; Belize; Botswana; Brazil; China; Colombia; Costa Rica; Croatia; Dominican Republic; Ecuador; Fiji; Iraq; Jamaica; Kazakhstan; Malaysia; Maldives; Mauritius; Mexico; Montenegro; Namibia; Panama; Paraguay; Peru; Romania; Russian Federation; Serbia; South Africa; Thailand; Turkey
High-income countries	12	6	Chile, Estonia, Hungary, Kuwait, Latvia, Lithuania, Poland, Saudi Arabia, Seychelles, Slovak Republic, Slovenia, Uruguay	Chile; Latvia; Lithuania; Poland; Slovak Republic; Uruguay
Total	124	96		

Source: ASPIRE database.
Note: Economies are divided among income groups according to 2016 gross national income per capita, calculated using the World Bank Atlas method. The groups are as follows: low-income, US$1,005 or less; lower-middle-income, US$1,006–3,955; upper-middle-income, US$3,956–12,235; and high-income, US$12,236 or more. See appendix H for gross national income per capita statistics for individual countries. ASPIRE = Atlas of Social Protection: Indicators of Resilience and Equity.

gathering the required information/data, verifying classification, and checking quality. Continuous improvement to the data is ensured by close collaboration between the ASPIRE central team, the ASPIRE focal points in the regions, and the World Bank Social Protection and Jobs Global Practice staff at the country level, who have extensive program knowledge.

When estimating the amount a country spends on SSN programs, the book uses the latest-available-year approach. For the list of all active programs, the latest year for which updates are available (as mentioned) is considered the reference year for which expenditures are tallied. Unfortunately, for some countries, spending information for the latest year is not available for all active programs, but in many cases prior-year information on spending is available. In such cases, this prior-year spending (relative to the same-year gross domestic product, GDP) is used. In sorting out the data, the focus is always on updating the largest programs in terms of beneficiary numbers and spending amounts. The analysis of spending (see chapter 2) also distinguishes the inclusion/exclusion of the health fee waivers in total SSN spending whenever possible.[4]

Performance indicators are estimated using nationally representative household surveys. As of November of 2017, the ASPIRE database included 309 household surveys, corresponding to 123 developing countries. The book uses only the latest year for each country and only if the data are from at least 2008; under this criterion, 20 countries were excluded. In addition, several countries whose surveys did not have SSN information were excluded: Cambodia (2013), Mali (2009), Myanmar (2009), Samoa (2008), Togo (2011), and Tonga (2009).[5] As a result, the performance indicators are based on 96 countries (see appendix B for a full list of the household surveys used).

The ASPIRE team carefully reviews different household surveys to identify relevant SPL program information. Typically, the surveys include household income and expenditure surveys; household budget surveys; living standards measurement surveys; integrated, multipurpose, and socioeconomic surveys; or any other survey that is nationally representative and captures information on social protection and labor programs. In some cases, this work also leads to recommendations made to government counterparts on how the design of the survey instrument/module can be changed to better capture SPL programs.

Individual variables are generated for each SSN program captured in the survey; they are then grouped into the eight harmonized program categories.[6] The performance indicators are generated using these harmonized program categories. These indicators, in turn, can be disaggregated by quintiles of welfare before and after transfers, extreme poverty status (defined as US$1.90/day in terms of purchasing power parity, PPP), and rural/urban populations. Household weights are used to expand results to the total population of each country.

For cross-country comparability, all monetary variables are expressed in 2011 prices and daily PPP in U.S. dollars. This also facilitates the PPP US$1.90/day poverty-line metric to determine the poverty status for each country/survey. Note that 2011 is used as a base year because this is the year when the most recent comprehensive global price statistics were collected as a part of the International Comparison Program.[7] The consumption or income aggregates used to rank households by their welfare distribution are validated by the World Bank's regional poverty teams.

There are important considerations to keep in mind when going through the performance analysis. First, this analysis is limited to the programs captured in the household surveys. Most household surveys capture only a fraction of the programs administered in a given country. Thus the data do not always include a comprehensive list of programs (which are likely to appear in administrative data) implemented in each country. Accordingly, coverage indicators are underestimated with respect to overall social spending. To illustrate this point, the ASPIRE team conducted a matching exercise, looking at program overlap between the administrative data and household surveys for several countries (see table 1.4). A few key messages emerge from this exercise:

1. *There is generally little overlap between administrative and household data.* In the sample of counties (see table 1.4), on average only about 20 percent of programs can be found in both administrative and household survey data; for some countries, the matching rate is less than 10 percent.
2. *Household surveys tend to capture larger programs, although only in part.* On average, the matching programs capture about 50 percent of the SSN budget, as seen by summing up the budget for the matching programs on the basis of administrative budget data.
3. *Every country case is unique.* There are significant variations across countries in terms of how many programs are captured in the household survey (as a percentage of the total number of programs) and what percent of the total budget they account for in the administrative data. For example, in Chile, 14 out of 135 programs (10 percent) match, accounting for 30 percent of SSN programs' total budget; in Romania, 10 out of 65 (15 percent) match, accounting for 96 percent of the total budget; and in South Africa, 6 out of 16 (40 percent) match, accounting for 85 percent of the total budget (see table 1.4).

TABLE 1.4 Matching of Administrative and Household Survey Data for Social Safety Net Programs for Selected Countries/Economies

Country/Economy	Reference year (latest) for administrative data	Number of SSN programs in administrative data	Reference year for HH survey data	Number of SSN programs/categories in HH survey data	Number of SSN programs/categories matching in both sources	Share of matched programs in the total number of programs (administrative data)	Share of all SSN budgets captured (in administrative data) by the matched programs (max = 1)
Sub-Saharan Africa							
Ethiopia	2016	8	2010–11	3	1	0.13	0.68
Mauritania	2016	7	2014	12	1	0.14	0.23
Mozambique	2015	20	2014	3	2	0.10	0.41
Rwanda	2016	14	2014	10	4	0.29	0.55
South Africa	2015	16	2010	8	6	0.38	0.85
Tanzania	2016	14	2012–13	7	3	0.21	0.25
East Asia and Pacific							
Indonesia	2015	28	2014	8	3	0.11	0.46
Vietnam	2015	58	2014	16	7	0.12	0.20
Europe and Central Asia							
Armenia	2014	12	2014	8	3	0.25	0.62
Georgia	2013	18	2011	14	6	0.33	0.77
Lithuania	2016	15	2008	16	9	0.60	0.70
Poland	2013	45	2012	14	11	0.24	0.60
Romania	2014	65	2012	14	10	0.15	0.96
Ukraine	2014	52	2013	20	13	0.25	0.61
Latin America and the Caribbean							
Chile	2015	135	2013	23	14	0.10	0.32
Colombia	2015	37	2014	9	3	0.08	0.18
Guatemala	2013	10	2014	16	3	0.30	0.89
Middle East and North Africa							
Iraq	2013	5	2012	5	1	0.20	0.15
Morocco	2016	22	2009	12	5	0.23	0.10
West Bank & Gaza	2014	13	2009	3	1	0.08	0.10
South Asia							
India	2016	20	2010–12	2	1	0.05	0.53
Nepal	2014	57	2010–11	16	2	0.04	0.32
Pakistan	2016	30	2013–14	3	2	0.07	0.61
Sri Lanka	2015	40	2012	7	3	0.08	0.68

Source: ASPIRE team calculations, 2017.
Note: For Vietnam, out of 58 programs, 21 are under Decree 136 (also called Program 136). Hence, Program 136 is a breakdown into 21 programs. ASPIRE = Atlas of Social Protection: Indicators of Resilience and Equity; HH = household; SSN = social safety net.

Also, some surveys collect information only on program participation without including transfer amounts. In such cases, only coverage and beneficiary incidence indicators can be estimated. Last, because household surveys differ in the method for collecting SPL information across countries, the quality of the information varies.

For example, some surveys collect information on social programs mixed with private transfers, making it difficult to isolate individual SPL programs. Despite these limitations, household surveys have unique advantages (see box 1.1) and are the sole source for calculating most performance indicators presented in this book.

BOX 1.1 Leveraging Household Survey Data to Monitor and Measure Social Protection and Labor Program Performance

Household surveys have great potential as instruments to monitor and assess the performance of social protection and labor (SPL) programs. However, not all countries use household surveys to estimate SPL program trends or generate basic performance indicators (such as coverage, benefit level, benefits and beneficiary incidence, and effects on poverty). A main factor behind the low use of household data is the inadequate SPL information captured in most national household surveys. Thus there is a need to improve data collection and the quality of SPL information in household surveys to better inform social policy.

Why are household surveys necessary to measure SPL performance? Household surveys are the only source of information regarding potential beneficiaries and the basis for ex ante simulations for policy reform. By including information representative of the total population, household surveys allow the identification of populations that, because of their characteristics, may be eligible for an SPL program (for example, the poor, disabled, and unemployed). Ex ante assessments can be conducted for policy reforms by simulating the effect of a newly introduced program or parameter-adjusted existing programs. In addition, ex post assessments facilitate evaluating whether SPL programs are reaching intended objectives. The availability of total household income or consumption in household surveys also enables analysis of the distributional effects of SPL programs and their effects on poverty and inequality.

How can household surveys be leveraged to become key instruments for monitoring and evaluating social policy? Leite et al. (forthcoming) propose a series of recommendations to improve

the collection of SPL information in survey instruments, including the following:

1. **Review existing SPL programs in the country.** Obtaining a full list of programs and their specifications (for example, target population, benefit level, frequency of payments, and program size) will help make the list of SPL programs in the questionnaire more complete and better formulate the survey questions to capture adequate information. In addition, information about the program size will help evaluate whether a program is large enough to be captured by the sample frame or if oversampling is needed.

2. **Identify and coordinate with key partners.** Coordination between policy makers, program implementers, and National Statistical Office officials is crucial to design a good set of questions and sampling frame. The survey's representation of programs can be imprecise if the sample does not overlap with areas where the programs are implemented.

3. **Design the best format to collect SPL program information.** Whenever possible, survey questions should be specific for each program, keeping answers at the individual level if the programs are provided to the individual (and not to the household). In addition, recording the value of the benefit (or an estimated value) makes performance analysis richer because monetary-based indicators (such as benefits. incidence, benefit size, and effects on poverty and inequality) can be estimated. Moreover, different collection formats can be explored, such as designing modules specific to social safety net programs and/or placing questions in sector-specific modules, given that SPL programs tend to be multisectorial.

Source: Leite et al., forthcoming.

Despite data limitations, the global SPL landscape today is much more accurate than even a few years ago because of advances in the identification, capture, and harmonization of ASPIRE data. This global accumulation of knowledge is reflected in this book, which builds on more extensive data (more countries/programs captured) and adds sophistication of analysis relative to the 2015 book on the state of social safety nets (Honorati, Gentilini, and Yemtsov 2015). Furthermore, for the first time, this book attempts to look at SSN programs over time when the data allow intertemporal comparisons.

HOW IS THE PERFORMANCE OF SOCIAL SAFETY NET PROGRAMS MEASURED?

Performance measurement is the process of collecting, analyzing, and/or reporting information regarding the performance of an individual, group, organization, system, or program component. The objective is to determine if the results/outputs align with the intention or the intended achievement. Performance measurement estimates the parameters under which programs are reaching the targeted results. By measuring performance, decisions can be made and interventions carried out to improve programs.

The analysis of SSN programs presented in this book relies on a number of key terms/parameters. These parameters include spending/budget, number of beneficiaries, coverage, beneficiary/benefit incidence, benefit size/adequacy, and poverty/inequality impact. This book focuses on the core performance indicators found in the ASPIRE database. Accordingly, the effects of SSN programs in such areas as health or education outcomes, saving behavior, labor supply, fertility, and migration are not considered; these effects can be measured only through rigorous impact evaluations.[8] The main contribution of this book is to present a set of comparable core indicators for many programs/countries, allowing a global picture of social safety nets to evolve.

"Spending" indicates the program budget

In most cases, the costs of benefits provided account for most spending. While most programs have administrative costs (which are the costs of running/implementing the program), those are rarely available and/or cannot be separated from the amount spent on benefits.

"Number of beneficiaries" is simply how many people or households benefit from the program

Usually, this information is available in the administrative data. The intricacy here is related to what the beneficiary unit is. Many programs are targeted at households as a beneficiary unit. In this case, it is often assumed that all household members benefit from the program/benefit, and hence the number of individual beneficiaries is simply the number of individuals living in the beneficiary households. For some programs, such as conditional cash transfers, very often a subset of the household members is assumed to benefit directly from the program (for example, children who get vaccinations or go to school). In this case, the book simply uses the number of direct beneficiaries provided (through primary and secondary data, as described earlier), without any further calculations. For individual-level benefits (for example, old-age social pensions), the number of direct beneficiaries is reported (even though, indirectly, all household members may benefit from a household member receiving a benefit). In any case, in the administrative data, the original beneficiary units are always reported (see appendix C). For the household-level benefits, the number of recipient households and the number of individuals living in those households are reported.

"Coverage" indicates the absolute number of program beneficiaries or percentage of the population or a given population group that benefits from a given SSN program

Coverage is important because it indicates the size of the program "blanket" in both absolute and relative terms. In the ideal world, the number of beneficiaries from the administrative data could be closely matched by coverage (of the same program) from the household survey data (using population weights). However, as table 1.4 demonstrates, this ideal is elusive. For the purposes of the performance analysis (chapter 3), this book evaluates coverage relying on the household survey data. This approach is taken because it would be helpful to know how various population groups (for example, poor versus nonpoor) are covered by the same program (that can be found in the household survey).

This level of analysis is simply not possible using administrative data. Coverage, in combination with benefit size/adequacy, is very often related to the program's impact.

"Beneficiary/benefit incidence" shows which segment of the population receives the program benefits

The beneficiary/benefit incidence can indicate what percentage of the total number of beneficiaries/total amount of benefits go to the poorest quintile of the welfare distribution. The calculation of this indicator requires the use of household survey data that include the welfare indicator. Moreover, the household survey needs to have the information about the SSN programs for which the benefit incidence is being assessed. Thus, the data demands are very high when it comes to estimating this parameter.

"Benefit level" indicates the amount of the benefit, whereas "benefit adequacy" is a measure of the relative benefit level

The main purpose of estimating *benefit adequacy* is to get some idea of to what extent the benefit size is small or large in comparison to a benchmark (for example, average income/consumption in a country, poverty line, minimum subsistence level, minimum wage, per capita GDP). The impact evaluation literature (cited later in this book) often finds that fragmented/small benefits fall short of achieving desired developmental effects.

"Poverty/inequality impact" reveals the distributional effects of the benefit

Regarding poverty impact, two indicators are often looked at: percentage reduction in the poverty headcount (prevalence) as a result of the benefit; and percentage reduction in the poverty depth (distance to the poverty line). The cost–benefit ratio can also be calculated. It indicates how much money, in U.S. dollars, it costs to reduce a poverty gap by US$1. As empirical evidence around the world suggests, many SSN benefits help poor people become less poor (that is, reduce the poverty gap/depth) rather than graduate entirely from poverty. Many SSN benefits also often help make societies more equal. This is estimated empirically by looking at the reduction in the measures of welfare (income/consumption) inequality, such as the Gini coefficient.

NOTES

1. Appendix C presents information available in the ASPIRE database on the biggest programs (in terms of numbers of beneficiaries) in 142 countries by aggregate program categories. Countries differ significantly in the number of SSN programs operating in the country, ranging from fewer than 10–15 (such as in Bolivia, Croatia, or Timor-Leste), to more than 50 programs (such as in Burkina Faso, Chile, or Vietnam). Thus, for some countries with a large number of programs, appendix C does not present the full picture of coverage or versatility of programs and should be treated with caution.

2. Data availability here refers to the most recent data available to the ASPIRE team. In some cases, more recent household survey data may be available for a given country, but these data have not been properly processed yet, or the welfare aggregate has not yet been derived, rendering the data unusable for calculating the performance indicators.

3. To calculate total spending as a percentage of GDP, program-level spending is divided by GDP using the GDP data from the corresponding year. In this chapter and in appendix D, the World Development Indicators database (July 2017 version) is used for all GDP data except for Timor-Leste, which uses the World Economic Outlook database (April 2017 version). The World Bank income group classification as of July of 2017 is used.

4. To make clear which categories of spending are presented in chapter 2, the figures and notes to each relevant figure indicate whether the data cover total SSN spending (including health fee waivers) or "core" SSN spending (excluding health fee waivers). This technique could potentially be used with other categories, such as educational fee waivers.

5. For the household survey data to be included in the analysis: (i) household surveys need to be nationally representative; (ii) they need to include information on social protection; (iii) there is a clearly defined welfare aggregate (either income or consumption). On the basis of these criteria, the household surveys for Azerbaijan and Lesotho, for example, were not used in the analysis. In the case of Azerbaijan, the survey is a nonrandom sample of the applicants to Targeted Social Assistance; in the case of Lesotho, it is the only country in the sample where the asset index (rather than consumption or income) is used for welfare rankings.

6. SSN/SA includes eight harmonized program categories, whereas a broader SPL includes 12 harmonized program categories. See appendix A for further details.

7. See http://siteresources.worldbank.org/ICPEXT
   /Resources/ICP_2011.html/.

8. Chapter 3 reviews some of these studies on the role of
   SSN in enhancing productive inclusion.

REFERENCES

ASPIRE (Atlas of Social Protection: Indicators of Resilience and Equity). 2017. "Data Sources and Methodology." Database, World Bank, Washington, DC. http://data topics.worldbank.org/aspire/~/documentation/.

Daidone, S., S. Asfaw, B. Davis, S. Handa, and P. Winters. 2016. "The Household and Individual-Level Economic Impacts of Cash Transfer Programs in Sub-Saharan Africa." Food and Agriculture Organization of the Unitd Nations, Rome.

Honorati, M., U. Gentilini, and R. Yemtsov. 2015. *The State of Social Safety Nets 2015*. Washington, DC: World Bank.

Leite, P., C. Rodríguez Alas, and V. Reboul. Forthcoming. "Measuring Social Protection and Labor Programs through Household Surveys." Policy Research Working Paper, World Bank, Washington, DC.

World Bank. 2012. "Resilience, Equity, and Opportunity: The World Bank Social Protection Strategy 2012–2022." World Bank, Washington, DC.

CHAPTER 2
Spending on Social Safety Nets

This chapter aims to answer four main questions: How much do countries spend on social safety net (SSN)/social assistance (SA) programs in relative terms, as a percentage of gross domestic product (GDP), and in absolute terms?[1] Do higher-income countries spend more, in relative and absolute terms, compared to lower-income countries? How has SSN spending changed over time? What is the composition of SSN spending in terms of the main spending categories and instruments?

HOW MUCH DO REGIONS AND COUNTRIES SPEND ON SOCIAL SAFETY NETS?

Developing countries spend, on average, 1.5 percent of GDP on SSN programs. Aggregate spending on SSNs, excluding general price subsidies, was examined for a sample of 124 developing countries for which data are available. SSN spending is higher than the global average in Europe and Central Asia, at 2.2 percent of GDP, and about the global average in Sub-Saharan Africa, at 1.5 percent, and in Latin America and the Caribbean, at 1.5 percent. East Asia and Pacific, the Middle East and North Africa, and South Asia spend 1.1 percent, 1.0 percent, and 0.9 percent of GDP, respectively (figure 2.1).

Countries in the Europe and Central Asia region spend on average the highest share of GDP on SSN globally. Georgia, at 7 percent of GDP on SSN, spends the most in the region (see appendix B). Spending in this country is driven by the universal old-age social pension scheme,

which is part of the SSN system, as well as the targeted social assistance program.

Countries in Sub-Saharan Africa spend around the global average on SSN. However, many programs in the Africa region are donor-funded (see figure 2.2).[2] About two-thirds of the United Nations High Commission on Refugees budget is allocated to programs in Africa, and this humanitarian assistance is counted as SSN spending.[3] The country with the highest share of GDP spent on SSN is South Sudan (10 percent of GDP), which has only two emergency assistance programs, both of which are fully financed by donors, reflecting the fragile environment in the country.[4]

The Africa region is very heterogenous in its SSN spending. Some of the world's top spenders, such as Lesotho (7 percent of GDP) and South Sudan (10 percent), are in Sub-Saharan Africa; but so are many countries that spend very little on SSN as a percentage of GDP. Those include Cameroon, Republic of Congo, Côte d'Ivoire, Guinea-Bissau, Madagascar, São Tomé and Príncipe, Somalia, and Togo, which spend less than 0.2 percent of GDP on SSN.

In the Latin America and Caribbean region, the mean SSN spending is 1.5 percent of GDP, or 1.3 percent, excluding heath fee waivers. The highest spender is Chile (3.5 percent of GDP), whereas the median country spends 1.5 percent of GDP (1.1 percent, excluding health fee waivers). Guatemala (0.19 percent of GDP) and

FIGURE 2.1 Average Global and Regional Spending on Social Safety Nets

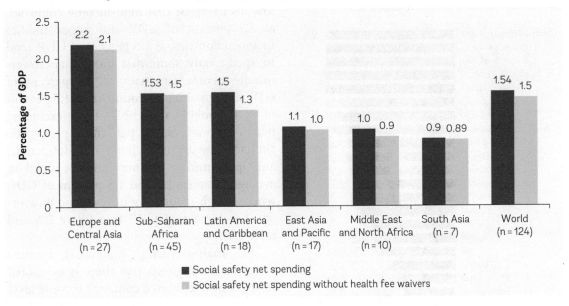

Source: ASPIRE database.

Note: The number of countries in each region appears in parentheses. The difference in the regional average for Africa in this report as opposed to the Africa regional report (Beegle, Coudouel, and Monsalve, forthcoming) is that in the regional report, average social safety net spending (1.3 percent of GDP) does not include South Sudan as an outlier in terms of spending. The regional numbers presented in this figure are simple averages across countries. See appendix B for details. The conceptual treatment of health fee waivers is not straightforward because it depends on how countries arrange and report their provision of health care. Although in some cases the health fee waivers are reported under public health expenditures, in other cases they are counted under social protection expenditures. ASPIRE = Atlas of Social Protection: Indicators of Resilience and Equity.

St. Lucia (0.48 percent of GDP) are the lowest SSN spenders (see appendix D).

The East Asia and Pacific region spends on average 1 percent of GDP on SSN, but significant variation in spending exists across countries. SSN spending ranges from 0.2 percent of GDP in Lao PDR and 0.3 percent in Myanmar to 2.0 percent in Mongolia and 6.5 percent in Timor-Leste (see appendix D). Timor-Leste spends the most on SSN in the region (figure 2.3). The median East Asia and Pacific country spends 0.8 percent of GDP on SSNs, or 0.7 percent, excluding health fee waivers (see table 2.1).

The median SSN spending across the globe is 1.1 percent of GDP, or 1 percent, excluding health fee waivers. The regions form two clusters in terms of median SSN spending. In Latin America and the Caribbean and in Europe and Central Asia, the median country spends 1.5–1.9 percent of GDP on SSN, whereas in East Asia and Pacific, Middle East and

North Africa, South Asia, and Sub-Saharan Africa, the median country spends almost 1 percentage point less, around 0.7–0.8 percent of GDP (see table 2.1).

Countries with very high SSN spending levels are often those that contend with fragility, conflict, and violence. For example, Timor-Leste introduced a universal social pension for war veterans in 2008 as a response to violent conflicts in the mid-2000s. In South Sudan, as mentioned, all SSN spending consists of two large programs financed and implemented by the World Food Programme. These programs are in-kind and include multiple components, such as general food distributions, blanket supplementary feeding programs, and targeted supplementary feeding programs for internally displaced persons and returnees.

Another common explanation for the observed high spending levels is the inclusion of universal programs in the SSN portfolio in

FIGURE 2.2 Share of Donor-Funded Safety Nets in Sub-Saharan African Countries

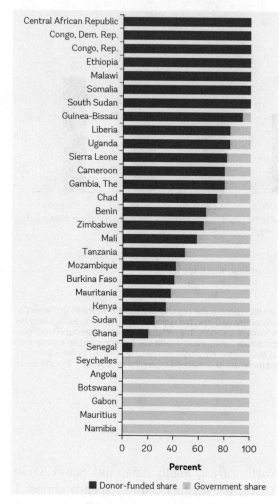

Source: Beegle, Coudouel, and Monsalve, forthcoming.

the countries. For example, Georgia and Lesotho are among the top spenders because their SSN programs include a universal old-age minimum social pension. In Georgia, spending of 4.6 percent of GDP on universal old-age pensions contributes more than 60 percent of total SSN spending. Lesotho spends 2 percent of GDP on old-age social pensions (see appendix D). Mongolia also spends significantly more than the regional average because of its universal child benefit, called the Child Money Program, which accounts for almost 80 percent of total SSN spending.

DO HIGHER-INCOME COUNTRIES SPEND MORE ON SOCIAL SAFETY NETS?

Globally, country income levels appear to be weakly associated with SSN spending as a percentage of gross domestic product. The data suggest that high-income countries, at 1.9 percent of GDP, and upper-middle-income countries, at 1.6 percent of GDP, tend to spend only somewhat more than lower-middle-income countries, at 1.4 percent of GDP, and low-income countries, at 1.5 percent of GDP. Looking at spending levels excluding health fee waivers, the patterns appear to be similar. Low-income, lower-middle-income, and upper-middle-income countries spend on average between 1.3 and 1.5 percent of GDP, whereas high-income countries spend on average 1.9 percent of GDP (see figure 2.5 and table 2.2).

The analysis using individual country observations suggests that there is no global relationship between a country's income level and SSN spending as a percentage of GDP. In the Latin America and the Caribbean region, spending appears weakly, positively associated with income levels, whereas in other regions, spending is either negatively associated with income levels or has no correlation (figure 2.6). Globally, it appears that countries with the same GDP per capita levels choose different levels of spending on SSNs reflecting different policy preferences rather than economic conditions.

Globally, the median country spends around US$80 (US$66, excluding health fee waivers) in purchasing parity power (PPP) terms annually per person (considering the total population, not just beneficiaries), while the mean country spends around US$157 (US$150, excluding health fee waivers). As a complement to the relative spending analysis, absolute annual (PPP US$) spending per capita can more accurately assess actual spending on SSNs in a country. For example, in absolute terms per person annually, the Latin America and the Caribbean countries spend PPP US$158 (US$139, excluding health fee waivers), whereas African countries spend PPP US$16 (figures 2.7 and 2.8). Even though the Africa region is the second-largest spending region in the world in relative terms (percentage of GDP), in absolute terms it is last among the regions (figure 2.9).

The absolute benefit level per household also differs significantly across country income groups. In a subsample of 36 countries that

FIGURE 2.3 Social Safety Net Spending Variations across Countries and Regions: East Asia and Pacific, Latin America and the Caribbean, and Europe and Central Asia

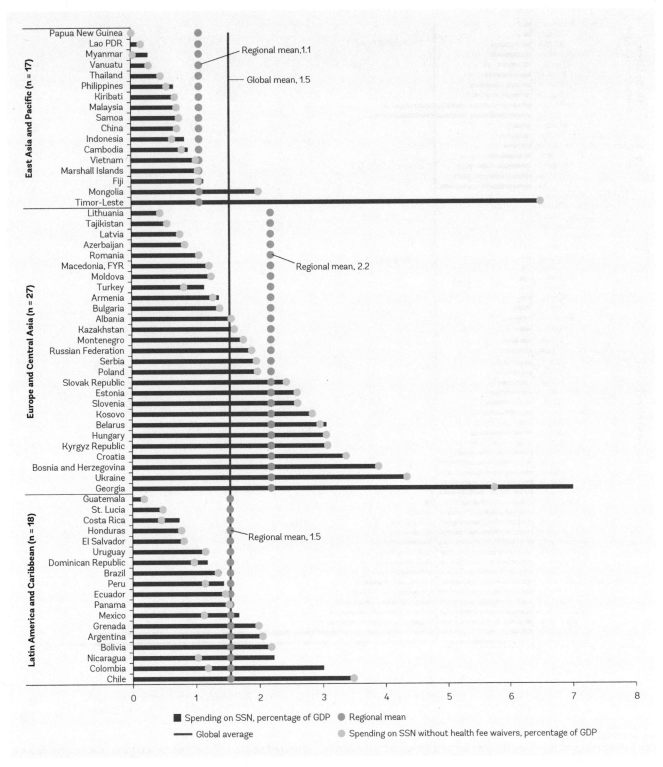

■ Spending on SSN, percentage of GDP   ● Regional mean
── Global average   ● Spending on SSN without health fee waivers, percentage of GDP

Source: ASPIRE database.
Note: Based on the most recent spending data available between 2010 and 2016 (except for the following four countries, for which only total spending data are available for years before 2010: Bhutan, Jordan, Marshall Islands, and Vanuatu). See appendix D for details. The number of countries in each region appears in parentheses. ASPIRE = Atlas of Social Protection: Indicators of Resilience and Equity.

FIGURE 2.4 Social Safety Net Spending Variations across Countries and Regions: Africa, Middle East and North Africa, and South Asia

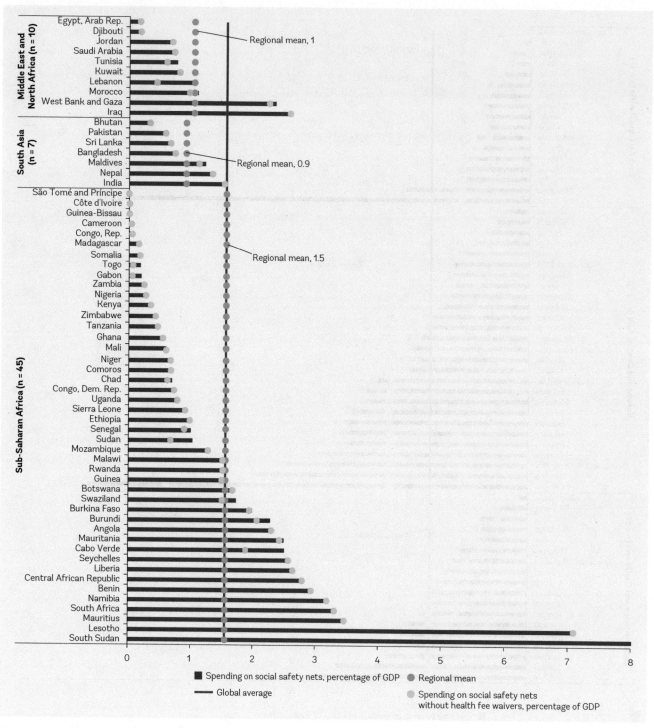

Source: ASPIRE database.
Note: Based on the most recent spending data available between 2010 and 2016 (except for the following four countries, for which only total spending data are available for years before 2010: Bhutan, Jordan, Marshall Islands, and Vanuatu). See appendix D for details. The number of countries in each region appears in parentheses. The scale is restricted for convenience; the true value for South Sudan is 10.1 percent. ASPIRE = Atlas of Social Protection: Indicators of Resilience and Equity.

THE STATE OF SOCIAL SAFETY NETS 2018

TABLE 2.1 Social Safety Net Spending across and within Regions

Percentage of GDP

Region	Spending on SSNs	Mean	Median	Minimum	Maximum
Europe and Central Asia (n = 27)	Total SSN	2.2	1.9	0.5	7.0
	Excluding health fee waivers	2.1	1.9	0.5	5.7
Sub-Saharan Africa (n = 45)	Total SSN	1.5	1.0	..	10.1
	Excluding health fee waivers	1.5	0.9	..	10.1
Latin America and the Caribbean (n = 18)	Total SSN	1.5	1.5	0.2	3.5
	Excluding health fee waivers	1.3	1.1	0.2	3.5
East Asia and Pacific (n = 17)	Total SSN	1.1	0.8	..	6.5
	Excluding health fee waivers	1.0	0.7	..	6.5
Middle East and North Africa (n = 10)	Total SSN	1.0	0.8	0.2	2.6
	Excluding health fee waivers	0.9	0.7	0.2	2.6
South Asia (n = 7)	Total SSN	0.9	0.7	0.3	1.5
	Excluding health fee waivers	0.9	0.7	0.3	1.5

Source: ASPIRE database.
Note: See appendix D for details. The number of countries in each region appears in parentheses. ASPIRE = Atlas of Social Protection: Indicators of Resilience and Equity; SSN = social safety net; .. = values below 0.01.

FIGURE 2.5 Social Safety Net Spending across Country Income Groups versus the OECD

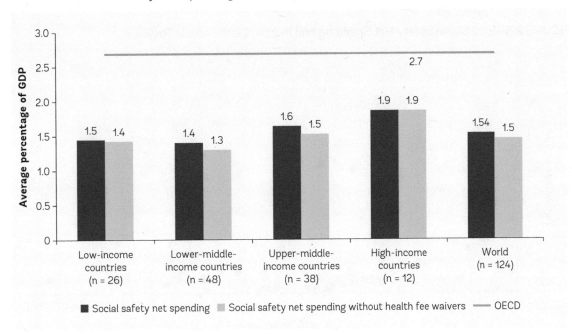

Source: ASPIRE database.
Note: The number of countries in each country income group appears in parentheses. High-income countries included in the analysis are Chile, Estonia, Hungary, Kuwait, Latvia, Lithuania, Poland, Saudi Arabia, Seychelles, Slovak Republic, Slovenia, and Uruguay. Data for OECD countries refer to 2013 and are based on the Social Expenditure Database. Social safety net spending for OECD countries here is approximated by the sum of the "family" and "other social policy" social protection functions, as defined in the Social Expenditure Database. ASPIRE = Atlas of Social Protection: Indicators of Resilience and Equity; OECD = Organisation for Economic Co-operation and Development.

have flagship (main) programs with the household as a beneficiary unit (see appendix E for details), the benefit amount (in PPP US$) per household is four time greater in upper-middle-income countries than in low-income countries—PPP US$106 versus PPP US$27, respectively (figure 2.10).

Median values of the monthly transfer for these large programs illustrate similar dispersion across country income groups. Median

TABLE 2.2 Variations in Social Safety Net Spending across Country Income Groups
Percentage of GDP

Region	Spending on SSNs	Mean	Minimum	Maximum	Median
Low-income countries (n = 26)	Total SSN	1.5	..	10.1	1.0
	Without health fee waivers	1.4	..	10.1	0.9
Lower-middle-income countries (n = 48)	Total SSN	1.4	..	7.1	0.8
	Without health fee waivers	1.3	..	7.1	0.7
Upper-middle-income countries (n = 38)	Total SSN	1.6	0.2	3.9	1.4
	Without health fee waivers	1.5	0.1	3.9	1.2
High-income countries (n = 12)	Total SSN	1.9	0.5	3.5	2.0
	Without health fee waivers	1.9	0.5	3.5	2.0
OECD countries (n = 34)	Family and other social protection areas	2.7	0.4	5.0	2.7

Source: ASPIRE database.
Note: The number of countries in each country income group appears in parentheses. High-income countries included in the analysis are Chile, Estonia, Hungary, Kuwait, Latvia, Lithuania, Poland, Saudi Arabia, Seychelles, Slovak Republic, Slovenia, and Uruguay. Data for OECD countries refer to 2013 and are based on the Social Expenditure Database. SSN spending for OECD countries here is approximated by the sum of the "family" and "other social policy" social protection functions, as defined in the Social Expenditure Database. ASPIRE = Atlas of Social Protection: Indicators of Resilience and Equity; OECD = Organisation for Economic Co-operation and Development; SSN = social safety net; .. = values below 0.01.

FIGURE 2.6 Total Social Safety Net Spending and Income Levels across Regions

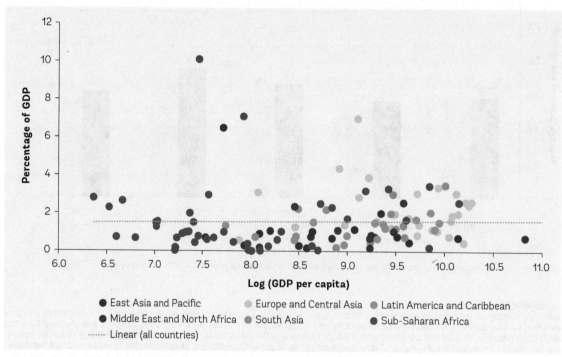

Sources: ASPIRE database; World Development Indicators for GDP per capita, PPP US$.
Note: ASPIRE = Atlas of Social Protection: Indicators of Resilience and Equity; PPP = purchasing power parity.

FIGURE 2.7 Absolute Annual Spending on Social Safety Nets per Capita across Countries and Regions: East Asia and Pacific, Europe and Central Asia, and Latin America and the Caribbean

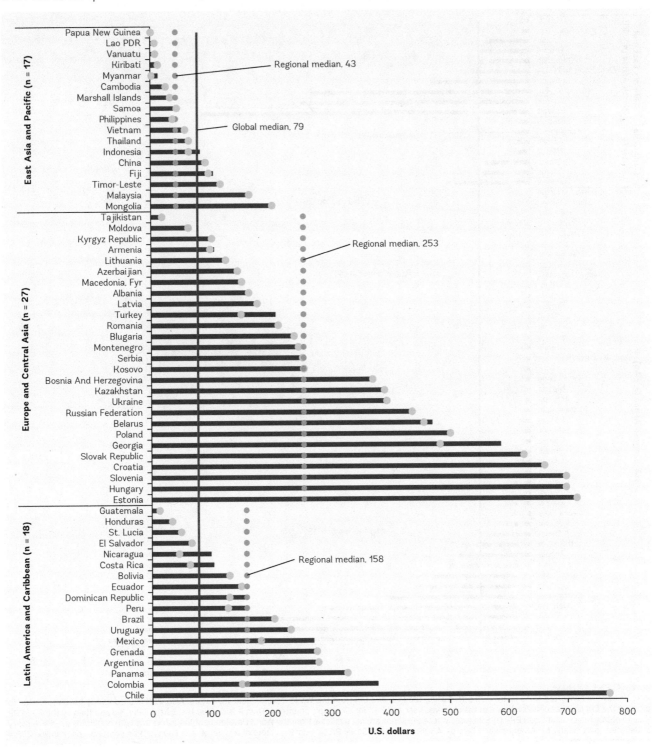

Source: ASPIRE database.
Note: Values are converted to constant 2011 prices using the PPP and CPI from the World Development Indicators. Also, 2011 is used as the base year value to calculate the CPI ratio, as deflator, between the observed year and 2011 for all sample countries. Then it is divided first by the CPI ratio and then by the 2011 PPP value to obtain the constant 2011 PPP US$. In cases where CPI series are not available from the World Development Indicators, the GDP deflator is used as a proxy for deflation, particularly for Argentina and Belarus. ASPIRE = Atlas of Social Protection: Indicators of Resilience and Equity; CPI = consumer price index; PPP = purchasing power parity.

FIGURE 2.8 Absolute Annual Spending on Social Safety Nets per Capita across Countries, Economies, and Regions: Middle East and North Africa, Sub-Saharan Africa, and South Asia

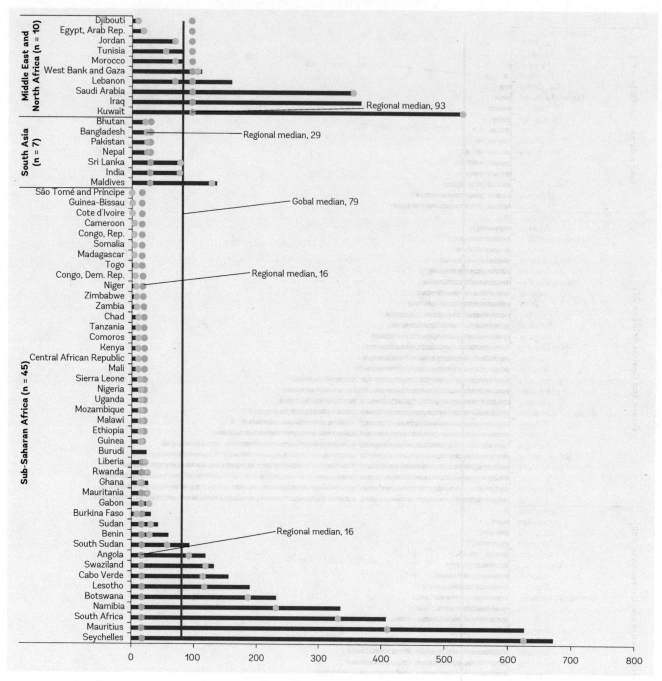

Source: ASPIRE database.
Note: Values are converted to constant 2011 prices using the PPP and CPI from the World Development Indicators. Also, 2011 is used as the base year value to calculate the CPI ratio, as deflator, between the observed year and 2011 for all sample countries. Then it is divided first by the CPI ratio and then by the 2011 PPP value to obtain the constant 2011 PPP US$. In cases where CPI series are not available from the World Development Indicators, the GDP deflator is used as a proxy for deflation, particularly for Argentina and Belarus. ASPIRE = Atlas of Social Protection: Indicators of Resilience and Equity; CPI = consumer price index; PPP = purchasing power parity.

FIGURE 2.9 Regional Median Annual Social Safety Net Spending per Capita

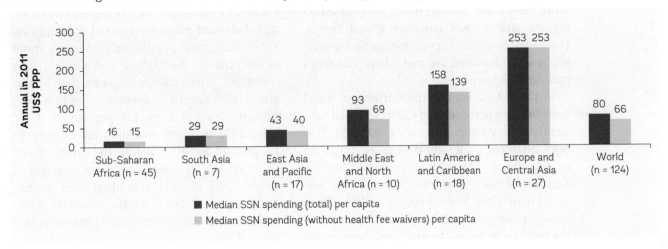

Source: ASPIRE database.
Note: The number of countries in each region appears in parentheses. ASPIRE = Atlas of Social Protection: Indicators of Resilience and Equity; PPP = purchasing power parity; SSN = social safety net.

FIGURE 2.10 Transfer Amount for Cash Transfer Programs, by Income Group

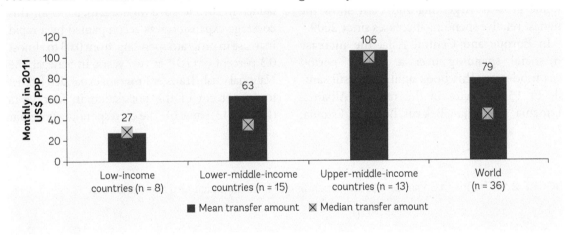

Source: ASPIRE database (see appendix E for details).
Note: The number of countries (one program per country) appears in parentheses. The largest, or flagship, cash transfer program is selected per country. See the full list of selected programs in appendix E. Transfer amount values (as designed) are converted to constant 2011 prices using the PPP and CPI from the World Development Indicators. Also, 2011 is used as the base year value to calculate the CPI ratio, as deflator, between the observed year and 2011 for all sample countries. Then it is divided first by the CPI ratio and then by the 2011 PPP value to obtain constant 2011 PPP US$. In cases where CPI series are not available from the World Development Indicators, the GDP deflator is used as a proxy for deflation, particularly for Argentina and Belarus. High-income countries are excluded from this analysis because of a small sample. ASPIRE = Atlas of Social Protection: Indicators of Resilience and Equity; CPI = consumer price index; PPP = purchasing power parity.

transfer amounts in low-income countries and lower-middle-income countries do not differ significantly (averaging about PPP US$30). However, the median upper-middle-income country provides more than three times the median benefits of low-income countries and lower-middle-income countries (a little less than PPP US$100), as figure 2.10 indicates.

HOW HAS SPENDING CHANGED OVER TIME?

In general, SSN spending fluctuates a lot over time in some countries, while it remains relatively stable in others. This section largely focuses on time trends in SSN spending in the Latin America and the Caribbean and the Europe and Central Asia regions because the other regions lack consistent spending data for 10 years or more. Hence, the findings reflect only these two regions and do not represent global trends. However, the expansion in coverage and spending is also illustrated for many large (flagship) programs globally.

In Latin America and the Caribbean, social spending as a percentage of GDP increased substantially over the past decade (2005–15). This book analyzed a subsample of seven countries in the region (Argentina, Brazil, Colombia, Ecuador, Mexico, Peru, and Uruguay) with balanced panel time-series spending on SSN. Their total population represents about 75 percent of the total Latin American and Caribbean population. The analysis suggests that in this group of countries, average SSN spending increased from 0.43 to 1.26 percent of GDP from 2003 to 2015 (see figure 2.11). The increase in SSN spending accelerated around the time of the 2008 financial crisis, despite a reduction in the rate of economic growth. Argentina and Peru show the highest relative spending increases since 2009.

In Europe and Central Asia, the increase in social spending over a similar period was moderate. This book analyzed a subsample of 15 countries in the region (Albania, Armenia, Azerbaijan, Belarus, Bulgaria, Estonia,

Kazakhstan, Latvia, Macedonia, Montenegro, Poland, Romania, Serbia, Turkey, and Ukraine) with balanced panel time-series spending on SSN.[5] Their total population represents about 60 percent of the Europe and Central Asia countries.[6] The analysis suggests that in this group of countries, average spending rose steadily, from 1.2 to 1.8 percent of GDP from 2003 to 2009, and then fell slightly, to 1.6 percent in 2014. Before the financial crisis, the region seems to have reached a steady level of SSN spending; then spending grew in response to the financial crisis; and now it is converging to the prior level (see figure 2.12).

Many countries in Sub-Saharan Africa and Asia are introducing flagship SSN programs and are rapidly expanding coverage. However, these initiatives come at a fiscal cost. In Tanzania, the Productive Safety Net Program expanded from 0.4 to 10 percent of the population from its launch in 2013 to 2016 (figure 2.13, panel a). This coverage expansion was accompanied by a rapid increase in program spending, from 0.03 to almost 0.3 percent of GDP in two years. In Senegal, the National Cash Transfer Program expanded from 3 to 16 percent of the population in four years (figure 2.13, panel b). The corresponding program

FIGURE 2.11 Trends in Social Safety Net Spending in Latin America and the Caribbean

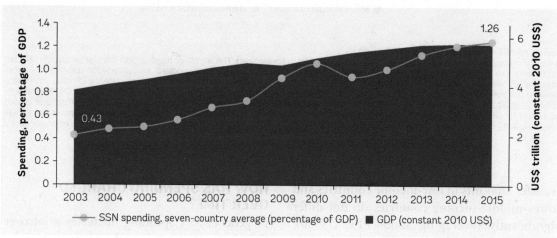

Source: ASPIRE database.
Note: GDP in Latin America and the Caribbean constitutes member countries of the International Development Association and International Bank for Reconstruction and Development. A balanced panel of seven countries (Argentina, Brazil, Colombia, Ecuador, Mexico, Peru, and Uruguay) is used. The average social safety net spending in Latin America and the Caribbean before 2010 should be interpreted with caution because data availability was more problematic, particularly for program-based disaggregated data up to 2009. Social safety net spending excludes health fee waivers. ASPIRE = Atlas of Social Protection: Indicators of Resilience and Equity; GDP = gross domestic product; SSN = social safety net.

FIGURE 2.12 Trends in Social Safety Net Spending in Europe and Central Asia, 2003–14

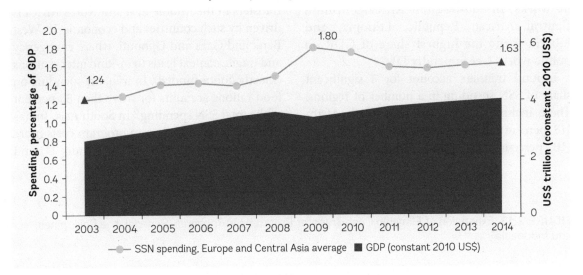

Source: ASPIRE database.
Note: GDP in Europe and Central Asia constitutes International Development Association and International Bank for Reconstruction and Development countries. Social safety net spending data do not include a data point for Poland in 2003 or for Montenegro, Poland, Serbia, and Turkey in 2014. The averages for these years should be interpreted with caution. ASPIRE = Atlas of Social Protection: Indicators of Resilience and Equity; SSN = social safety net.

spending increased from 0.05 to 0.2 percent of GDP during 2013–15. In Indonesia, the Program Keluarga Harapan increased its coverage from 1 to 9 percent of the population between 2008 and 2016, and the respective budget also increased (figure 2.13, panel c). In the Philippines, the flagship conditional cash transfer program called 4Ps increased its coverage from 4 to 20 percent of the population between 2008 and 2015, and the respective budget increased from 0.1 to 0.5 percent of GDP (figure 2.13, panel d). The global inventory of the biggest SSN programs (by category) per country can be found in appendix C.

WHICH SOCIAL SAFETY NET INSTRUMENTS DO COUNTRIES FUND?

Beyond the heterogeneity in total spending, countries and regions also differ in their preferences for various SSN instruments. The legacy of SSNs, cultural differences, demographic conditions, the socioeconomic context, political will, and other factors shape the structure of countries' SSN portfolios. Figure 2.14 maps the distribution of SSN budgets across different program types, by region.

The analysis suggests that cash transfers take up more than half of all SSN spending. Europe

and Central Asia has the largest cash transfer budget share among regions (with cash transfers consisting of unconditional and conditional cash transfers and social pensions). Cash transfers in Europe and Central Asia account for 76 percent of the total SSN spending portfolio. At the same time, the Middle East and North Africa countries, on average, allocate just over 40 percent of their budget to cash transfers (see figure 2.14).

The Latin America and Caribbean region has the largest conditional cash transfer budget share. The region spends around 21 percent of its total SSN budget on this instrument. However, the Latin America and Caribbean region is not alone in its substantial reliance on conditional cash transfers. It is followed closely by Sub-Saharan Africa, where conditional cash transfers account for around 18 percent of the SSN budget. East Asia and Pacific spends 12 percent of GDP on conditional cash transfers (figure 2.14).

The public works spending budget share is the highest in South Asia, where this type of program is commonly implemented. South Asia spends 25 percent of its SSN budget on public works. In South Asia, Bangladesh and India spend the highest share (see appendix D). Sub-Saharan Africa spends on average 12 percent of the SSN budget on public works. In Sub-Saharan Africa, Burundi, Central African Republic, Ethiopia, and Liberia spend the highest share of GDP on public works (see appendix D).

In-kind transfers account for a significant share of SSN spending in a number of regions. These include Middle East and North Africa (18 percent), Africa (11 percent), South Asia (10 percent), and Latin America and the Caribbean (9 percent). The spending on in-kind transfers in the Middle East and North Africa is driven by such countries and economies as West Bank and Gaza and Djibouti, where emergency and fragile context leads to in-kind interventions (mostly donor funded). In Iraq, the spending on food rations accounts for more than 85 percent of the total SSN spending.[7] In South Asia, India's Public Distribution System program costs more than 1 percent of GDP (see appendix D) and

FIGURE 2.13 Expansion of Flagship Cash Transfer Programs in Tanzania, Senegal, the Philippines, and Indonesia

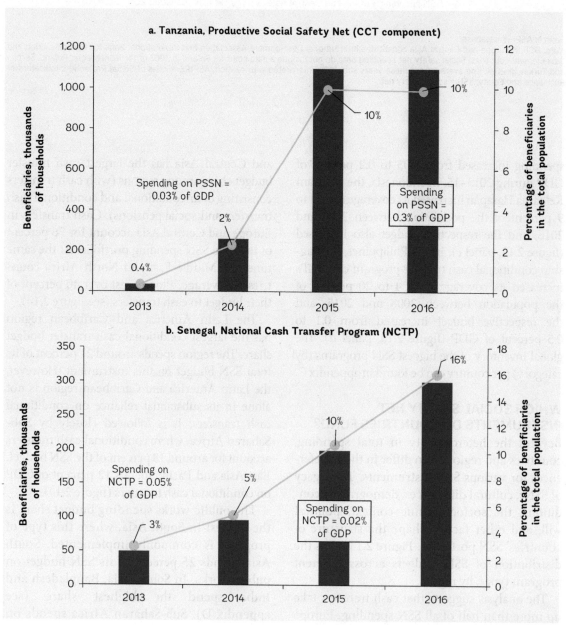

(figure continues next page)

THE STATE OF SOCIAL SAFETY NETS 2018

FIGURE 2.13 Expansion of Flagship Cash Transfer Programs in Tanzania, Senegal, the Philippines, and Indonesia *(Continued)*

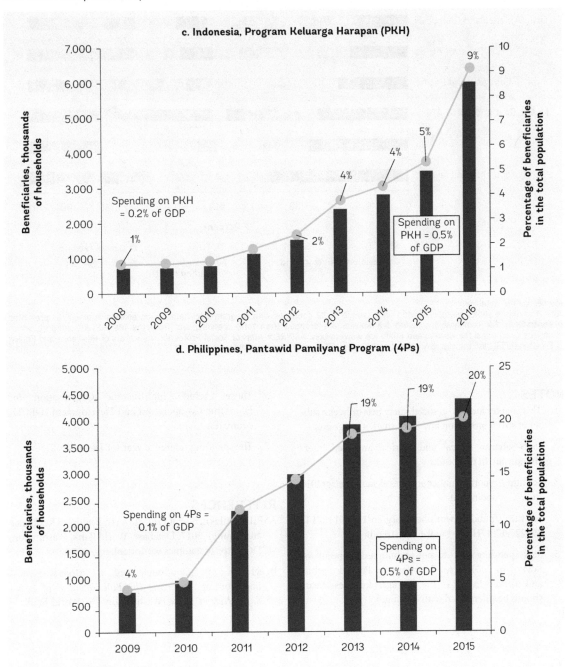

c. Indonesia, Program Keluarga Harapan (PKH)

Spending on PKH = 0.2% of GDP

Spending on PKH = 0.5% of GDP

d. Philippines, Pantawid Pamilyang Program (4Ps)

Spending on 4Ps = 0.1% of GDP

Spending on 4Ps = 0.5% of GDP

Source: ASPIRE database.
Note: Data for Tanzania include Zanzibar. ASPIRE = Atlas of Social Protection: Indicators of Resilience and Equity; CCT = conditional cash transfer.

contributes almost 70 percent of the total SSN budget captured in administrative data. Regions allocate between 4 and 9 percent to school feeding programs (see figure 2.14).

As this chapter has illustrated, SSN programs take many forms, and their budgets tend to expand across space and time. The next chapter explores the performance of SSN programs around the world. It looks at what countries achieve in terms of coverage, benefit incidence, and poverty/inequality impact for the SSN budget they spend.

FIGURE 2.14 Social Safety Net Spending across Regions, by Instrument

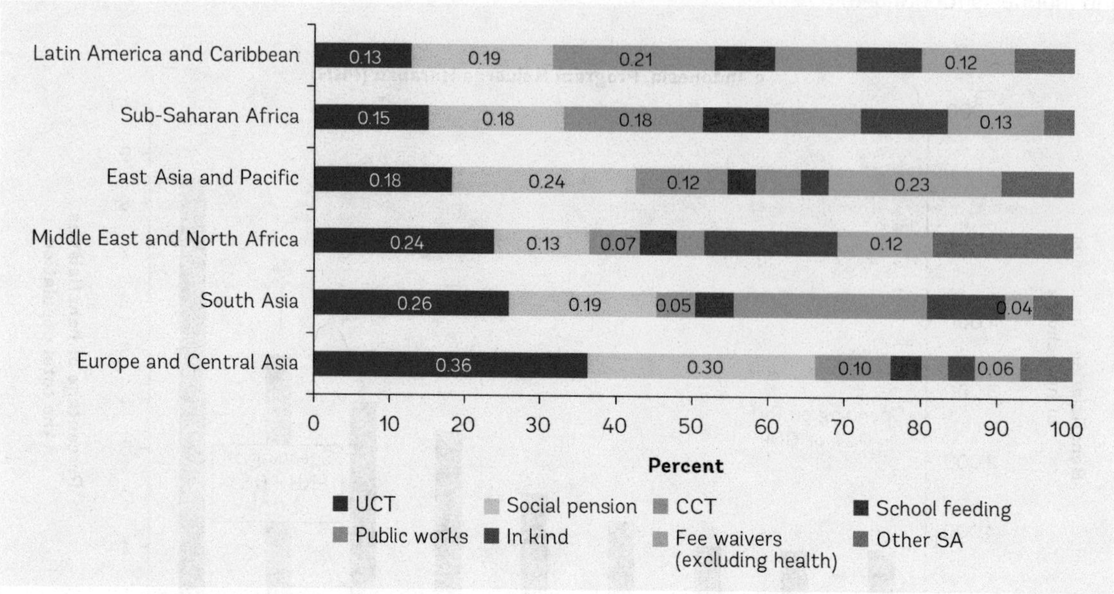

Source: ASPIRE database.
Note: This figure shows estimates based on a sample of 112 countries with program-level data disaggregation available, as presented in appendix D. For comparability, health fee waivers are dropped from total spending and from the fee waivers category, which comprises educational fee waivers and utility fee waivers only. ASPIRE = Atlas of Social Protection: Indicators of Resilience and Equity; CCT = conditional cash transfer; SA = social assistance; UCT = unconditional cash transfer.

NOTES

1. This chapter focuses on social safety nets only, as a subset of social protection and labor market programs.

2. "Sub-Saharan Africa" and "Africa" are used interchangeably in this book.

3. See http://reporting.unhcr.org/sites/default/files/gr2016/pdf/02_Funding.pdf.

4. See http://pubdocs.worldbank.org/en/154851467143896227/FY17HLFS-Final-6272016.pdf.

5. SSN spending data do not include a data point for Poland in 2003 or for Montenegro, Poland, Serbia, and Turkey in 2014. The averages for these years should be interpreted with caution.

6. Those exclude high-income Organisation for Economic Co-operation and Development (OECD) countries.

7. The spending reference year for Iraq is 2012.

REFERENCES

ASPIRE (Atlas of Social Protection: Indicators of Resilience and Equity). 2017. Database, World Bank, Washington, DC. http://datatopics.worldbank.org/aspire/.

Beegle, K., A. Coudouel, and E. Monsalve, eds. Forthcoming. *Realizing the Full Potential of Social Safety Nets in Africa*. Washington, DC World Bank.

CHAPTER 3

Analyzing the Performance of Social Safety Net Programs

This chapter analyzes the performance of social safety net (SSN)/social assistance (SA) programs using four indicators: coverage, beneficiary incidence, level of benefits, and impact on poverty and inequality. To set the stage, the first section of this chapter presents an overview of the coverage of social protection and labor (SPL) programs in general that encompasses SSN/SA programs, social insurance, and labor market programs. Within this framework, this chapter then analyzes the role of SSN programs as a main SPL instrument. Performance indicators provide answers to very important development questions. Coverage indicates what percentage of the total population or a specific population group benefits from SSN programs. Among all possible population groups, the poor have the greatest need for social protection and are particularly the focus of SSNs aimed at assisting the poor. Beneficiary incidence sheds light on how the total number of beneficiaries are distributed along the welfare distribution of the population. The level of benefits indicates the proportion of the benefits with respect to the household's total income or consumption. Impact on poverty and inequality shows the reduction in the poverty headcount, poverty gap, and inequality (as measured by the Gini index) because of the SPL transfers.

The performance indicators presented in this chapter represent only a first step at monitoring SSN program performance and do not replace results from impact evaluations. Performance indicators from household survey data help monitor SSN programs' performance over time as information from household surveys becomes available. Given that significant resources are being invested by governments in the implementation of SSN programs, it is important to continuously monitor the effectiveness of these programs and inform social policy.

Performance indicators derived from household surveys assess the effect of the transfers on the welfare of beneficiaries (in terms of income or consumption) and their distributional effects. Impact evaluations, on the other hand, are designed to measure a broader specific set of outcomes, such as the effects on beneficiaries' level of consumption, production, labor supply, human capital, and risk management (see highlight 1 at the end of this chapter). The effects attributed to the program are evaluated by using a counterfactual to determine the potential outcomes for the beneficiaries in the absence of the program. However, impact evaluations are not conducted very frequently and are not available for all programs; accordingly, household surveys play a crucial role in monitoring programs, given that they are systematically conducted across years and may include a larger set of programs for which impact evaluations are not available. Therefore, performance indicators from household surveys and impact evaluations provide a complementary picture of what social protection programs are achieving.

This chapter first presents evidence on coverage, then on beneficiary incidence, followed by benefit size, and impacts on poverty and inequality. In addition, a highlight focuses on productive outcomes of SSN programs in Sub-Saharan Africa based on impact evaluations. The analysis uses a subset of the most recent household surveys (2008–16) from the Atlas of Social Protection: Indicators of Resilience and Equity (ASPIRE) database, corresponding to 96 countries with information about SSN programs. The full sample of countries is used for coverage and beneficiary incidence indicators; however, for assessing benefits level and impacts on poverty and inequality, only 79 countries are used, for which the monetary value of the transfers is provided in the household surveys. This chapter also provides country-level key performance indicators of SPL programs in appendix F.1 and key performance indicators solely for SSN/SA programs in appendix F.2.

WHO IS COVERED BY SOCIAL PROTECTION AND LABOR PROGRAMS?

Coverage is expressed as the percentage of the population receiving a given type of SPL program. In this analysis, coverage includes direct and indirect beneficiaries (all household members where at least one member receives a benefit). The analysis first presents the global picture of SPL coverage by region and country income group, and then zooms in on country-level coverage rates by the type of SSN program. In discussing the coverage of the poor, the poor are defined as individuals who belong to the bottom 20 percent of the welfare distribution (in terms of household total income or consumption per capita). In all subsequent figures and in appendix F, the pretransfer welfare indicator is used to rank households, except for the indicator that expresses the social transfers as a share of total beneficiary welfare, which includes transfers.

The analysis reveals that SPL programs cover on average 44 percent of the total population. SPL programs cover more than half the population in East Asia and Pacific, Europe and Central Asia, Latin American and the Caribbean, and

Middle East North Africa (see figure 3.1).[1] In terms of coverage of the poorest, Europe and Central Asia has the highest coverage of individuals in the poorest quintile (86 percent), followed by Latin American and the Caribbean (76 percent). In all regions, a higher percentage of the poorest quintile (compared to the total population) is covered.

The coverage rates presented in the first three figures (see figures 3.1–3.3) are particularly high because they include all types of SPL programs, not only SSN/SA programs. In other words, the figures include any type of social insurance (old-age pension and other social security), active and passive labor market programs, and SSNs (unconditional cash transfers [UCTs], conditional cash transfers [CCTs], social pensions, public works, fee waivers and targeted subsidies, school feeding, in-kind transfers, and other SA programs).[2] In addition, other methodological factors drive this high coverage. Specifically, the calculation includes direct and indirect beneficiaries, and the poorest quintile is estimated using pre-transfer welfare.

In a sample of countries capturing all country income groups, the average SPL coverage rate of the poorest quintile is 56 percent. The coverage of SPL programs is highly correlated with the countries' level of income. Figure 3.2 shows that high- and upper-middle-income countries cover 97 percent and 77 percent of the poorest quintile, respectively. In contrast, lower-middle- and low-income countries cover 54 and 19 percent of the poorest quintile, respectively. These coverage figures should be interpreted with caution because coverage rates derived from household surveys are likely to be underestimated.[3] As a response to observed coverage gaps for the poor, such initiatives as universal social protection (USP) have emerged (see box 3.1).

In terms of the coverage of the poor, low-income countries lag in all three areas of social protection. Figure 3.3 shows that social insurance programs are more prevalent in high-income countries, covering 60 percent of the poorest quintile; in contrast, in low-income countries only 2 percent of the poorest quintile is covered by this program type. SSN/SA programs account for most SPL program coverage of the poor in all country income groups. Yet, high-income countries report the highest

FIGURE 3.1 Share of Total Population and the Poorest Quintile That Receives Any Social Protection and Labor Programs, as Captured in Household Surveys, by Region

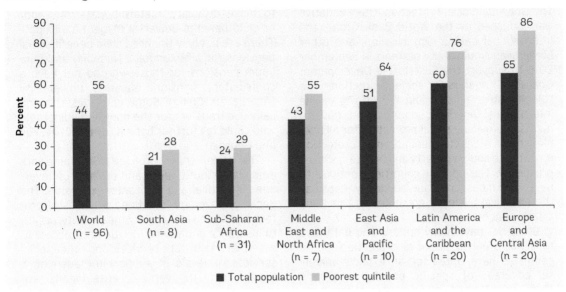

Source: ASPIRE database.
Note: The total number of countries per region included in the analysis appears in parentheses. Aggregated indicators are calculated using simple averages of country-level social protection and labor coverage rates across regions. Coverage is determined as follows: (number of individuals in the total population or poorest quintile who live in a household where at least one member receives the transfer)/(number of individuals in the total population). This figure underestimates total social protection and labor coverage because household surveys do not include all programs that exist in each country. The poorest quintile is calculated using per capita pretransfer welfare (income or consumption). ASPIRE = Atlas of Social Protection: Indicators of Resilience and Equity.

FIGURE 3.2 Share of Total Population and the Poorest Quintile That Receives Any Social Protection and Labor Programs, as Captured in Household Surveys, by Country Income Group

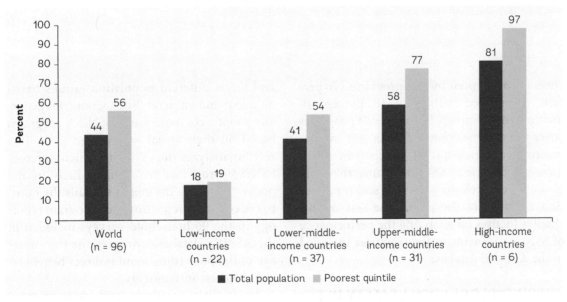

Source: ASPIRE database.
Note: The total number of countries per country income group included in the analysis appears in parentheses. Aggregated indicators are calculated using simple averages of country-level social protection and labor coverage rates across country income groups. Coverage is determined as follows: (number of individuals in the total population or poorest quintile who live in a household where at least one member receives the transfer)/(number of individuals in the total population). This figure underestimates total social protection and labor coverage because household surveys do not include all programs that exist in each country. The poorest quintile is calculated using per capita pretransfer welfare (income or consumption). ASPIRE = Atlas of Social Protection: Indicators of Resilience and Equity.

BOX 3.1 Universal Social Protection

The Universal Social Protection (USP) Initiative was launched by the World Bank Group, the International Labour Organisation, and other bilateral and multilateral partners in September 2016 to support the Sustainable Development Goal (SDG) agenda for social protection.[a] The USP Initiative aims to join the efforts of the international agencies, donors, and governments in providing social protection for all people in need. Access to adequate social protection is central to ending poverty and boosting shared prosperity. The poorest countries continue to have enormous coverage/adequacy gaps, as the empirical evidence presented in this book clearly suggests.

Countries have many options and pathways to achieve universal social protection. Some countries have opted for an explicit universal coverage of specific population groups (Botswana, Timor-Leste), whereas others have used a more gradual and progressive approach to building up coverage (Brazil, Thailand). Some countries have the principles of universalism (universal rights) embedded in their national constitutions (Bolivia, South Africa), whereas others have pursued those principles without constitutional provisions (Swaziland, Uruguay). Universal social protection is most commonly started with (universal) old-age pensions (see chapter 4), but some countries have opted to make disability, maternity/paternity, and/or child benefits universal (Argentina, Nepal). There are publicly financed child benefit social pensions for all (Mongolia, Namibia) and minimum pensions for those who do not have a contributory pension, ensuring universality (Azerbaijan, China). Some countries strategically use transfers for the poor and vulnerable who could fall further behind (Brazil, Chile, Fiji, and Georgia).

The implementation of the USP Framework emphasizes both depth and breadth of coverage, or vertical and horizontal expansion. The depth of coverage is defined as areas of protection and can include income security, access to insurance and saving instruments, access to essential health care services, and other social services or levels of support (or adequacy). Expansion in the vertical sense means providing more protection to the same covered groups. In terms of horizontal expansion, there are different population groups with respect to the stage in the life cycle (children, working age, and elderly) or level of income (poor, vulnerable, middle class, rich). The evidence suggests that countries tend to gradually expand coverage both vertically and horizontally. The degree of coverage of the poor is highly correlated with the degree of coverage of the general population.

a. See http://www.ilo.org/global/topics/social-security/WCMS_378991/lang--en/index.htm.

coverage of the poor by SSN programs (76 percent), compared with only 18 percent in low-income countries. Labor market programs cover the poor at a rate of 2 percent in low-income countries and 8 percent in high-income countries.[4] SSN programs therefore play a pivotal role in achieving social protection coverage of the poor.[5] The rest of this chapter focuses on analyzing the performance of SSN instruments in the countries included in the ASPIRE database.

WHICH TYPES OF SOCIAL SAFETY NET PROGRAMS COVER THE POOR?

Different countries focus on different SSN instruments. There is no one-size-fits-all approach to SSN/SA programs. These noncontributory programs address different issues and target different population groups based on needs and vulnerabilities. Countries generally adopt a combination of SSN/SA programs based on their social policy objectives. This section analyzes the extent to which different SSN/SA programs cover individuals in the poorest quintile. The analysis details the number of countries reporting each program typology in the 96 household surveys included in the ASPIRE database and presents the coverage of the poor (direct and indirect beneficiaries) by these instruments.

To facilitate analysis and cross-country comparisons, the programs are grouped into eight standard SSN categories. Therefore, the coverage indicator corresponds to the aggregated program category and not necessarily to an individual program. For example,

FIGURE 3.3 Share of Poorest Quintile That Receives Any Social Protection and Labor Program, as Captured in Household Surveys, by Type of Social Protection and Labor Area and Country Income Group

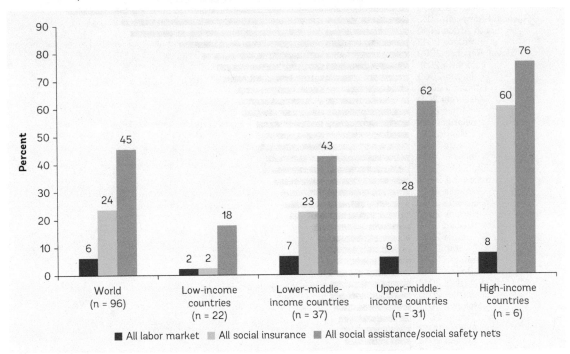

■ All labor market ■ All social insurance ■ All social assistance/social safety nets

Source: ASPIRE database.
Note: The total number of countries per country income group included in the analysis appears in parentheses. Aggregated indicators are calculated using simple averages of country-level coverage rates for social insurance, social assistance, and labor market programs, across country income groups. Indicators do not count for overlap among programs types (people receiving more than one program); therefore, the sum of percentages by type of program may add up to more than 100 percent. Coverage is determined as follows: (number of individuals in the total population or poorest quintile who live in a household where at least one member receives the transfer)/(number of individuals in the total population). This figure underestimates total social protection and labor coverage because household surveys do not include all programs that exist in each country. The poorest quintile is calculated using per capita pretransfer welfare (income or consumption). ASPIRE = Atlas of Social Protection: Indicators of Resilience and Equity.

Latvia includes 10 programs under UCTs, which embrace the means-tested Guaranteed Minimal Income Allowance, together with more universal child and family benefits. On the other hand, Belize includes only one program, the social welfare transfer, under UCTs. Complete documentation of the programs that are included in each SSN category, per country, is available in the ASPIRE online portal.[6] In the discussion that follows, coverage of the poor is presented by each SSN program category, illustrating different patterns in the use of specific SSN interventions, the degree of variation in coverage rates across countries, and the benchmarking of country results against global program averages.[7]

UCTs constitute some of the most popular safety net tools and are included in most household surveys in all regions. They cover 23 percent of the poorest quintile, on average. In the ASPIRE database, UCT programs are reported in the household surveys of 63 countries, compared with 103 countries where the administrative data report having at least one program in this category.[8] The most UCTs are found in the household surveys for Europe and Central Asia and Sub-Saharan Africa (20 and 17 countries, respectively). Figure 3.4 shows the distribution of UCT programs covering from 0.6 to almost 100 percent of the poorest quintile. Among the programs that achieve almost 100 percent coverage of the poor are the Child Money Program in Mongolia,[9] and the social transfers in Malaysia (94 percent coverage of the poor), which may reflect the performance of the Bantuan Rakyat 1 Program,

FIGURE 3.4 Share of the Poorest Quintile That Receives Unconditional Cash Transfer Programs, as Captured in Household Surveys

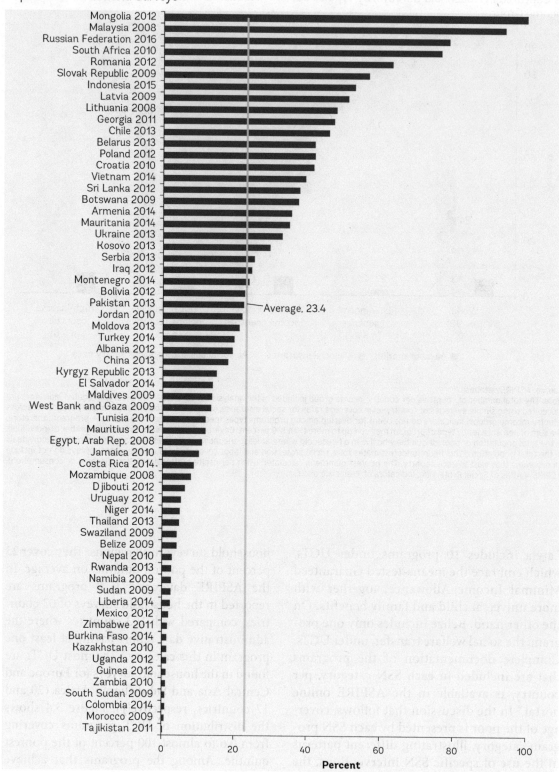

Source: ASPIRE database.

Note: The number of countries per region is as follows: total (n = 63); Europe and Central Asia (n = 20); Sub-Saharan Africa (n = 17); Latin America and the Caribbean (n = 9); Middle East and North Africa (n = 7); East Asia and Pacific (n = 6); and South Asia (n = 4). Unconditional cash transfers include any of the following: poverty alleviation and emergency programs, guaranteed minimum-income programs, and universal or poverty-targeted child and family allowances. They do not include social pensions or targeted subsidies in cash. The average coverage of unconditional cash transfers is estimated as the simple average of these programs' coverage rates across countries. Coverage is determined as follows: (number of individuals in the total population or poorest quintile who live in a household where at least one member receives the transfer)/(number of individuals in the total population). This figure underestimates total coverage because household surveys do not include all programs that exist in each country. The poorest quintile is calculated using per capita pretransfer welfare (income or consumption). ASPIRE = Atlas of Social Protection: Indicators of Resilience and Equity.

the country's flagship cash transfer program for the poor.[10] In Europe and Central Asia, Russian Federation's cash transfer programs show the largest coverage of the poor (79 percent).

CCTs typically aim to reduce poverty and increase human capital by requiring beneficiaries to comply with conditions such as school attendance and health checkups. The average coverage of the poorest quintile by CCTs in the sample of surveys is 40 percent. Pioneered by Brazil and Mexico in the late 1990s, CCTs spread to other countries in the region and worldwide. Yet, few household surveys outside of

Latin America and the Caribbean capture CCT information. Only 19 countries in ASPIRE include information on CCT programs in their household surveys (of which 16 are in Latin America and the Caribbean), compared with 64 programs observed in the administrative database. This instrument covers from 2.4 to 75 percent of the poor (see figure 3.5). Asignaciones Familiares in Uruguay has the largest coverage of the poor (75 percent), followed by Bonos Juancito Pinto and Juana Azurduy in Bolivia (73 percent), and Prospera in Mexico (63 percent). The CCT with large coverage outside Latin America and the Caribbean is the Pantawid Pamilyang Pilipino

FIGURE 3.5 Share of the Poorest Quintile That Receives Conditional Cash Transfer Programs, as Captured in Household Surveys

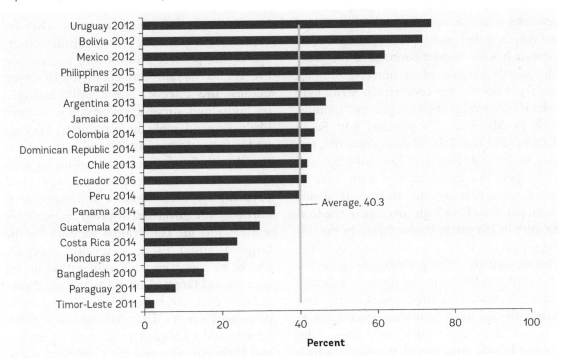

Source: ASPIRE database.
Note: The number of countries per region included in the analysis is as follows: total (n = 19); Latin America and the Caribbean (n = 16); East Asia and Pacific (n = 2); South Asia (n = 1); Europe and Central Asia (n = 0); Middle East and North Africa (n = 0); and Sub-Saharan Africa (n = 0). Conditional cash transfer programs include the following: Argentina 2013: Asignación Universal por Hijo. Bangladesh 2010: Maternity allowance; Program for the Poor Lactating; Stipend for Primary Students (MOPMED); Stipend for Dropout Students; Stipend for Secondary and Higher Secondary/Female Student. Bolivia 2012: Bono Juancito Pinto; and Bono Juana Azurduy. Brazil 2015: Bolsa Família. Chile 2013: Subsidio Familiar (SUF); Bono de Protección Familiar y de Egreso; Bono por control del niño sano; Bono por asistencia escolar; and Bono por logro escolar. Colombia 2014: Familias en Acción. Costa Rica 2014: Avancemos. Dominican Republic 2014: Solidaridad Program and other transfers. Ecuador 2016: Bono de Desarrollo Humano. Guatemala 2014: Programa Mi Bono Seguro. Honduras 2013: Asignaciones Familiares-Bonos PRAF and otro tipo de bonos. Jamaica 2010: Program of Advancement Through Health and Education (PATH)–child 0–71 months; 6–17 years; and pregnant and lactating women. Mexico 2012: Oportunidades. Panama 2014: Red de Oportunidades. Paraguay 2011: Tekopora. Peru 2014: Programa Juntos. Philippines 2015: Pantawid Pamilyang Pilipino Program (4Ps). Timor Leste 2011: Bolsa da Mae. Uruguay 2012: Asignaciones Familiares. The average coverage of conditional cash transfers is estimated as the simple average of these programs' coverage rates across countries. Coverage is determined as follows: (number of individuals in the total population or poorest quintile who live in a household where at least one member receives the transfer)/(number of individuals in the total population). This figure underestimates total coverage because household surveys do not include all programs that exist in each country. The poorest quintile is calculated using per capita pretransfer welfare (income or consumption). ASPIRE = Atlas of Social Protection: Indicators of Resilience and Equity.

Program (4Ps) in the Philippines, which covers 60 percent of the poor (see figure 3.5), demonstrating its focus on ensuring coverage of the poorest.

For individuals who do not have access to social insurance benefits, social pensions aim to overcome loss of income because of old age, disability, or death of the bread winner. In the sample of countries, social pensions cover, on average, 20 percent of the poorest quintile. Social pensions presented here include noncontributory disability and survivor pensions, and thus represent a broader category than old-age social pensions (featured in chapter 4). Only 36 countries in the ASPIRE household survey database capture any form of social pensions, compared with 75 countries in the administrative database. Most surveys with social pension information are found in Europe and Central Asia (n = 13) and Latin America and the Caribbean (n = 10). In the sample, social pensions cover between 0.6 and 81 percent of individuals in the poorest quintile (see figure 3.6). Georgia has the highest coverage of the poorest quintile because of its universal old-age social pensions. A few countries in Africa have extensive coverage of the poorest quintile, such as Mauritius (79 percent) and South Africa (62 percent). In all these countries, formal social insurance has low coverage and social pensions constitute the main form of social protection for the elderly. Thailand's social pensions have high coverage of the lowest quintile (58 percent), also driven by providing support to the elderly and disabled, taking into account their living arrangements within extended families.[11] On the opposite extreme, some countries in Europe and Central Asia have extended social insurance systems; therefore, social pensions cover only those who do not benefit from social insurance, which constitute rather narrow population groups. Hence the coverage is low (Latvia, Montenegro, Russian Federation, and Serbia).

Public works programs typically condition the transfer on participating in a community project/activity. Very few public works programs are captured in the sample of household surveys, and their coverage of the poorest quintile is limited, at 11 percent. Public works are implemented for many reasons, such as to provide employment of last resort or to mitigate covariate and idiosyncratic shocks. Public works programs include cash-, food-, and inputs-for-work (Andrews et al. 2012). They are more often implemented in Sub-Saharan Africa and South Asia, although respective information/data are not often captured in household surveys. Only 9 countries in ASPIRE have specific information about public works in the household surveys, as compared with 96 countries in the administrative database. In these countries, public works cover between 1 and 27 percent of the poorest quintile (figure 3.7); the largest coverage rates are observed for the MGNREG program in India (27 percent), a flagship national social safety net program with a history going back decades; and MASAF in Malawi (21 percent), the social fund program that has become the cornerstone of the national SSN system.

Fee waivers and targeted subsidies typically subsidize services or provide access to low-priced food staples to the poor. They are common but generally provide limited coverage of the poorest quintile—13 percent, on average, in the sample of countries. However, because this category is not easily collected by household surveys, this average is most likely a considerable underestimate. Services under this category usually relate to education, health, housing, transportation, or utilities. When a beneficiary is exempt from payment for such services and the cost is borne by the government program, such fee waivers provide conditional support for the targeted group using a specific service.[12] Out of 82 countries with information on fee waivers and targeted subsidies in the administrative database, only 22 are observed in the household survey data. Among the regions, Europe and Central Asia (n = 10 countries) and Latin America and the Caribbean countries (n = 8 countries) capture this typology of programs in the surveys most often. The program covers between 0.4 and 56 percent of the poor (see figure 3.8). Coverage rates for targeted subsidies and fee waivers in Europe and Central Asia tend to be smaller because these programs focus only on a subset of the poor, but tend to include several different forms of benefits (for example, subsidized housing; and fee waivers for kindergartens, health care, public transportation).

FIGURE 3.6 Share of the Poorest Quintile That Receives Social Pensions, as Captured in Household Surveys

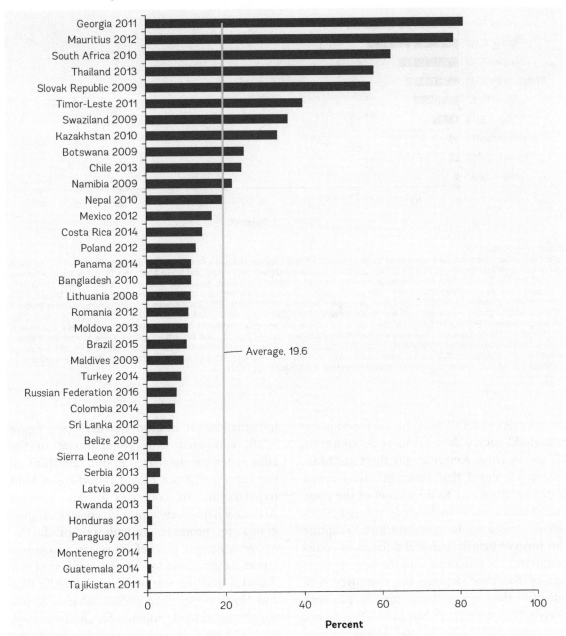

Source: ASPIRE database.
Note: The number of countries per region is as follows: total (n = 36); Europe and Central Asia (n = 13); Latin America and the Caribbean (n = 10); Sub-Saharan Africa (n = 7); South Asia (n = 4); East Asia and Pacific (n = 2); and Middle East and North Africa (n = 0). Social pensions include any of the following: noncontributory old-age pensions; disability pensions; and survivor pensions. Social pensions average coverage is the simple average of social pensions coverage rates across countries. Coverage is determined as follows: (number of individuals in the total population or poorest quintile who live in a household where at least one member receives the transfer)/(number of individuals in the total population). This figure underestimates total coverage because household surveys do not include all programs that exist in each country. The poorest quintile is calculated using per capita pretransfer welfare (income or consumption). ASPIRE = Atlas of Social Protection: Indicators of Resilience and Equity.

School feeding programs provide meals to students generally in poor and food-insecure areas, with the aim of improving nutrition, health, and educational outcomes. In the sample, these programs are found, on average, to benefit a significant share of the poor—37 percent. Even though school feeding is a common safety net program, it is not always captured in household surveys. Of the 117 countries reporting school feeding in administrative data, only

FIGURE 3.7 Share of the Poorest Quintile That Receives Public Works, as Captured in Household Surveys

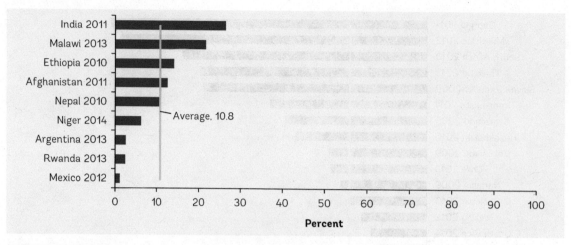

Source: ASPIRE database.
Note: The number of countries per region is as follows: total (n = 9); Sub-Saharan Africa (n = 4); Latin America and the Caribbean (n = 2); South Asia (n = 3); East Asia and Pacific (n = 0); Europe and Central Asia (n = 0); and Middle East and North Africa (n = 0). Public works programs included: Afghanistan 2011: Cash-for-work programs; food-for-work programs; or income-generating program/projects. Argentina 2013: Plan de Empleo. Ethiopia 2010: Productive Safety Net Program (PSNP). India 2011: MGNREG and other public works. Malawi 2013: MASAF; PWP; Inputs-for-work program. Mexico 2012: Programa de Empleo Temporal (PET). Nepal 2010: Rural Community Infrastructure Works Program (RCIW) and other food-for-work and cash for work programs. Niger 2014: Public works. Rwanda 2013: Public works from the Vision 2020 Umurenge Program. Public works average coverage is the simple average of public works coverage rates across countries. Coverage is determined as follows: (number of individuals in the total population or poorest quintile who live in a household where at least one member receives the transfer)/(number of individuals in the total population). This figure underestimates total coverage because household surveys do not include all programs that exist in each country. The poorest quintile is calculated using per capita pretransfer welfare (income or consumption). ASPIRE = Atlas of Social Protection: Indicators of Resilience and Equity.

26 countries with this program are found in the household survey data. Of these 26 countries, 15 are in Latin America and the Caribbean. Figure 3.9 shows that coverage varies across countries from 2.21 to 86 percent of the poor. Such variation is more likely to reflect the differences in survey designs and efforts to capture this form of benefit than real differences across countries. The programs with the largest coverage of the poor, among the countries with adequate data, are in Botswana (86 percent), Bolivia (73 percent), El Salvador (69 percent), Nicaragua (67 percent), and Honduras and Panama (66 percent).

In-kind transfers consist of food rations, clothes, school supplies, shelter, fertilizers, seeds, agricultural tools or animals, and building materials, among others. They are a very common SSN instrument, and in the sample cover, on average, 27 percent of the poorest quintile. Their objectives are usually to provide food security, improve nutrition, increase agricultural productivity, and deliver emergency relief. Forty-five countries in the ASPIRE household survey database capture

information on in-kind transfers (see figure 3.10), compared with 90 countries in the administrative database. About one-third of the surveys (14 out of 45) reporting in-kind transfers are in countries in Sub-Saharan Africa, where they typically consist of programs to promote agricultural productivity or emergency relief. However, programs report larger coverage of the poor in Latin America and the Caribbean and Middle East and North Africa than in Sub-Saharan Africa. Supplemental food programs for children, pregnant and nursing women, and the elderly are common in Latin America and the Caribbean, as well as school supplies and uniforms. In a few countries, these programs cover a high percentage of the poor, including Peru (84 percent), Ecuador (74 percent), and El Salvador and Paraguay (70 percent). Coverage in Peru is particularly large because the in-kind category encompasses seven in-kind programs captured in the survey, including nutritional programs, school supplies, uniforms, and shoes and laptops to school children. In Middle East and North Africa, in-kind transfers take the form of food

FIGURE 3.8 Share of the Poorest Quintile That Receives Fee Waivers and Targeted Subsidies, as Captured in Household Surveys

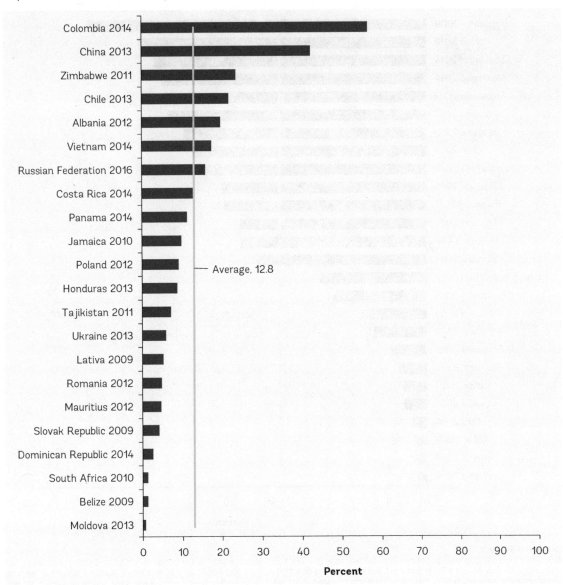

Source: ASPIRE database.
Note: The number of countries per region is as follows: total (n = 22); Europe and Central Asia (n = 10); Latin America and the Caribbean (n = 8); Sub-Saharan Africa (n = 2); East Asia and Pacific (n = 2); Middle East and North Africa (n = 0); and South Asia (n = 0). Fee waivers and targeted subsidies include any of the following: energy products; education; utilities; housing or transportation fees waivers to specific households; or such fees discounted below the market cost. They do not include health fee waivers/subsidies, except for Zimbabwe. Fee waivers and targeted subsidies program coverage is the simple average of these programs' coverage rates across countries. Coverage is determined as follows: (number of individuals in the total population or poorest quintile who live in a household where at least one member receives the transfer)/(number of individuals in the total population). This figure underestimates total coverage because household surveys do not include all programs that exist in each country. The poorest quintile is calculated using per capita pretransfer welfare (income or consumption). ASPIRE = Atlas of Social Protection: Indicators of Resilience and Equity.

and in-kind aid. They cover about 81 percent of the poor in Iraq and 56 percent in the Arab Republic of Egypt (see figure 3.10). In East Asia and Pacific, Indonesia's Rastra Program (rice subsidies) has the largest coverage of the poor (71 percent).[13]

WHAT IS THE BENEFICIARY INCIDENCE OF VARIOUS SOCIAL SAFETY NET INSTRUMENTS?

Beneficiary incidence indicates to what extent a given population group benefits from a program. For this analysis, individuals are ranked

FIGURE 3.9 Share of the Poorest Quintile That Receives School Feeding Programs, as Captured in Household Surveys

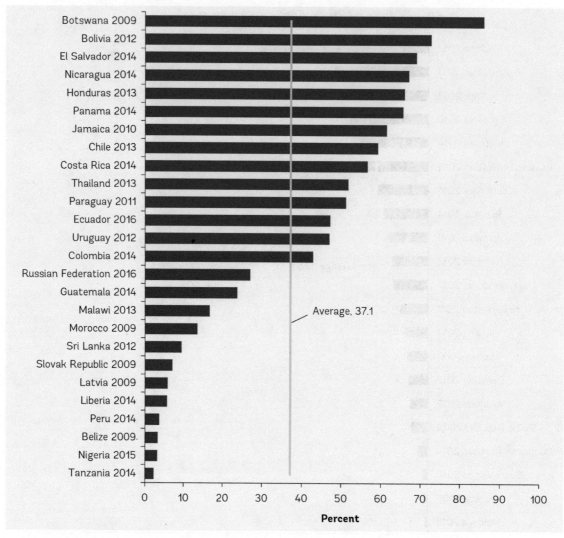

Source: ASPIRE database.
Note: The number of countries per region is as follows: total (n = 26); Latin America and the Caribbean (n = 15); Sub-Saharan Africa (n = 5); Europe and Central Asia (n = 3); Middle East and North Africa (n = 1); East Asia and Pacific (n = 1); and South Asia (n = 1). School feeding programs encompass any type of meals or food items provided at school. School feeding average coverage is the simple average of school feeding coverage rates across countries. Coverage is determined as follows: (number of individuals in the total population or poorest quintile who live in a household where at least one member receives the transfer)/(number of individuals in the total population). This figure underestimates total coverage because household surveys do not include all programs that exist in each country. The poorest quintile is calculated using per capita pretransfer welfare (income or consumption). ASPIRE = Atlas of Social Protection: Indicators of Resilience and Equity.

according to their position in the welfare distribution, based on quintiles of per capita pretransfer income or consumption; the proportion of program beneficiaries belonging to each quintile is presented. Another corresponding indicator is benefits incidence, which shows the proportion of program benefits transferred to individuals in each quintile.[14] A program is considered propoor if more than 20 percent of its total beneficiaries belong to the bottom

20 percent of the distribution (or if more than 40 percent of its total beneficiaries belong to the bottom 40 percent of the distribution).[15] Beneficiary incidence and benefits incidence help determine which population groups are benefiting from the program, and thus are useful indicators to analyze the performance of SPL programs. Propoor beneficiary and benefits incidence is the only way to ensure that a program within a given budget achieves greater

FIGURE 3.10 Share of the Poorest Quintile That Receives In-Kind Transfers, as Captured in Household Surveys

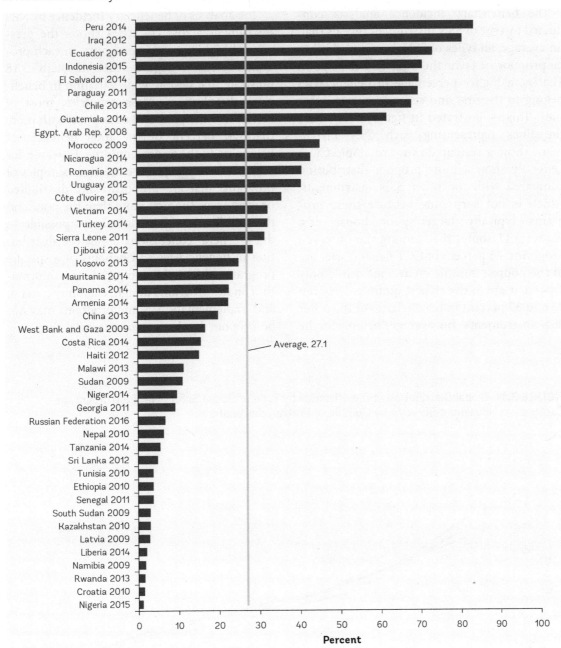

Source: ASPIRE database.
Note: The number of countries per region is as follows: total (n = 45); Sub-Saharan Africa (n = 14); Latin America and the Caribbean (n = 11); Europe and Central Asia (n = 9); Middle East and North Africa (n = 6); East Asia and Pacific (n = 3); and South Asia (n = 2). In-kind transfers include any of the following: food aid; agricultural inputs; clothes; school supplies; and building materials. In-kind transfers average coverage is the simple average of in-kind transfer coverage rates across countries. Coverage is determined as follows: (number of individuals in the total population or poorest quintile who live in a household where at least one member receives the transfer)/(number of individuals in the total population). This figure underestimates total coverage because household surveys do not include all programs that exist in each country. The poorest quintile is calculated using per capita pretransfer welfare (income or consumption). ASPIRE = Atlas of Social Protection: Indicators of Resilience and Equity.

impact in terms of poverty reduction (Yemtsov et al., forthcoming).

The beneficiary incidence analysis conducted by type of SSN instrument reveals that, on average, all types of SSN programs tend to be propoor or favor the poor and near-poor. That is, a higher percentage of beneficiaries belong to the first and second poorest quintiles. This is illustrated in figure 3.11, where the lines representing each SSN instrument show a similar downward slope. CCTs generally show a more propoor distribution compared with the other SSN instruments, which is not surprising because these programs typically target poor households. Figure 3.11 shows that, among the observed programs, 45 percent of CCT beneficiaries are in the poorest quintile on average, while only 4 percent are in the richest quintile. Between 33 and 37 percent of beneficiaries of the other SSN instruments, on average, belong to the

poorest quintile, which indicates that those instruments are still propoor.

The analysis of beneficiary incidence by SSN instrument across countries shows the presence of highly propoor programs in each program category. Figures 3.12 through 3.18 illustrate that despite wide variation in beneficiary distribution across countries, most of them favor the poor and near-poor, with more than 20 percent of the total beneficiaries belonging to the poorest quintile. However, for every SSN category, there are also examples of programs that are proportionally distributed or even favor the rich more than the poor and the middle class. It is not always possible to draw general conclusions about the distribution of beneficiaries and benefits of a specific program without knowing detailed information on the program's design, eligibility criteria, and implementation. Some programs may not be propoor by design; for example, they may

FIGURE 3.11 Global Distribution of Beneficiaries by Type of Social Safety Net Instrument, as Captured in Household Surveys, by Quintile of Pretransfer Welfare

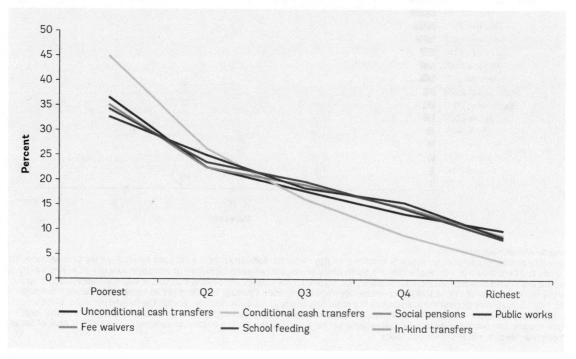

Source: ASPIRE database.
Note: The total number of countries where the social safety net instrument is captured in household surveys is as follows: unconditional cash transfers (n = 63), conditional cash transfers (n = 19); social pensions (n = 36); public works (n = 9); fee waivers and targeted subsidies (n = 22); school feeding (n = 26); and in-kind transfers (n = 45). Beneficiaries' incidence is calculated as follows: (number of direct and indirect beneficiaries [people who live in a household where at least one member receives the transfer] in a given quintile)/(total number of direct and indirect beneficiaries). The sum of percentages across quintiles per given instrument equals 100 percent. Aggregated indicators are calculated using simple averages of program instrument beneficiaries' incidence rates across countries. Quintiles are calculated using per capita pretransfer welfare (income or consumption). ASPIRE = Atlas of Social Protection: Indicators of Resilience and Equity; Q = quintile.

not be addressed specifically to the poor but to the general population (that is, in the case of universal programs). Or their eligibility criteria may be categorical (for example, in terms of disability, ethnicity, and war victims) and not means-tested. In those cases, beneficiaries meeting the categorical requirements may not belong to the poor.

UCTs are characterized by a wide range of beneficiary incidence across countries, but on average, 37 percent of UCT beneficiaries belong to the poorest quintile and 23 to the second-poorest quintile (figure 3.12). One reason for this large variation of results across countries is the fact that ASPIRE—in some countries—aggregates many types of UCTs, and the respective programs may have very different objectives and eligibility criteria. However, for other countries, this category captures only one program, making it easier to interpret the observed beneficiary incidence results. Universal programs have an even distribution. For instance, for the Child Money Program in Mongolia, the participation

FIGURE 3.12 Distribution of Unconditional Cash Transfer Beneficiaries, as Captured in Household Surveys, by Quintile of Pretransfer Welfare

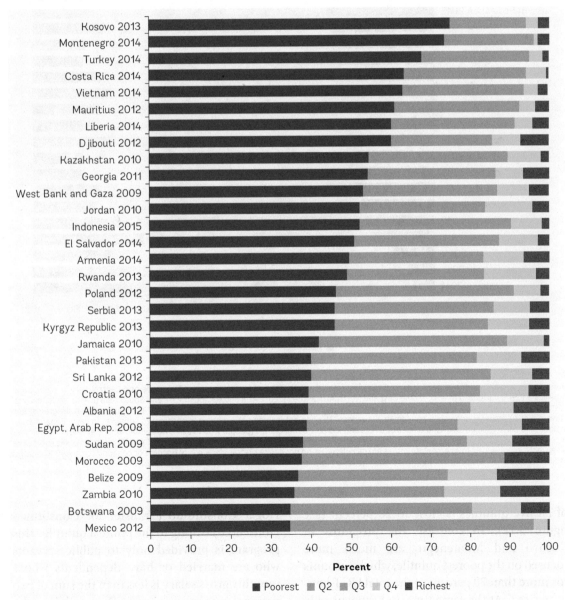

(Figure continues next page)

FIGURE 3.12 Distribution of Unconditional Cash Transfer Beneficiaries, as Captured in Household Surveys, by Quintile of Pretransfer Welfare *(Continued)*

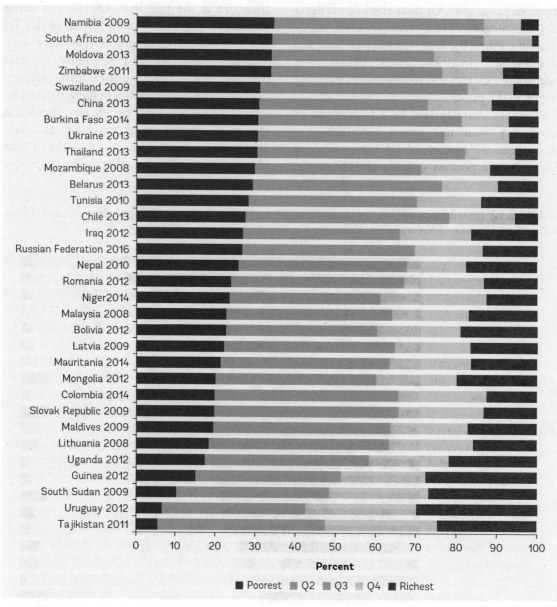

Source: ASPIRE database.
Note: The number of countries per region is as follows: total (n = 63); Sub-Saharan Africa (n = 17); Europe and Central Asia (n = 20); Latin America and the Caribbean (n = 9); Middle East and North Africa (n = 7); East Asia and Pacific (n = 6); and South Asia (n = 4). Unconditional cash transfers include any of the following: poverty alleviation and emergency programs; guaranteed minimum-income programs; and universal or poverty-targeted child and family allowances. They do not include social pensions or targeted subsidies in cash. Beneficiaries' incidence is calculated as follows: (number of direct and indirect beneficiaries [people who live in a household where at least one member receives the transfer] in a given quintile)/(total number of direct and indirect beneficiaries). The sum of percentages across quintiles per given instrument equals 100 percent. Quintiles are calculated using per capita pretransfer welfare (income or consumption). ASPIRE = Atlas of Social Protection: Indicators of Resilience and Equity; Q = quintile.

of all five quintiles is close to 20 percent (see figure 3.12). In contrast, the programs in Kosovo and Montenegro are much more focused on the poorest quintile, which accounts for more than 70 percent of the total UCT beneficiaries.[16] At the same time, in Uruguay, only 7 percent of the beneficiaries of Prima por Hogar Constituido (Transfer for Constituted Household) belong to the poorest quintile. This program is provided only to public servants who are married or have dependents whose monthly gross salary is less than the sum of two national minimum wages. This explains why the program is not propoor by design.

In general, CCTS are, as has been mentioned already, more propoor than other SSN program types. Among all 19 CCT programs included in the ASPIRE database, the average beneficiary incidence is 45 percent for the poorest quintile and 26 percent for the second-poorest quintile. Panama's conditional cash transfer program, Red de Oportunidades, has an incidence of participants from the poorest quintile of 75 percent. More than 65 percent of the beneficiaries of Programa Juntos in Peru, belong to the poorest 20 percent. Timor-Leste's Bolsa da Mae has the lowest beneficiary incidence rate for the poorest quintile, at 21 percent (see figure 3.13).

Social pensions also have a very propoor distribution of beneficiaries. An average of 35 percent of beneficiaries belong to the poorest quintile and 22 percent to the second-poorest

quintile. The State Social Maintenance Benefit in Latvia has the highest proportion of beneficiaries belonging to the poorest quintile (59 percent). In contrast, Programa Adulto Mayor in Guatemala and Bono por Tercera Edad in Honduras have only 8 and 9 percent of their beneficiaries coming from the poorest quintile, respectively (see figure 3.14). Part of the propoor performance shown by some countries may be related to the way the pretransfer indicator is constructed. If social pensions cover a sizable part of the poor and their benefit level is high, most beneficiaries may tend to depend on them and hence group in the lowest quintile of the welfare distribution once such transfers are removed. On the other hand, social pensions in Honduras tend to cluster further up the income distribution, reflecting

FIGURE 3.13 Distribution of Conditional Cash Transfer Beneficiaries, as Captured in Household Surveys, by Quintile of Pretransfer Welfare

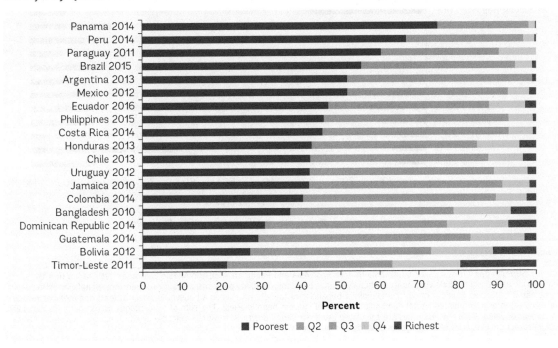

Source: ASPIRE database.
Note: The number of countries per region is as follows: total (n = 19); Latin America and the Caribbean (n = 16); East Asia and Pacific (n = 2); South Asia (n = 1); Europe and Central Asia (n = 0); Middle East and North Africa (n = 0); and Sub-Saharan Africa (n = 0). Conditional cash transfer programs include the following: Argentina 2013: Asignación Universal por Hijo. Bangladesh 2010: Maternity allowance, Program for the Poor Lactating, Stipend for Primary Students (MOPMED), Stipend for Drop Out Students, Stipend for Secondary and Higher Secondary/ Female Student. Bolivia 2012: Bono Juancito Pinto and Bono Juana Azurduy. Brazil 2015: Bolsa Família. Chile 2013: Subsidio Familiar (SUF), Bono de Protección Familiar y de Egreso, Bono por control del niño sano, Bono por asistencia escolar and Bono por logro escolar. Colombia 2014: Familias en Acción. Costa Rica 2014: Avancemos. Dominican Republic 2014: Solidaridad Program and other transfers. Ecuador 2016: Bono de Desarrollo Humano. Guatemala 2014: Programa Mi Bono Seguro. Honduras 2013: Asignaciones Familiares-Bonos PRAF and otro tipo de bonos. Jamaica 2010: Program of Advancement Through Health and Education (PATH)—child (0-71 months); 6-17 years; and pregnant and lactating women. Mexico 2012: Oportunidades. Panama 2014: Red de Oportunidades. Paraguay 2011: Tekopora. Peru 2014: Programa Juntos. Philippines 2015: Pantawid Pamilyang Pilipino Program (4Ps). Timor-Leste 2011: Bolsa da Mae. Uruguay 2012: Asignaciones Familiares. Beneficiaries' incidence is calculated as follows: (number of direct and indirect beneficiaries [people who live in a household where at least one member receives the transfer] in a given quintile)/(total number of direct and indirect beneficiaries). The sum of percentages across quintiles per given instrument equals 100 percent. Quintiles are calculated using per capita pretransfer welfare (income or consumption). ASPIRE = Atlas of Social Protection: Indicators of Resilience and Equity; Q = quintile.

FIGURE 3.14 Distribution of Social Pensions Beneficiaries, as Captured in Household Surveys, by Quintile of Pretransfer Welfare

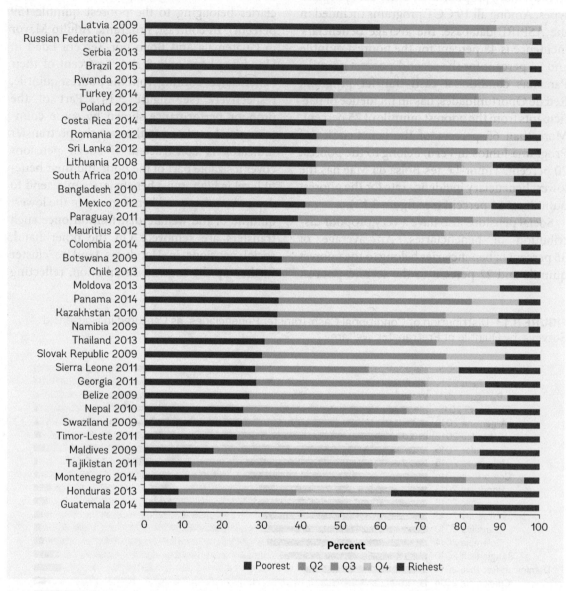

Source: ASPIRE database.
Note: The number of countries per region is as follows: total (n = 36); Europe and Central Asia (n = 13); Latin America and the Caribbean (n = 10); Sub-Saharan Africa (n = 7); South Asia (n = 4); East Asia and Pacific (n = 2); and Middle East and North Africa (n = 0). Social pensions include any of the following: noncontributory old-age pensions; disability pensions; and survivor pensions. Beneficiaries' incidence is calculated as follows: (number of direct and indirect beneficiaries [people who live in a household where at least one member receives the transfer] in a given quintile)/(total number of direct and indirect beneficiaries). The sum of percentages across quintiles per given instrument equals 100 percent. Quintiles are calculated using per capita pretransfer welfare (income or consumption). ASPIRE = Atlas of Social Protection: Indicators of Resilience and Equity; Q = quintile.

this instrument's bias in coverage toward richer areas of the country.

The beneficiary incidence of public works for the poorest quintile is 33 percent, on average. Yet, when looking at the two bottom quintiles, all 10 public works programs analyzed have a beneficiary incidence rate of at least 45 percent for the poorest 40 percent, which still makes it a

somewhat propoor instrument. Public works are limited only to households with able-bodied, unemployed members who are willing to work. Because many public works rely on self-selection and are oversubscribed, especially in low-income countries (more people want to work in these programs than they have employment positions), there is a lot of sharing and

FIGURE 3.15 Distribution of Public Works Beneficiaries, as Captured in Household Surveys, by Quintile of Pretransfer Welfare

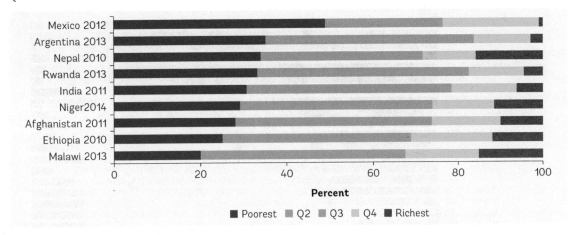

Source: ASPIRE database.
Note: The number of countries per region is as follows: total (n = 9); Sub-Saharan Africa (n = 4); Latin America and the Caribbean (n = 2); South Asia (n = 3); East Asia and Pacific (n = 0); Europe and Central Asia (n = 0); and Middle East and North Africa (n = 0). Public works programs include the following: Afghanistan 2011: Cash-for-work, food-for-work programs, or income-generating program/projects. Argentina 2013: Plan de Empleo. Ethiopia 2010: Productive Safety Net Program (PSNP). India 2011: MGNREG and other public works. Malawi 2013: MASAF, PWP, Inputs-for-work program. Mexico 2012: Programa de Empleo Temporal (PET). Nepal 2010: Rural Community Infrastructure Works Program (RCIW) and other food-for-work and cash for work programs. Niger 2014: Public works. Rwanda 2013: Public works from the Vision 2020 Umurenge Program. Beneficiaries' incidence is calculated as follows: (number of direct and indirect beneficiaries [people who live in a household where at least one member receives the transfer] in a given quintile)/(total number of direct and indirect beneficiaries). The sum of percentages across quintiles per given instrument equals 100 percent. Quintiles are calculated using per capita pretransfer welfare (income or consumption). ASPIRE = Atlas of Social Protection: Indicators of Resilience and Equity; Q = quintile.

capture of the program by the not so poor. Mexico's Programa de Empleo Temporal shows the most propoor distribution, with 49 percent of beneficiaries coming from the poorest quintile (see figure 3.15).

Fee waivers and targeted subsidies have a somewhat flatter beneficiary incidence along the welfare distribution, compared with other instruments. On average, 33 percent of their beneficiaries belong to the poorest quintile and 24 percent to the second-poorest quintile. In Panama, most of the beneficiaries (82 percent) of food supplements and agricultural subsidies belong to the poorest quintile, followed by Vietnam, where nearly three-quarters (73 percent) of beneficiaries of housing, petroleum, and kerosene subsidies and tuition fee exceptions are in the poorest quintile. In South Africa, by contrast, the rich capture most of these benefits (see figure 3.16).

Beneficiary incidence of school feeding programs varies substantially by country. On average, 34 percent of beneficiaries of school feeding programs belong to the poorest quintile and 24 percent to the second-poorest quintile (see figure 3.17). The most propoor programs are found in the Slovak Republic and Latvia, where

82 and 73 percent of the beneficiaries are drawn from the poorest quintile, respectively. All these programs are rather narrow in coverage, and stand out from a typical universal school feeding program, with different objectives that are often not focused on alleviating poverty. In addition, in universal programs with high coverage, the incidence of school feeding will depend on the access to schooling across quintiles, which may be skewed in favor of the nonpoor, and is not a design feature of the program itself.

In-kind transfers are generally quite propoor. In the sample of observed programs, 34 percent of beneficiaries of in-kind transfers belong to the poorest quintile and 23 percent to the second-poorest quintile. Food aid in Djibouti and food and nutritional programs in Uruguay have especially propoor distributions, with 71 and 70 percent of the recipients belonging to the poorest quintile, respectively (see figure 3.18).[17]

WHAT ARE THE BENEFIT LEVELS OF SOCIAL SAFETY NET PROGRAMS?

The level of benefits is measured by two indicators: per capita average transfer (monetary value) and share of benefits with respect to per

FIGURE 3.16 Distribution of Fee Waivers and Targeted Subsidies Beneficiaries, as Captured in Household Surveys, by Quintile of Pretransfer Welfare

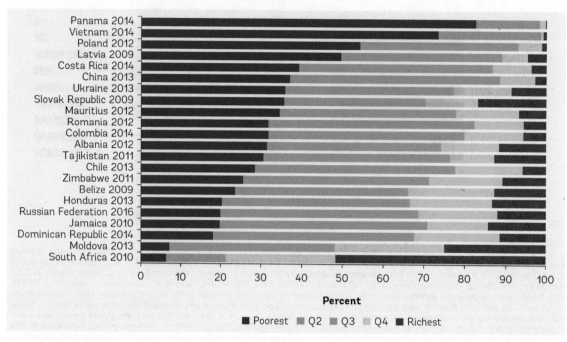

Source: ASPIRE database.
Note: The number of countries per region is as follows: total (n = 22); Europe and Central Asia (n = 10); Latin America and the Caribbean (n = 8); Sub-Saharan Africa (n = 2); East Asia and Pacific (n = 2); Middle East and North Africa (n = 0); and South Asia (n = 0). Fee waivers and targeted subsidies include any of the following: energy products; education; utilities; housing or transportation fees waivers to specific households; or such fees discounted below the market cost. They do not include health benefits or subsidies, except for Zimbabwe. Beneficiaries' incidence is calculated as follows: (number of direct and indirect beneficiaries [people who live in a household where at least one member receives the transfer] in a given quintile)/(total number of direct and indirect beneficiaries). The sum of percentages across quintiles per given instrument equals 100 percent. Quintiles are calculated using per capita pretransfer welfare (income or consumption). ASPIRE = Atlas of Social Protection: Indicators of Resilience and Equity; Q = quintile.

capita household income or consumption (adequacy ratio).[18] The per-capita average transfer is an absolute measure of benefit size and can be compared with social minimums, such as the poverty line or minimum wage. Benefits as a share of household welfare (income or consumption), on the other hand, are a relative measure that allows the importance of the transfers in proportion to household per capita welfare to be assessed.

The level of benefits is set to achieve program objectives within budget constraints. There are no standard rules to set benefits levels, given that they need to be calibrated to fulfill program objectives and meet budget constraints. Contributory old-age pensions, for example, are based on the amount of contributions individuals make during their active working life. In poverty reduction programs, the size of the transfers may be calibrated to reduce the poverty gap of the target population; programs that aim to address food security will set their benefits to meet nutritional needs.[19] For example, Kenya's Hunger Safety Net

Program sets transfer levels based on the five-year average price of cereals, whereas Zambia's Social Cash Transfer Program sets its benefits close to the price of a 50-pound bag of maize (corn) monthly, which would allow a household to eat a second meal each day (Schüring 2010; Garcia and Moore 2012).

The size of the benefit is a determining factor to achieve positive impacts on household well-being. The way program administrators set benefit levels varies across countries; some programs use flat benefits, whereas others adjust benefits based on household size, number of dependents, and so forth. Flat benefits raise the issue that the per capita transfer will decrease with household size and program impacts will vary across beneficiary households. Inflation is another factor that can erode the real value of the transfers over time, unless regular adjustment mechanisms are applied. In Kenya's Cash Transfer Program for Orphans and Vulnerable Children, for example, the value of the transfer decreased by almost 60 percent because of

FIGURE 3.17 Distribution of School Feeding Beneficiaries, as Captured in Household Surveys, by Quintile of Pretransfer Welfare

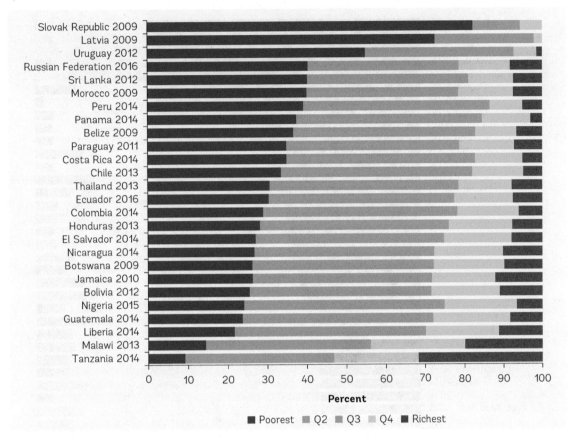

Source: ASPIRE database.
Note: The number of countries per region is as follows: total (n = 26); Latin America and the Caribbean (n = 15); Sub-Saharan Africa (n = 5); Europe and Central Asia (n = 3); Middle East and North Africa (n = 1); East Asia and Pacific (n = 1); and South Asia (n = 1). School feeding programs encompass any type of meals or food items provided at school. Beneficiaries' incidence is calculated as follows: (number of direct and indirect beneficiaries [people who live in a household where at least one member receives the transfer] in a given quintile)/(total number of direct and indirect beneficiaries). The sum of percentages across quintiles per given instrument equals 100 percent. Quintiles are calculated using per capita pretransfer welfare (income or consumption). ASPIRE = Atlas of Social Protection: Indicators of Resilience and Equity; Q = quintile.

inflation between 2007 to 2011 (Daidone et al. 2016). Therefore, having flexibility to adjust benefit levels is important to maximize positive impacts on household well-being, granted there is budget space to do so.

How large should a transfer be to achieve meaningful impacts? The higher the share of the transfers with respect to household welfare, the greater the impacts on poverty and inequality are likely to be.[20] Given budget constraints, however, larger transfers may imply fewer beneficiaries. There are concerns that larger transfer values can create disincentives to work. However, most impact evaluations have found that transfers in general do not reduce labor supply, but they do influence the allocation of labor and time. Therefore, determining the size of the transfers is usually a delicate balance

between the benefit amount needed to achieve objectives, needs for program coverage, and the available budget. Given these considerations, the evidence gathered from impact evaluations suggests that most successful cash transfers programs, for example, transfer at least 20 percent of household consumption to beneficiaries (Handa et al. 2013).

Empirical analysis indicates that the benefit level expressed as a share of beneficiary welfare among recipients varies greatly across SPL areas. Figures 3.19 and 3.20 show that on average the benefit level for social insurance programs is greater than the benefit level for SSN programs. This is expected because social insurance programs are designed to replace beneficiaries' working earnings. The global average for social insurance programs as a share of

FIGURE 3.18 Distribution of In-Kind Transfer Beneficiaries, as Captured in Household Surveys, by Quintile of Pretransfer Welfare

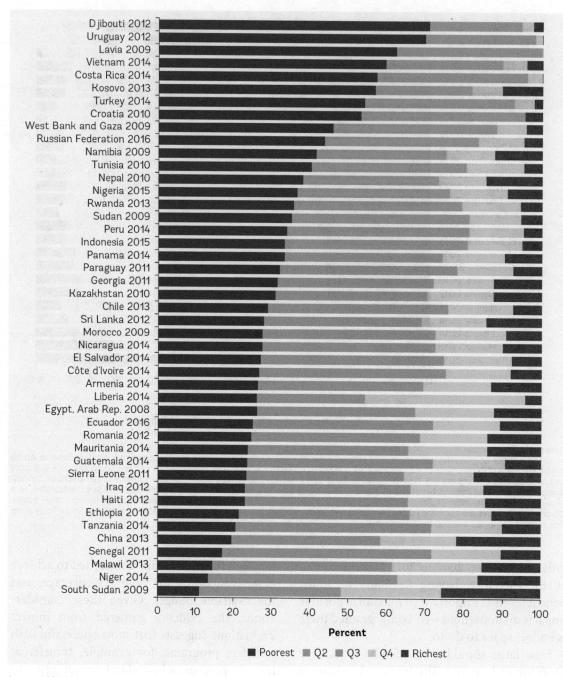

Source: ASPIRE database.

Note: The number of countries per region is as follows: total (n = 45); Sub-Saharan Africa (n = 14); Latin America and the Caribbean (n = 11); Europe and Central Asia (n = 9); Middle East and North Africa (n = 6); East Asia and Pacific (n = 3); and South Asia (n = 2). In-kind transfers include any of the following: food aid; agricultural inputs; clothes; school supplies; and building materials. Beneficiaries' incidence is calculated as follows: (number of direct and indirect beneficiaries [people who live in a household where at least one member receives the transfer] in a given quintile)/(total number of direct and indirect beneficiaries). The sum of percentages across quintiles per given instrument equals 100 percent. Quintiles are calculated using per capita pretransfer welfare (income or consumption). ASPIRE = Atlas of Social Protection: Indicators of Resilience and Equity; Q = quintile.

beneficiary welfare is 32 percent for the total population, whereas the share of SSN benefits is only 10 percent (see figure 3.19).[21]

The proportion of social insurance benefits with respect to beneficiary welfare, for the total population, increases with income, from 18 percent in low-income countries to 49 percent in high-income countries. This is not the case for SSN programs, for which the relative level of benefits differs less accros country

FIGURE 3.19 Social Protection and Labor Transfer Value Captured in Household Surveys, as a Share of Beneficiaries' Posttransfer Welfare among the Total Population

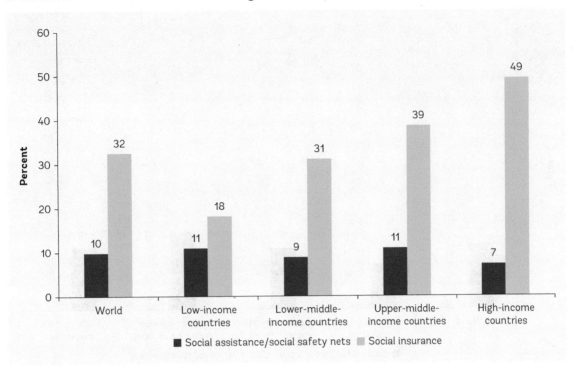

Source: ASPIRE database.
Note: The number of countries per country income group with monetary values for social assistance is as follows: total (n = 79), high-income countries (n = 5), upper-middle-income countries (n = 30), lower-middle-income countries (n = 30), and low-income countries (n = 14). The number of countries with monetary values for social insurance is as follows: total (n = 79), high-income countries (n = 6), upper-middle-income countries (n = 28); lower-middle-income countries (n = 29), and low-income countries (n = 16). Transfers as a share of a beneficiary's welfare can be generated only if monetary values are recorded in the household survey; for this reason, the sample of countries used in this figure is smaller than the one used to estimate coverage and beneficiary incidence. Labor market programs were not included because they encompass mostly active labor market programs for which only participatory variables (vs. monetary) are observed in the surveys. The sample of countries that include monetary variables (mostly for unemployment insurance) is too small to derive any meaningful conclusion (n = 18). The share of transfers is determined as follows: (transfer amount received by all direct and indirect beneficiaries in a population group)/(total welfare aggregate of the direct and indirect beneficiaries in that population group). Aggregated indicators are calculated using simple averages of country-level social assistance and social insurances transfers' shares, across country income groups. ASPIRE = Atlas of Social Protection: Indicators of Resilience and Equity.

income groups; SSN benefits as share of beneficiary welfare is 7 percent for high-income countries, for example, whereas for low-income countries and upper-middle-income countries it is 11 percent (see figure 3.19). The relatively high level of SSN benefits for low-income countries could also reflect the fact that many of the SSN programs in those countries are donor/externally funded. However, the available data do not make it possible to test this hypothesis.

SPL transfers make up a significant proportion of the welfare of individuals in the poorest quintile. For the surveys included in ASPIRE, the average share of the transfers in the welfare of the poorest quintile is 46 percent for social insurance and 19 percent for SSNs (see figure 3.20), compared with 32 and 10 percent observed in the total population (see figures 3.19). For the

poor, the share of social insurance benefits is still higher than the share of SSNs, but there is not a clear correlation between the magnitude of this share and country income groups. For example, social insurance makes up 48 percent of beneficiary welfare in low- and upper-middle-income countries, higher than the share observed for lower-middle-income countries (39 percent). Likewise, SSN programs make up 22 percent of beneficiary welfare in upper-middle-income countries, which is higher than the share in lower-middle- and high-income countries (18 percent) (see figure 3.20).

On average, SSN transfers account for 19 percent of the welfare of the poorest quintile. However, transfer levels vary greatly across SSN instruments and across countries. These differences reflect, in part, different program objectives and the degree of transfer values captured

FIGURE 3.20 Social Protection and Labor Transfer Value Captured in Household Surveys, as a Share of Beneficiaries' Posttransfer Welfare among the Poorest Quintile

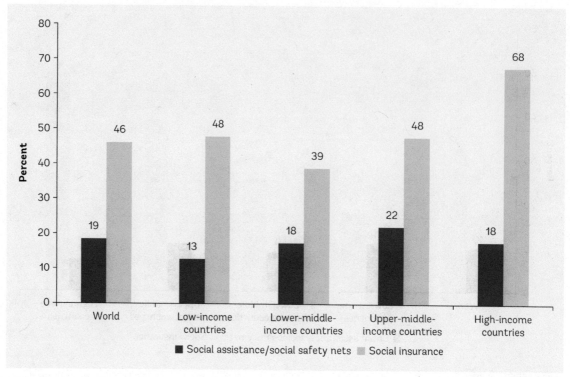

Source: ASPIRE database.

Note: The number of countries per country income group with monetary values for social assistance is as follows: total (n = 79), high-income countries (n = 5), upper-middle-income countries (n = 30), lower-middle-income countries (n = 30), and low-income countries (n = 14). The number of countries with monetary values for social insurance is as follows: total (n = 79), high-income countries (n = 6), upper-middle-income countries (n = 28), lower-middle-income countries (n = 29), and low-income countries (n = 16). Transfers as a share of a beneficiary's welfare can be generated only if monetary values are recorded in the household survey; for this reason, the sample of countries used in this figure is smaller than the one used to estimate coverage and beneficiary incidence. Labor market programs were not included because they encompass mostly active labor market programs for which only participatory variables (vs. monetary) are observed in the surveys. The sample of countries that include monetary variables (mostly for unemployment insurance) is too small to derive any meaningful conclusion (n = 18). The share of transfers is determined as follows: (transfer amount received by all direct and indirect beneficiaries in a population group)/(total welfare aggregate of the direct and indirect beneficiaries in that population group). Aggregated indicators are calculated using simple averages of country-level social assistance and social insurance transfers' shares, across country income groups. The poorest quintile is calculated using per capita posttransfer welfare (income or consumption). ASPIRE = Atlas of Social Protection: Indicators of Resilience and Equity.

in household surveys. Figures 3.21 to 3.25 illustrate the proportion of SSN benefits with respect to beneficiary welfare by type of SSN instrument and by country.[22] Social pensions and CCTs tend to make up, on average, a higher proportion of beneficiary welfare—while the share is much lower for public works, fee waivers, and targeted subsidies. However, this indicator varies greatly across countries within each SSN instrument.

On average, UCT transfers as a share of beneficiary welfare for the poorest quintile amount to 19 percent. To estimate this indicator, 52 surveys with monetary values were used out of 63 surveys with UCT information and out of a total of 79 surveys with monetary data for SSNs (see figure 3.21). As mentioned, in the case of UCTs, this indicator could be imprecise because

various cash transfers implemented with different objectives may be aggregated: for example, poverty alleviation programs and universal family allowances. However, in a few countries, a single program is included in the UCT typology; thus, results can be attributed to that particular program.

Some UCT programs with a poverty alleviation objective tend to have a higher benefit level. For example, UCT programs make up the largest share of the welfare of the poor (49 percent) in Georgia and Rwanda (figure 3.21). Several programs are aggregated into the UCT categories for Georgia, but the results are mainly driven by the Targeted Social Assistance (TSA) program.[23] In the case of Rwanda, the result corresponds to the Direct Support from the Vision 2020 Umurenge Programme (VUP),

FIGURE 3.21 Unconditional Cash Transfer Value Captured in Household Surveys, as a Share of Beneficiaries' Posttransfer Welfare among the Poorest Quintile

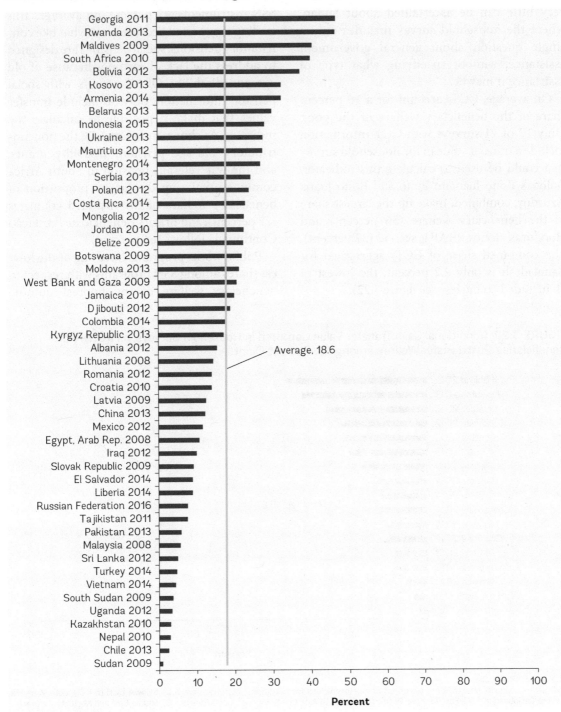

Source: ASPIRE database.
Note: The number of countries per region with monetary values for unconditional cash transfers is as follows: total (n = 52); Europe and Central Asia (n = 20); Sub-Saharan Africa (n = 10); Latin America and the Caribbean (n = 8); East Asia and Pacific (n = 5); Middle East and North Africa (n = 5); and South Asia (n = 4). Unconditional cash transfers include any of the following: poverty alleviation and emergency programs; guaranteed minimum-income programs; and universal or poverty-targeted child and family allowances. They do not include social pensions or targeted subsidies in cash. Transfers as a share of a beneficiary's welfare can be generated only if monetary values are recorded in the household survey; for this reason, the sample of countries used in this figure is smaller than the one used to estimate coverage and beneficiary incidence. The share of transfers is determined as follows: (transfer amount received by all direct and indirect beneficiaries in a population group)/(total welfare aggregate of the direct and indirect beneficiaries in that population group). Unconditional cash transfer average share is the simple average of unconditional cash transfers' shares across countries. The poorest quintile is calculated using per capita posttransfer welfare (income or consumption). ASPIRE = Atlas of Social Protection: Indicators of Resilience and Equity.

ANALYZING THE PERFORMANCE OF SOCIAL SAFETY NET PROGRAMS

the only UCT captured in the household survey. On the other side of the spectrum, very little can be ascertained about Sudan, where the household survey includes only a single question about general government assistance, without specifying what type of assistance it may be.

On average, CCTs account for a 16 percent share of the beneficiary welfare of the poor. Only 17 of 21 surveys with CCT information include a transfer value in the household survey that could be used to calculate this indicator. Bolivia's Bono Juancito Pinto and Bono Juana Azurduy, combined, make up the largest share of the beneficiary welfare (36 percent) and Honduras' Bonos PRAF is second (32 percent). The combined share of CCTs aggregated for Bangladesh is only 2.2 percent, the lowest of all included countries (see figure 3.22).

Social pensions make up a higher proportion of the welfare of the poor compared with other SSN instruments: 27 percent, on average. This finding is expected because somewhat like contributory pensions, social pensions are designed to address the lack of earnings because of old age and disability. Of 37 surveys with social pension information, only 30 include transfer values that make it possible to calculate the indicator. As shown in figure 3.23, the noncontributory old-age pension, disability grants, and the war veterans pension in South Africa combined make up the largest proportion of beneficiary welfare of the included countries (77 percent), and Brazil's Benefício de Prestação Continuada follows (66 percent).

Public works programs have one of the lowest shares among SSN programs with respect to beneficiary welfare of the poorest quintile

FIGURE 3.22 Conditional Cash Transfer Value Captured in Household Surveys, as a Share of Beneficiaries' Posttransfer Welfare among the Poorest Quintile

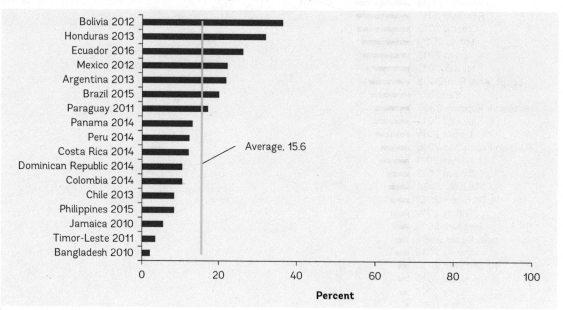

Source: ASPIRE database.

Note: The number of countries per region with monetary values for conditional cash transfers is as follows: total (n = 17), Latin America and the Caribbean (n = 14), East Asia and Pacific (n = 2), South Asia (n = 1), Sub-Saharan Africa (n = 0), Middle East and North Africa (n = 0), and Europe and Central Asia (n = 0). Conditional cash transfer programs include the following: Argentina 2013: Asignación Universal por Hijo. Bangladesh 2010: Maternity allowance, Program for the Poor Lactating, Stipend for Primary Students (MOPMED), Stipend for drop out students, Stipend for Secondary and Higher Secondary/Female Student. Bolivia 2012: Bono Juancito Pinto and Bono Juana Azurduy. Brazil 2015: Bolsa Família. Chile 2013: Subsidio Familiar (SUF), Bono de Protección Familiar y de Egreso, Bono por control del niño sano, Bono por asistencia escolar and Bono por logro escolar. Colombia 2014: Familias en Acción. Costa Rica 2014: Avancemos. Dominican Republic 2014: Solidaridad Program and other transfers. Ecuador 2016: Bono de Desarrollo Humano. Honduras 2013: Asignaciones Familiares-Bonos PRAF and otro tipo de bonos. Jamaica 2010: Program of Advancement Through Health and Education (PATH)–Child 0-71 months, 6-17 years and pregnant and lactating women. Mexico 2012: Oportunidades. Panama 2014: Red de Oportunidades. Paraguay 2011: Tekopora. Peru 2014: Programa Juntos. Philippines 2015: Pantawid Pamilyang Pilipino Program (4Ps). Timor-Leste 2011: Bolsa da Mae. Transfers as a share of a beneficiary's welfare can be generated only if monetary values are recorded in the household survey; for this reason, the sample of countries used in this figure is smaller than the one used to estimate coverage and beneficiary incidence. The share of transfers is determined as follows: (transfer amount received by all direct and indirect beneficiaries in a population group)/(total welfare aggregate of the direct and indirect beneficiaries in that population group). Conditional cash transfer average share is the simple average of conditional cash transfers' shares across countries. The poorest quintile is calculated using per capita posttransfer welfare (income or consumption). ASPIRE = Atlas of Social Protection: Indicators of Resilience and Equity.

FIGURE 3.23 Social Pensions' Value Captured in Household Surveys, as a Share of Beneficiaries' Posttransfer Welfare among the Poorest Quintile

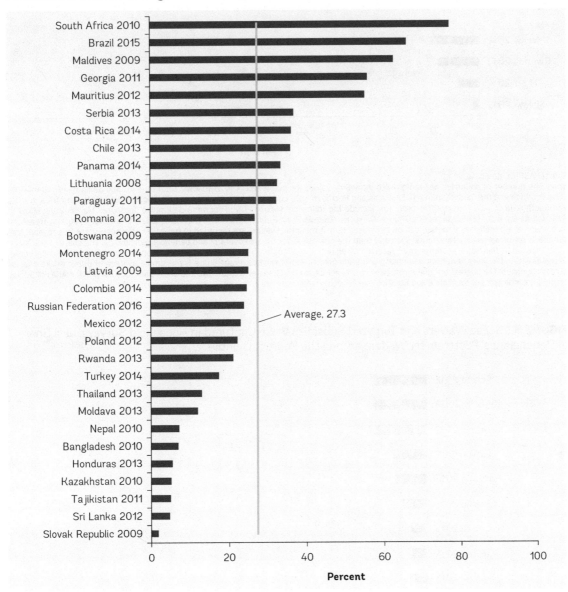

Source: ASPIRE database.
Note: The number of countries per region with monetary values for social pensions is as follows: total (n = 30), Europe and Central Asia (n = 13), Latin America and the Caribbean (n = 8), South Asia (n = 4), Sub-Saharan Africa (n = 4), East Asia and Pacific (n = 1), and Middle East and North Africa (n = 0). Social pensions include any of the following: noncontributory old-age pensions; disability pensions; and survivor pensions. Transfers as a share of a beneficiary's welfare can be generated only if monetary values are recorded in the household survey; for this reason, the sample of countries used in this figure is smaller than the one used to estimate coverage and beneficiary incidence. The share of transfers is determined as follows: (transfer amount received by all direct and indirect beneficiaries in a population group)/(total welfare aggregate of the direct and indirect beneficiaries in that population group). Social pensions average share is the simple average of social pensions' shares across countries. The poorest quintile is calculated using per capita posttransfer welfare (income or consumption). ASPIRE = Atlas of Social Protection: Indicators of Resilience and Equity.

(7 percent). However, little can be concluded from the public works average indicator because only 4 out of 10 surveys with public works information include monetary values (see figure 3.24). This indicator cannot be estimated for some flagship public works programs (for example, the Productive Safety Net Program in Ethiopia or MGNREG in India),

because they do not have monetary values in household surveys.

Fee waivers and targeted subsidies have the lowest share of beneficiary welfare among SSN programs: 6.7 percent, on average—much lower than the SSN global average of 19 percent (see figure 3.25). This finding is not surprising because fee waivers and targeted subsidies

FIGURE 3.24 Public Works' Value Captured in Household Surveys as a Share of Beneficiaries' Posttransfer Welfare among the Poorest Quintile

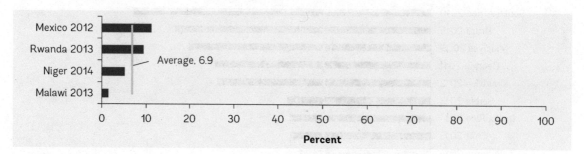

Source: ASPIRE database.
Note: The number of countries per region with monetary values for public works is as follows: total (n = 4), Sub-Saharan Africa (n = 3), Latin America and the Caribbean (n = 1), East Asia and Pacific (n = 0), Europe and Central Asia (n = 0), Middle East and North Africa (n = 0), and South Asia (n = 0). Public works programs include the following: Mexico 2012: Programa de Empleo Temporal. Malawi 2013: MASAF, PWP, Inputs for Work Program. Niger 2014: Public works. Rwanda 2013: Public works from the Vision 2020 Umurenge Program. Transfers as a share of a beneficiary's welfare can be generated only if monetary values are recorded in the household survey; for this reason, the sample of countries used in this figure is smaller than the one used to estimate coverage and beneficiary incidence. The share of transfers is determined as follows: (transfer amount received by all direct and indirect beneficiaries in a population group)/(total welfare aggregate of the direct and indirect beneficiaries in that population group). Public works average share is the simple average of public works' shares across countries. The poorest quintile is calculated using per capita posttransfer welfare (income or consumption). ASPIRE = Atlas of Social Protection: Indicators of Resilience and Equity.

FIGURE 3.25 Fee Waivers and Targeted Subsidies Value Captured in Household Surveys, as a Share of Beneficiaries' Posttransfer Welfare among the Poorest Quintile

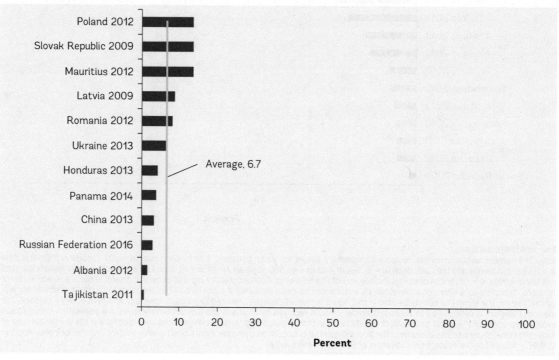

Source: ASPIRE database.
Note: The number of countries per region with monetary values for few waivers and targeted subsidies is as follows: total (n = 12); Europe and Central Asia (n = 8); Latin America and the Caribbean (n = 2); East Asia and Pacific (n = 1); Sub-Saharan Africa (n = 1); Middle East and North Africa (n = 0); and South Asia (n = 0). Fee waivers and targeted subsidies include any of the following: food, energy products, education, utilities, housing or transportation fees waivers to specific households, or discounted below the market cost. They do not include health benefits or subsidies. Transfers as a share of a beneficiary's welfare can be generated only if monetary values are recorded in the household survey; for this reason, the sample of countries used in this figure is smaller than the one used to estimate coverage and beneficiary incidence. The share of transfers is determined as follows: (transfer amount received by all direct and indirect beneficiaries in a population group)/(total welfare aggregate of the direct and indirect beneficiaries in that population group). Fee waivers and targeted subsidies average share is the simple average of these programs' shares across countries. The poorest quintile is calculated using per capita posttransfer welfare (income or consumption). ASPIRE = Atlas of Social Protection: Indicators of Resilience and Equity.

included under this category are typically aimed at helping the poor offset the cost of some services rather than support main earnings. In addition, the values captured in surveys and used to build this indicator are only a subset of this type of benefits: merely subsidies paid in cash. Many of these benefits are, by design, in the form of fee waivers, and thus monetary values are not available in the surveys. This indicator was calculated using only 12 out of 24 surveys with fee waivers and targeted subsidy information.

WHAT ARE THE POVERTY AND INEQUALITY IMPACTS OF SOCIAL SAFETY NET PROGRAMS?

This section provides an analysis of the ability of SSN monetary transfers to reduce poverty and inequality. The reduction in poverty and inequality is simulated by comparing beneficiaries' welfare recorded in the survey before and after SSN transfers. Using information from surveys, the analysis computes what household per capita income or consumption would be without SSN transfers (see box 3.2). In other words, the transfer value is subtracted from the observed welfare (posttransfer welfare) to determine who would fall into poverty (using the absolute or relative poverty lines) if the transfer is eliminated (pretransfer welfare). The proportion of individuals who are lifted out of poverty as a direct effect of the transfer is estimated and illustrated in figure 3.26, along with the poverty gap reduction.[24]

On the basis of the information observed in household surveys, the analysis shows that SSN

BOX 3.2 Measuring the Impact of Social Protection and Labor Programs

Household surveys provide a unique opportunity to measure the impact of the social protection and labor (SPL) programs on poverty or inequality because they contain information on the household aggregated income or consumption (welfare). This information makes it possible to determine, in each country, who the poor are. To allow international comparability, the Atlas of Social Protection: Indicators of Resilience and Equity (ASPIRE) database adopts two measures of poverty: the international absolute poverty line of US$1.90 a day per capita in purchasing power parity (PPP) terms; and a relative poverty line set at the bottom 20 percent of the pretransfer welfare distribution.

This chapter measures impacts on poverty and inequality by comparing households' per capita welfare before and after the transfers. For example, assume that the threshold for the bottom 20 percent in a given country is US$2.50 PPP per capita per day. The survey reports that a household has a per capita income (or consumption) of US$3.00 PPP a day, which includes a transfer of US$1.00 PPP a day. The US$3.00 PPP welfare level constitutes the posttransfer welfare for that household. Then the analysis subtracts the transfer from that welfare (3.00 − 1.00 = 2.00). The US$2.00 PPP a day amount constitutes the pretransfer welfare. Because US$2.00 is lower than the quintile threshold of US$2.50, it can be determined that this household was lifted out of poverty thanks to the transfers. By replicating this calculation for the universe of households/individuals receiving transfers and applying the population expansion factors, the book is able to estimate the direct poverty and inequality reduction rates from the transfers for any given country.

This chapter uses three indicators to measure impacts on poverty and inequality: poverty headcount, poverty gap, and inequality reductions (in percent or relative terms). Poverty headcount provides the number of people living under the poverty line in a given country. The poverty headcount reduction is the percentage reduction in poverty because of the transfer. However, not all program beneficiaries become nonpoor after receiving a transfer; this depends on their position under the poverty line and if the transfer helped the beneficiary reach or surpass the poverty line. For those who do not overcome poverty, the simple headcount does not provide information on how much "less poor" beneficiaries are after the transfer. For this reason, the poverty gap is an important indicator to estimate the depth of poverty or how far below, on average, the welfare of poor individuals is from the poverty line. The poverty gap reduction thus provides information on the ability of SPL programs to bridge this gap. The Gini coefficient measures the inequality among values of the welfare distribution. Inequality reduction thus provides the percentage reduction in the Gini index because of the SPL transfer (Yemtsov et al., forthcoming).

transfers are making a substantial contribution in the fight against poverty. Whether an absolute poverty line (measured as US$1.90 per capita per day in purchasing power parity [PPP] terms) or a relative poverty line (measured in terms of the poorest 20 percent) is used, the analysis suggests that individuals are escaping poverty or decreasing their depth of poverty because of the SSN transfers.[25] For the 79 countries that have monetary information, transfers reduce the incidence of absolute poverty (US$1.90 PPP per day) by 36 percent, whereas relative poverty (the bottom 20 percent) is reduced by 8 percent (see figure 3.26).

On average, SSN transfers are reducing the poverty gap more than the poverty headcount. In other words, even if SSN transfers are not lifting the poor and near-poor above the poverty line, they significantly reduce the poverty gap. As shown in figure 3.26, SSN transfers reduce the absolute poverty gap by 45 percent and the relative poverty gap by 16 percent.

These results are remarkable considering that these figures are underestimated because household surveys do not capture the whole universe of SSN programs implemented in those countries. Therefore, it can be inferred that the real impacts are likely to be even larger.

The reductions in the poverty headcount, poverty gap, and inequality by SSN transfers are observed in all country income groups. In the sample of 79 surveys, the relative poverty headcount is reduced by 8 percent, the poverty gap by 16 percent, and the Gini inequality index by 2 percent (see figure 3.27). Across country income groups, the average reduction in relative poverty headcount is only 2 percent in low-income countries, 7 percent in lower-middle-income countries, 11 percent in upper-middle-income countries, and 15 percent in high-income countries. In terms of the poverty gap, the average reduction is 3 percent for low-income countries, 14 percent for lower-middle-income countries, 21 percent for

FIGURE 3.26 World Reductions in Poverty from Social Safety Net Transfers, as Captured in Household Surveys, as a Share of Pretransfer Indicator Levels, by Relative and Absolute Poverty Lines

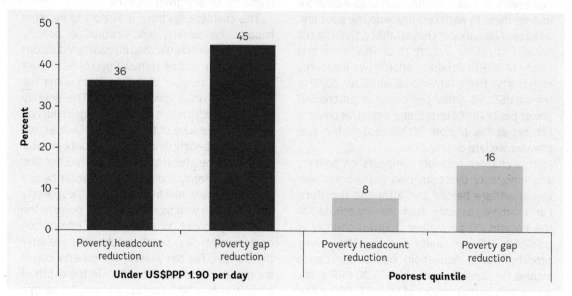

Source: ASPIRE database.
Note: The number of countries per region with monetary values for social safety nets is as follows: world (n = 79); Sub-Saharan Africa (n = 23); Europe and Central Asia (n = 20); Latin America and the Caribbean (n = 16); East Asia and Pacific (n = 10); Middle East and North Africa (n = 6); and South Asia (n = 4). This figure uses a relative measure of poverty defined as the poorest 20 percent of the welfare distribution (income or consumption) and absolute measure of poverty defined as US$1.90 PPP per day. Impacts on poverty and inequality can be estimated only if monetary values are recorded in the household survey; for this reason, the sample of countries used in this figure is smaller than the one used to estimate coverage and beneficiary incidence. Percentages of poverty and inequality reduction are calculated as follows: (poverty headcount pre-transfer – poverty headcount posttransfer)/(poverty headcount pretransfer). Same calculations apply for poverty gap percentage reductions. Aggregated indicators are calculated using simple averages of country-level percentage reductions of the indicator across country income groups. The reductions in poverty are underestimated because ASPIRE does not include data for every single country in the country income groups, and even for a given country the survey does not include all existing social safety net programs or provide monetary values for them. For example, India and the impact of its flagship program MNREGA are not included in the calculation because only participatory information is available for the program. ASPIRE = Atlas of Social Protection: Indicators of Resilience and Equity; PPP = purchasing power parity.

FIGURE 3.27 Reductions in Poverty and Inequality from Social Safety Net Transfers, as Captured in Household Surveys, as a Share of Pretransfer Indicator Levels, by Country Income Group Using Relative Poverty Line

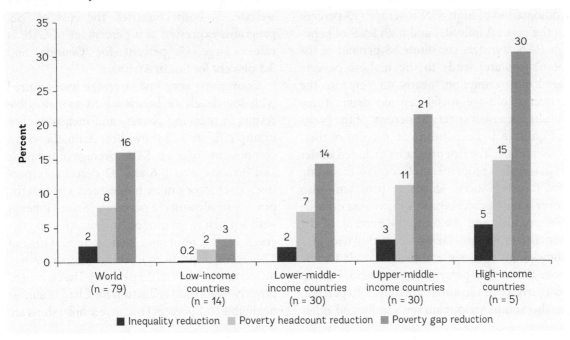

Source: ASPIRE database.
Note: The total number of countries per country income group included in the analysis appears in parentheses. This figure uses a relative measure of poverty defined as the poorest 20 percent of the welfare distribution (income or consumption). Impacts on poverty and inequality can be estimated only if monetary values are recorded in the household survey; for this reason, the sample of countries used in this figure is smaller than the one used to estimate coverage and beneficiary incidence. Percentages of poverty and inequality reduction are calculated as follows: (poverty headcount pretransfer – poverty headcount posttransfer)/(poverty headcount pretransfer). The same calculations apply for the Gini index and poverty gap percentage reductions. Aggregated indicators are calculated using simple averages of country-level percentage reduction of the indicator across country income groups. The reductions in poverty and inequality are underestimated because ASPIRE does not include data for every single country in the country income groups, and even for a given country the survey does not include all existing social safety net programs or provide monetary values for them. ASPIRE = Atlas of Social Protection: Indicators of Resilience and Equity.

upper-middle-income countries, and 30 percent for high-income countries. The Gini inequality index is less affected by SSN transfers, but reductions are still observed, ranging from 0.2 percent in low-income countries to 5 percent in high-income countries.

The lower reduction in poverty and inequality observed for low-income countries is likely driven by several factors. First, fewer low-income countries have recent household survey data available compared with other country income groups. Second, of the 22 low-income country surveys included in ASPIRE, only 14 surveys include monetary variables for SSN programs. Third, many low-income country surveys neither capture SSN-specific program information nor include the universe of programs that exist in the country. And fourth, less than 10 percent of the global population live in low-income countries; therefore, the number of individuals moving out of poverty (in percent terms) is

lower than in other country income groups.[26] See appendix F.3 for a list of poverty and inequality reductions from SSN programs by country.

WHAT FACTORS AFFECT THE IMPACT OF SOCIAL SAFETY NET TRANSFERS ON POVERTY AND INEQUALITY?

The extent to which SSN transfers have an impact on poverty and inequality depends on factors such as program coverage, transfer level, and the beneficiary/benefit incidence. Policy makers need to pay attention to the interaction of these factors when designing policies to reduce poverty/inequality. Figures 3.28 and 3.29 explore the reductions in poverty and inequality achieved by each country, given their degree of coverage of the poor and benefits levels.

The analysis reveals, in general, that very high coverage levels paired with high benefit levels lead to higher outcomes in poverty and inequality reduction. For example, Georgia and

South Africa display the highest poverty head-count reduction using the poorest quintile as the poverty measure (see figure 3.28). Georgia's combination of high SSN coverage (93 percent of the poorest quintile) and high level of bene-fits (SSN transfers constitute 68 percent of the poor's welfare) leads to the highest poverty headcount reduction, nearly 43 percent. The universal old-age social pension drives these results because it covers 81 percent of the poor-est quintile and constitutes 56 percent of their total welfare. The five programs included under cash transfers programs for Georgia—including the Targeted Social Assistance program—also cover a high percentage of the poorest quintile (46 percent) and make up 49 percent of the beneficiary welfare. Likewise, South Africa also shows high coverage and benefit levels for the poor (96 and 72 percent, respectively), leading to a poverty headcount reduction of 40 percent. In the South African survey, family and other

allowances are among the SSN benefits with high coverage of the poor; however, social pen-sions constitute higher shares of beneficiary welfare. In both countries, the cost of SSN programs expressed as a percentage of GDP is rather large (7 percent for Georgia and 3.3 percent for South Africa).

Conversely, very low coverage levels paired with low levels of benefits lead to negligible results in reducing poverty and inequality. For example, figure 3.28 shows how Armenia, with a combination of lower SSN coverage of the poor and benefits level (46 and 32 percent, respec-tively), achieves a more modest reduction in the poverty headcount (12 percent). SSNs in Liberia, with a much more modest combination of cov-erage of the poor and benefit level (10 and 17 percent, respectively), achieve a small poverty headcount reduction (2.5 percent). The estimated poverty headcount reduction for Chad is almost negligible (0.1 percent) because scholarships are

FIGURE 3.28 Poverty Headcount Reduction from Coverage and Level of Social Assistance Benefits for the Poorest Quintile, as Captured in Household Surveys

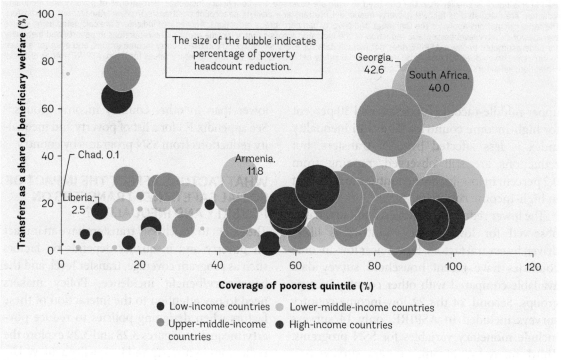

Source: ASPIRE database.
Note: The number of countries with monetary values for social safety nets is as follows: world (n = 79), high-income countries (n = 5), upper-middle-income countries (n = 30), lower-middle-income countries (n = 30), and low-income countries (n = 14). This figure uses a relative measure of poverty defined as the poorest 20 percent of the welfare distribution (income or consumption). Poverty headcount reductions can be estimated only if monetary values are recorded in the household survey; for this reason, the sample of countries used in this figure is smaller than the one used to estimate coverage and beneficiary incidence. Percentages of poverty headcount reduction are calculated as follows: (poverty headcount pretransfer − poverty headcount posttransfer)/(poverty headcount pretransfer). Poverty headcount reductions are underestimated because ASPIRE does not include data for every single country in the country income groups, and even for a given country the survey may not include all existing social safety net programs or provide monetary values for those programs. ASPIRE = Atlas of Social Protection: Indicators of Resilience and Equity.

the only SSN program captured in the survey. These scholarships have very low coverage of the poor (0.2 percent), although their contribution to beneficiary welfare is 23 percent.

In terms of the poverty gap reduction, the same interplay between coverage and benefit size is observed. In third place behind Georgia and South Africa, Mauritius also shows high coverage and benefit levels for the poorest quintile (84 percent and 55 percent, respectively), leading to a poverty gap reduction of 61 percent. The survey includes monetary information for eight programs, of which the noncontributory basic retirement pension has the highest coverage of the poor. Mauritius also reports high social spending according the administrative database (3.5 percent of GDP). In Poland, SSN programs captured in the household surveys report a relatively high level of coverage of the poor (65 percent), but the transfer as a share of beneficiary welfare is smaller

(27 percent), producing a more modest estimated poverty gap reduction (42 percent). In Montenegro, SSN programs provide modest coverage of the poor (25 percent) and represent a modest share of beneficiary welfare (28 percent); thus, Montenegro achieves a modest poverty gap reduction (23 percent). In the Maldives, the household survey includes only two SSN programs: unspecified government transfers and social pensions. Even though social pensions have a high benefit level, driving the Maldives' SSN average benefit to 76 percent of the beneficiary welfare, the coverage of both types of programs is small (15 percent) and thus the poverty gap reduction is modest (28 percent). In Burkina Faso, the poverty gap reduction is 0.1 percent, mostly because the survey does not capture a monetary value for government transfers, meaning that the estimation rests only on information on scholarships and other general transfers (figure 3.29).

FIGURE 3.29 Poverty Gap Reduction from Coverage and Level of Social Assistance Benefits for the Poorest Quintile, as Captured in Household Surveys

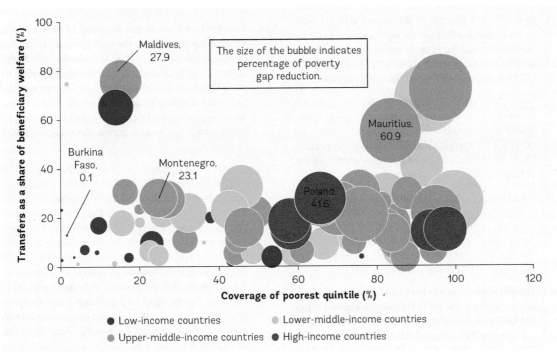

Source: ASPIRE database.
Note: The number of countries with monetary values for social safety nets is as follows: world (n = 79); high-income countries (n = 5); upper-middle-income countries (n = 30); lower-middle-income countries (n = 30); and low-income countries (n = 14). This figure uses a relative measure of poverty defined as the poorest 20 percent of the welfare distribution (in terms of income or consumption). Poverty gap reductions can be estimated only if monetary values are recorded in the household survey; for this reason, the sample of countries used in this figure (n = 79) is smaller than the one used to estimate coverage and beneficiary incidence (n = 96). Percentages of poverty gap reduction are calculated as follows: (poverty gap pretransfer − poverty gap post transfer)/(poverty gap pretransfer). Poverty gap reductions are underestimated because ASPIRE does not include data for every single country in the country income groups, and even for a given country, the survey may not include all existing social safety net programs or provide monetary values for those programs. ASPIRE = Atlas of Social Protection: Indicators of Resilience and Equity.

NOTES

1. SPL programs encompass social safety nets/social assistance, social insurance, and labor market programs.

2. For example, the household survey for El Salvador includes programs under the three areas of SPL. In this case, even though the most iconic programs in the country such as the CCT and social pensions are not adequately captured in the household survey, the in-kind transfers programs as well as the school feeding program drive the coverage of SSN programs up to 53 percent of the total population and 72 percent of the poorest quintile.

3. A source of potential bias is the fact that household surveys do not collect information from all social protection programs implemented in a country, but big flagship programs are likely to be captured.

4. A factor influencing this low coverage is that very little information on labor market interventions is captured in most household income and expenditure surveys; thus, it is difficult to draw meaningful conclusions regarding this program type.

5. The terms "social safety nets" and "social assistance" are used interchangeably in this book.

6. See http://datatopics.worldbank.org/aspire/~/documentation.

7. Aggregated variables with too few observations (less than 0.5 percent of the survey sample) were excluded because they are not representative to derive meaningful results. For example, the Livelihood Empowerment Against Poverty (LEAP), Ghana's UCT program, was excluded under this criterion.

8. Under ASPIRE, UCTs encompass interventions such as poverty alleviation or emergency programs, guaranteed minimum-income programs, and universal or poverty-targeted child and family allowances; UCTs do not include social pensions, public works, or targeted subsidies paid in cash.

9. The Child Money Program was introduced in Mongolia as a targeted program in 2005 and became universal in July of 2006. Although the program was discontinued temporarily, it was reintroduced in October 2012, with a benefit level of US$14.72 per month per child (Yeung and Howes 2015).

10. The BR1M program was launched in 2012 to provide a single transfer to the poor. Households earning below RM3,000 monthly receive RM1,200; households earning between RM3,001 amd RM4,000 monthly receive RM900; and single individuals, 21 years and older, earning less than RM2,000 per month, receive RM450 (BR1M's official website: https://ebr1m.hasil.gov.my). The Malaysian Household Income Survey does not identify the name of the cash transfer program in the questionnaire. However, it is likely capturing the BR1M program.

11. In many countries, elderly people tend to live within larger extended multigenerational families, whose members benefit indirectly from social pensions. Moreover, these pensions provide sizable benefits, and because the measure of welfare used in this book is pretransfer, many of the recipient families of social pensions tend to concentrate in the lowest quintile once this benefit is subtracted. This helps explain the high coverage of all the poor by social pensions in some countries featured in figure 3.6.

12. For this analysis, universal health schemes and universal general price subsidies are not included (most fuel subsidies or price support schemes for food are excluded). Instead, for commodities, only those subsidies that are targeted to specific individuals and families are included. One form of targeted subsidy is a lifeline (lower) tariff for a limited quantity of electricity, which is available only for eligible groups (as in Albania or the Russian Federation).

13. The Rastra Program, formerly called *Beras untuk Rakyat Miskin (Raskin)*, is a rice subsidy introduced in 1998 as an emergency food security program. It delivers rice for purchase at subsidized prices and prioritizes poor and near-poor households (World Bank 2012). Even though the program reports the highest coverage of the poor, the benefit has been diluted to 4 kg per household on average from the promised 15 kg. In light of this, the government is proceeding with significant reforms.

14. Benefits incidence is not included in this analysis because information on the transfer value is needed to estimate it. Because not all the surveys include the monetary value of the transfers, the report prefers to use a larger sample of surveys by analyzing only the distribution of beneficiaries. If the value of the transfers is similar across beneficiaries, the distribution of beneficiaries and benefit across income groups will be similar.

15. Whether a program is propoor can be determined by the Coady-Grosh-Hoddinott (CGH) indicator, which divides the share of the beneficiaries/benefits belonging to a certain population group (for example, the bottom 20 percent) by the population share of this group. If the result is higher than 1, the program is considered progressive toward this group. For instance, if the bottom 20 percent of the population accounts for 40 percent of beneficiaries, this indicator will be equal to 2, indicating that the program focuses on the poor. In the case of a universal program where benefits are equally distributed, the CGH indicator will be 1.

16. It is particularly interesting to observe that some programs with similar design features and institutional structures—such as the Family Material Support (MOP) and Family Allowances Program in Montenegro and Serbia, which have the same legacy of the Federal Republic of Yugoslavia, and preserve some core

features—have quite different distributions of beneficiaries. That implies that implementation matters a lot in how well the program is capable of targeting the poor.

17. In the case of Djibouti, these food distribution programs focus on rural areas where over half the population lives in poverty, according to the survey.

18. Transfers as a share of beneficiaries' welfare is estimated as the amount of transfers received by a quintile divided by the total income or consumption of beneficiaries in that quintile.

19. The poverty gap is the distance below the poverty line and the average income of the poor. It is typically expressed as the percentage shortfall in income of the poor with respect to the poverty line.

20. At the same time, the greater is the concern about potential disincentives to work.

21. To assess benefit levels, information on the actual value of the transfers is needed. Therefore, only 79 out of 96 surveys available in ASPIRE were analyzed because not all surveys include monetary information.

22. This analysis was done only for the types of programs that involve a monetary transfer. Thus, the indicator was not calculated for school feeding programs nor for in-kind transfers. The sample of countries is also different per SSN instrument, compared with the sample used for coverage and beneficiary incidence, depending on the availability of data about the transfer value in the survey for each of the SSN instruments analyzed.

23. These programs are Internally Displaced Persons Assistance, social assistance to multichildren families, social assistance to orphans, social assistance to children with disabilities, and Targeted Social Assistance (TSA).

24. Therefore, this is a first-level approximation of the direct impact of the monetary transfers observed in the surveys. It also does not assess any medium- or long-term effects of SSN transfers on their specific objectives, which are better measured by impact evaluations.

25. The absolute poverty line of US$1.90 PPP a day may not constitute a meaningful standard for many high-income countries that have a very small population, or may not even have anybody living under that threshold. In fact, countries such as Belarus, Croatia, Lithuania, Montenegro, and Romania are able to fully eradicate their poverty headcount at US$1.90 PPP a day, according to information provided by household surveys (see appendix F).

26. There are 3 billion people living in lower-middle-income countries and only 659 million in low-income countries. In lower-middle-income countries, 500 million people live below the US$1.90 PPP a day threshold, which is more than 75 percent of the total population of low-income countries. In India alone, 285 million people are living on less than US$1.90 PPP a day, as well as 120 million in Nigeria, and 49 million in China. In other words, most of the world's poor live outside low-income countries.

REFERENCES

Andrews, C., C. Del Ninno, C. Rodriguez Alas, and K. Subbarao. 2012. *Public Works as a Safety Net: Design, Evidence, and Implementation.* Directions in Development. Washington, DC: World Bank.

ASPIRE (Atlas of Social Protection: Indicators of Resilience and Equity). 2017. Database, World Bank, Washington, DC. http://datatopics.worldbank.org/aspire/.

Daidone, S., S. Asfaw, B. Davis, S. Handa, and P. Winters. 2016. "The Household and Individual-Level Economic Impacts of Cash Transfer Programmes in Sub-Saharan Africa. Synthesis Report." Food and Agricultural Organization of the United Nations, Rome.

Garcia, M., and C. Moore. 2012. *The Cash Dividend: The Rise of Cash Transfer Programs in Sub-Saharan Africa.* Directions in Development. Washington, DC: World Bank.

Handa, S., M. Park, R. Osei Darko, I. Osei-Akoto, B. Davis, and S. Daidone. 2013. "Livelihood Empowerment against Poverty Program: Impact Evaluation." Carolina Population Center, University of North Carolina at Chapel Hill.

Schüring, E. 2010. "Strings Attached or Loose Ends? The Role of Conditionality in Zambia's Social Cash Transfer Scheme." Maastricht Graduate School of Governance, Maastricht, Netherlands.

World Bank. 2012. "Raskin Subsidized Rice Delivery. Social Assistance Program and Public Expenditure Review No. 3." World Bank, Washington, DC.

Yemtsov, R. M. Honorati, B. Evans, Z. Sajaia, and M. Lokshin. Forthcoming. "An Analytical Approach to Assessing Social Protection Effectiveness: Concepts and Applications." World Bank, Washington, DC.

Yeung, Y., and S. Howes. 2015. "Resources-to-Cash: A Cautionary Tale from Mongolia." Development Policy Centre Discussion Paper #42, Crawford School of Public Policy, The Australian National University, Canberra., Australia.

A defining characteristic of the poor in Sub-Saharan Africa is they are trapped in low-productivity or low-paying jobs. An analysis using a sample of 28 low-income-country household surveys from the Atlas of Social Protection: Indicators of Resilience and Equity (ASPIRE) found that 73 percent of individuals in the poorest 20 percent are employed, of which 69 percent work in agriculture.[1] Of those employed, 49 percent are self-employed, whereas 30 percent are unpaid workers. Furthermore, many of the poor live in a context of poorly functioning or nonexistent labor and insurance/credit markets that affect household economic decisions (Handa et al. 2017). In this context, cash transfers may help households overcome these market failures and may enable them to spend more and to make productive investments. This in turn may generate household-level multiplier effects (Daidone et al. 2016), as well as spillover and income multiplier effects in local communities (Daidone et al. 2015; Thome et al. 2016).

This highlight summarizes new research on the broader impacts of unconditional cash transfers, particularly regarding economic impacts and productive inclusion in the context of Sub-Saharan Africa. The discussion draws largely on papers that synthesize and analyze the results from evaluations in eight Sub-Saharan African countries as part of The Transfer Project[2] and the From Protection to Production (PtoP) Project.[3,4] The narrative is complemented with the results of a metadata analysis of the impact evaluations available for 20 programs in 10 African countries (Ralston, Andrews, and Hsiao 2017); as well as a systematic review of 56 cash transfers programs (including unconditional cash transfers, conditional cash transfers, noncontributory social pensions, and enterprise grants) in low- and middle-income countries from 2000 to 2015 (Bastagli et al. 2016).

Findings from these evaluations consistently show statistically positive impacts of cash transfer programs on productive outcomes such as crop production, productive investments, employment, and more effective risk-coping mechanisms. The findings include income-multiplier effects for beneficiary and nonbeneficiary households and local economies. They debunk misconceptions like cash transfers being handouts that promote dependency and induce wasteful consumption. On the contrary, cash transfers have economic impacts beyond their intended objectives that strengthen beneficiary livelihoods and, if complemented with other instruments, can be leveraged to produce long-lasting benefits for beneficiaries, paving their way out of poverty.

WHAT ARE THE ECONOMIC IMPACTS OF CASH TRANSFERS ON BENEFICIARIES AND THEIR HOUSEHOLDS?

Household Production

Impact evaluations indicate that cash transfers increase household crop production, lead to changes in types of crops cultivated, and increase consumption and sales of homegrown production. The evaluation of programs in seven Sub-Saharan African countries found significant impacts in all these areas, even though their magnitude varied across countries (Daidone et al. 2016). Crop production increased in Zambia and Lesotho. The value of the overall production in Zambia almost doubled, boosting postprogram per capita consumption to a level 25 percent higher than the transfer itself (Davis et al. 2016). In Ethiopia, Malawi, and Zimbabwe, transfers led to changes in the types of crops cultivated. In Kenya and Malawi-Mchinji, the cash transfer increased consumption of the home-grown production (Davis et al. 2016).

Consumption and Productive Investments

Robust evidence indicates that households use transfers for basic needs and productive investments, dispelling myths of profligate spending. A meta-analysis conducted on impacts for seven African countries found that on average, household consumption increases by US$0.74 for each US$1 transferred (Ralston, Andrews, and Hsiao 2017). The magnitude of this impact varies across countries, with the largest impact experienced by programs targeted at the poor: the Malawi Social Cash Transfer Program reports the largest consumption impact, at 179 percent of the transfer value. In addition, a review of 19 programs and 11 studies using data from Africa, Asia, and Latin America found no evidence that transfers, conditional or unconditional, increase the use of alcohol and tobacco (Evans and Popova 2014).

The review by Bastagli et al. (2016) found that cash transfers improved household consumption in 25 of 35 studies looking at this effect. Their review also found an increase in livestock ownership/purchase, agricultural assets and inputs, and savings (although not for all programs or for all types of livestock, assets, or inputs). The Transfer Project found that five out of eight programs had significant impacts on the increase in livestock ownership. The effect of households investing in diverse types of animals was large in Malawi and Zambia, whereas more limited effects were observed in Kenya, Lesotho, and Zimbabwe, where small livestock were acquired. Impacts were not found in Ghana. The meta-data analysis by Ralston, Andrews, and Hsiao (2017) confirms these findings by estimating a combined average increase of 34 percent in livestock ownership across programs in seven countries (four were significant).

Most programs had significant impacts on the purchase/use of agricultural inputs such as seeds, fertilizer, and pesticides, although the magnitude of these impacts varied across countries. In terms of agricultural assets (for example, axes, hoes, picks, and other tools), positive impacts were observed in Ethiopia, Malawi, Zambia, and Zimbabwe. Impacts were not observed in Kenya, Lesotho, and Ghana. Even though all impacts were not always significant, all countries reported positive significant results for population subgroups, type of animal, or asset (Daidone et al. 2016; Davis et al. 2016; Handa et al. 2017).

Labor and Time Allocation

Impact evaluations generally show no evidence that cash transfers reduce the labor supply. In the African context, transfers have an impact on household decision making on labor allocation and time use, in terms of switching between different income-generating activities or between labor, domestic tasks, or leisure (Handa et al. 2017). In other words, cash transfers give households flexibility to allocate time and labor to these activities, leading to a switch from casual agricultural labor to on-farm labor (David et al. 2016). As a female beneficiary in Malawi expressed with respect to doing casual labor or *ganyu*: "I used to be a slave to *ganyu* but now I'm a bit free" (Barca

et al. 2015). In the context of informal rural labor markets, casual wage labor is a last-resort activity that households use to survive or when liquid funds are scarce. Therefore, for beneficiaries to increase work and time on their own farms is a preferred activity and a sign of improved economic conditions. These findings are consistent with other studies that have concluded that transfers do not reduce the labor supply or create dependency. For example, Banerjee et al. (2015), after conducting seven randomized control trials of cash transfers programs in six countries (Honduras, Indonesia, Mexico, Morocco, Nicaragua, and the Philippines), found no evidence that cash transfers have impacts on either the propensity to work or the overall number of hours worked.

Risk Management and Coping Strategies

Cash transfers, impact evaluations find, allow beneficiary households to manage risk more effectively by diversifying income-generating activities, increasing savings, and reducing detrimental coping strategies. In Zambia, the share of beneficiary households running nonfarm enterprises increased 16 percentage points, and the businesses reported 1.4 more months in operation, compared with the control group, after receiving cash transfers. In Zimbabwe, there was an increase of 5 percentage points in the share of households operating these businesses and an increase of 5 percentage points in the share reporting profits. Other countries do not report significant results (Daidone et al. 2016). In Ghana, a qualitative evaluation finds evidence of increased petty trading of small amounts of kerosene and the sale of cooked food (Barca et al. 2015).

Cash transfers often lead to increasing savings. Ghana and Zambia reported increases in savings of 11 and 24 percentage points, respectively. In Ethiopia, Ghana, and Malawi transfers led to a reduction of loans and debt repayments (Daidone et al. 2016). In Zambia and Zimbabwe, transfers contributed to an increase in households' creditworthiness; however, households were still risk averse and reluctant to take on new credit (Davis et al. 2016). Ralston, Andrews, and Hsiao (2017) found that beneficiary households are 20 percentage points more likely to save compared with the control group; this translates into an average increase of 92 percent in the number of households setting aside savings.

Studies also report a decrease in negative risk-coping strategies, such as distress sales of assets, begging, eating less, or putting children to work. Ethiopia, Lesotho, and Malawi reported less begging and changes in eating habits. Beneficiary households were less likely to take children out of school in almost all the countries analyzed by Davis et al. (2016) and Daidone et al. (2016). As an elderly beneficiary in Ethiopia said: "Hunger pushed me to do this [beg]. Since I started to receive the cash transfer I no longer have to. I feel happier" (Barca et al. 2015).

Qualitative evaluations also show that cash transfers programs increase social capital. They help beneficiaries reenter social networks, strengthening informal social protection systems and risk-sharing management arrangements (Davis et al. 2016). The very poor faced fewer stigmas, participated more fully in the community, and supported other households or institutions because of the transfers.

Spillover Effects in Local Economies

Cash transfer programs not only bring economic impacts to beneficiary individuals and households but also can create spillover effects that benefit nonbeneficiary households and local economies. When beneficiaries spend transfers, cash is injected into local markets, potentially creating income multipliers. That is, for each US$1 transferred to a beneficiary household, the total income of the local economy may increase by more than US$1. These spillovers are difficult to measure by experimental methods because they are second-order impacts that are diffused over a population greater than the beneficiary population (Thome et al. 2016). However, researchers developed the Local Economy-Wide Impact Evaluation (LEWIE) to simulate the effect of cash transfers in local economies. LEWIE measures the impact of cash transfers on the production activities of beneficiary and non-beneficiary households, how these effects change during programs scaled up, and the reasons these effects happen (Taylor 2012).[5]

In Ethiopia, Ghana, Kenya, Lesotho, Malawi, Zambia, and Zimbabwe, cash transfers have significant spillovers in the local economy and nominal income multipliers. Using the LEWIE model, income multipliers range from 1.27 in Malawi to 2.52 in Ethiopia (Hintalo region). The income spillover (multiplier minus 1) indicates that for every US$1 transferred to the beneficiary household, the local economy gains an additional US$0.27–1.25 (Thome et al. 2016).

After considering potential inflation, simulations find that the real income multiplier, even though lower than the nominal multiplier, is still greater than 1 for all seven countries. If producers in the local economy face constraints to increase production in response to the higher demand of goods led by the transfers, this may put upward pressure on prices and lower income multipliers. However, even after accounting for inflation, income multipliers are still greater than 1, ranging from 1.08 in Kenya (Nyanza Province) to 1.81 in Ethiopia (Hintalo). The elasticity of the supply of local goods largely drives the differences between real and nominal multipliers. In economies that can easily increase the supply of goods, the price increase is small and nominal and real multipliers are similar (Thome et al. 2016).

NOTES

1. ASPIRE generates country context indicators using 129 surveys standardized by the I2D2 Project (International Income Distribution Database).

2. The Transfer Project is a joint effort of the United Nations Children's Fund (UNICEF), Save the Children, and the University of North Carolina to support the implementation of impact evaluations of cash transfer programs in Sub-Saharan Africa. It focuses on the broad range of impacts of government-run cash transfer programs in Sub-Saharan Africa.

3. The From Protection to Production (PtoP) Project is part of the Transfer Project and focuses on exploring the linkages between social protection, agriculture, and rural development; http://www.fao.org/economic/ptop/home/en/.

4. Countries and cash transfer programs included under the PtoP Project include the following: Ethiopia: Tigray Social Cash Transfer Pilot Program (SCTPP); Ghana: Livelihood Empowerment Against Poverty Program (LEAP); Kenya: Cash Transfer Program for Orphans and Vulnerable Children (CT-OVC); Lesotho: Child Grants Program (CGP); Malawi: Social Cash Transfer (SCT); Zambia: Program Child Grant Program (CGP); and Zimbabwe: Harmonized Social Cash Transfer Program (HSCT).

5. To do this, LEWIE models link agricultural household models into a general-equilibrium model of the local economy, which is a treated village (Thome et al. 2016).

REFERENCES

ASPIRE (Atlas of Social Protection: Indicators of Resilience and Equity). 2017. Database, World Bank, Washington, DC. http://datatopics.worldbank.org /aspire/.

Banerjee, A., R. Hanna, G. Kreindler, and B. A. Olken. 2015. "Debunking the Stereotype of the Lazy Welfare Recipient: Evidence from Cash Transfer Programs Worldwide." Working Paper No. 308, Center for International Development, Harvard University, Cambridge, MA.

Barca, V., S. Brook, J. Holland, M. Otulana, and P. Pozarny. 2015. "Qualitative Research and Analyses of the Economic Impacts of Cash Transfer Programmes in Sub-Saharan Africa. Synthesis Report." Food and Agricultural Organization of the United Nations, Rome.

Bastagli, F., J. Hagen-Zanker, L. Harman, V. Barca, G. Sturge, and T. Schmidt. 2016. "Cash Transfers: What Does the Evidence Say? A Rigorous Review of Programme Impact and the Role of Design and Implementation Features." Overseas Development Institute, London. http://www.odi.org/projects /2797-social-protection-literature-review-poverty -impact.

Daidone, S., L. Pellerano, S. Handa, and B. Davis. 2015. "Is Graduation from Social Safety Nets Possible? Evidence from Sub-Saharan Africa." *IDS Bulletin* 46 (2): 93–102.

Daidone, S., S. Asfaw, B. Davis, S. Handa, and P. Winters. 2016. "The Household and Individual-Level Economic Impacts of Cash Transfer Programmes in Sub-Saharan Africa. Synthesis Report." Food and Agricultural Organization of the United Nations, Rome.

Davis, B., S. Handa, N. Hypher, N. Winder Rossi, P. Winters, and J. Yablonski, eds. 2016. *From Evidence to Action: The Story of Cash Transfers and Impact Evaluation in Sub-Saharan Africa.* Oxford, UK: Oxford University Press.

Evans, D., and A. Popova. 2014. "Cash Transfers and Temptation Goods: A Review of Global Evidence." Policy Research Working Paper 6886, World Bank, Washington, DC.

Handa, S., S. Daidone, A. Peterman, B. Davis, A. Pereira, T. Palermo, J. Yablonski. 2017. "Myth Busting? Confronting Six Common Perceptions about Unconditional Cash Transfers as a Poverty Reduction Strategy in Africa." Office of Research–Innocenti Working Paper 2017-11, UNICEF (United Nations Children's Fund).

Ralston, L., C. Andrews, and A. Hsiao. 2017. "A Meta-Analysis of Safety Net Programs in Africa." Working Paper, World Bank, Washington, DC.

Taylor, J. E. 2012. "A Methodology for Local Economy-Wide Impact Evaluation (LEWIE) of Cash Transfers." Food and Agricultural Organization of the United Nations, Rome.

Thome, K., J. Taylor, M. Filipski, B. Davis, and S. Handa. 2016. "The Local Economy Impacts of Social Cash Transfers: A Comparative Analysis of Seven Sub-Saharan Countries." Food and Agricultural Organization of the United Nations, Rome.

PART II
Special Topics

CHAPTER 4

Social Assistance and Aging

Most individuals will reach old age. If aging is almost a certainty for so many individuals, how can elderly people mitigate welfare risks or potential problems such as illness or disability? Social insurance programs can offer coverage of illness, disability, and other potential risks for a significant number of elderly people. However, in most developing countries, people with low income are more exposed to these risks. Social insurance might be restricted to a small group of workers, such as formal employees or employees in certain sectors. For those individuals who are not covered, the option of voluntary savings is close to impossible because a low income makes it difficult to save, and existing instruments for long-term savings are unavailable to them.

This chapter describes a key component that countries are rapidly introducing to support the special needs of elderly people: old-age social pensions.[1] This type of program is becoming an important policy tool to address issues of low social insurance coverage and, in some cases, to address aspects of poverty alleviation. This chapter provides the general characteristics of noncontributory old-age social pensions in different regions, describes recent trends, gives performance indicators, and includes a special highlight on policy and implementation discussions and considerations (see highlight 2).

WHAT ARE OLD-AGE SOCIAL PENSIONS, AND WHY ARE THEY ON THE RISE?

An aging population is a common trend across regions. For some regions, the onset of the trend will be sooner; for other regions, the effect of the trend will be much greater (see figure 4.1). Today, the Europe and Central Asia region has the largest percentage of elderly people; in the long term, Latin America and the Caribbean, South Asia, and East Asia and Pacific will experience the biggest increase. Although elderly people now represent 8 percent of the total population in Latin America and the Caribbean, their share is projected to grow nearly four times by the year 2100. While the share of elderly people now represents 5 and 8 percent of the total populations in South Asia and East Asia and Pacific, respectively, their shares are projected to grow over five times in South Asia (to 27 percent) and over 3.5 times in East Asia and Pacific (to 29 percent) by 2100 (United Nations Population Research Council 2017).

Despite the evident aging trend, most countries do not have systems and benefits that can fully cover elderly people or their special needs. Many countries have social insurance programs, but not everyone participates in those. In this context, very often the old-age social pension becomes a key instrument for providing social assistance coverage in old age.

Old-age social pensions are here defined as noncontributory cash benefits targeted at elderly people, generally provided and financed by governments, and not linked to past contributions, earnings, or years of service. Old-age social pensions take different forms, but their main parameters for eligibility include age, citizenship, residency, and, in some cases, means testing.

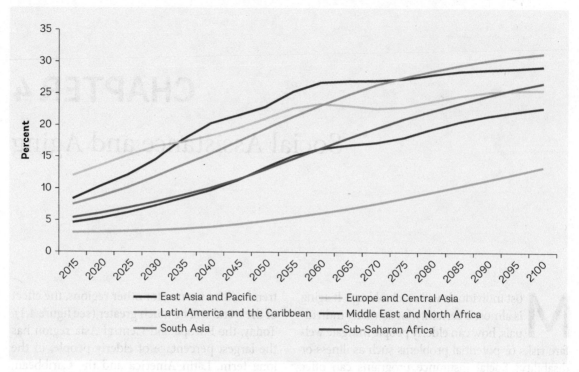

Source: Estimates based on UN Population Division data (https://www.un.org/development/desa/publications/world-population-prospects -the-2017-revision.html).

Three main characteristics of old-age social pensions set them apart from social insurance and some social assistance programs (Palacios and Knox-Vydmanov 2014). First, there is an important distinction between social pensions and minimum pensions. Minimum pensions are set up as the minimum guaranteed benefit provided by social insurance systems, while social pensions in countries with social insurance systems tend to be set below the minimum pension and to be accessible to those who have not made any contributions; have not participated in any mandatory scheme; and/or have an extremely low income. Second, old-age social pensions tend to be publicly financed out of government revenues (through general taxation). The third core distinction is between old-age social pensions and broader social assistance. Old-age social pensions are social assistance benefits exclusively targeted at older people. Social assistance programs can include and cover, but are not necessarily targeted at, elderly people.

Old-age social pensions were introduced in some countries almost as early as social insurance. In 1891, Denmark introduced a local

social pension for poor citizens 60 years of age and older. New Zealand (1898), Australia (1908), Iceland (1909), the United Kingdom (1909), and Sweden (1913) then followed this policy. The first social pensions were means-tested. It was not until 1938 that New Zealand, for example, introduced a universal pension for individuals age 65 years and older.[2] Figure 4.2 presents the evolution of old-age social pension systems around the world. Between 1940 and 1990, many countries introduced this type of social security benefit. Yet, around half of all old-age social pension programs have existed only since 1990.

Old-age social pensions have proliferated in the past two decades. Since 2001, 29 economies have introduced or expanded this social assistance/social safety net instrument (figure 4.3). Latin America and the Caribbean have led the trend, followed by East Asia and several African economies. In addition, economies that already had a social pension system (mostly contributory systems) introduced parallel benefits aimed at covering different groups (for example, the rural programs and "70 and Up" in Mexico). By 2014, an estimated 101 economies had

FIGURE 4.2 Number of Countries with Old-Age Social Pensions, 1898–2012

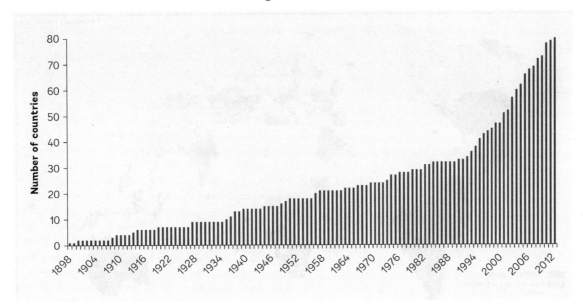

Source: HelpAge Social Pensions Database.

FIGURE 4.3 Introduction of Old-Age Social Pensions, 2001–13

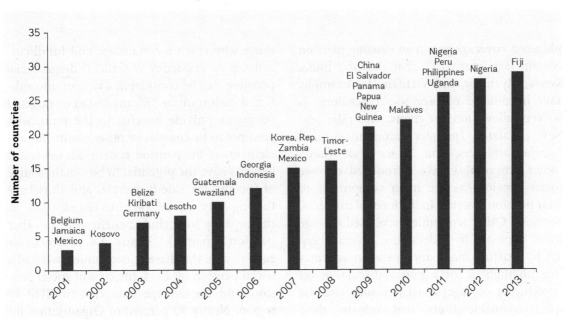

Source: HelpAge Social Pensions Database.
Notes: The height of each column indicates the cumulative number of countries with a social pension during this period. Germany: needs-based pension supplement (Grundsicherung im Alter); Mexico: "70 y Mas" regional scheme was introduced in 2001; Nigeria: Osun Elderly Persons Scheme. Papua New Guinea: Only one province (New Ireland) has an old-age social pension.

introduced old-age social pensions.[3] Almost all Latin American countries have them, whereas Sub-Saharan Africa economies have some of the largest old-age social pensions systems in terms of the share of the elderly population covered.

WHY DO COUNTRIES INTRODUCE OLD-AGE SOCIAL PENSIONS?

Old-age social pensions are introduced on the basis of an economy's needs and capacity, in particular to alleviate poverty, establish the main component of a pension system, or

MAP 4.1 Countries with Old-Age Social Pensions and Their Main Purpose

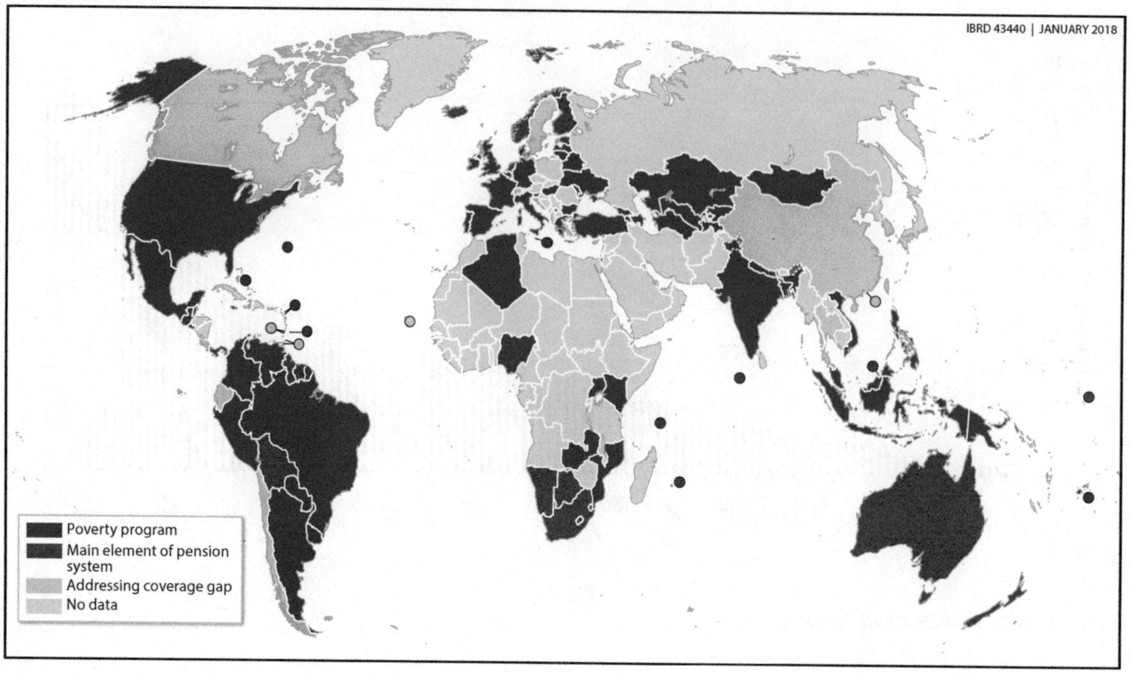

IBRD 43440 | JANUARY 2018

Legend:
- Poverty program
- Main element of pension system
- Addressing coverage gap
- No data

Source: World Bank 2017.

address a coverage gap in an existing pension system (see map 4.1). Bangladesh, India, Kenya, Myanmar, and Vietnam, for example, have introduced old-age social pensions as poverty alleviation programs. Australia and New Zealand (pioneer economies) and Bolivia, Maldives, and Timor-Leste (newcomer economies) have introduced old-age social pensions as the main component of their pension systems, in the form of universal pensions. Other economies have used old-age social pensions to address the coverage gap left by existing mandatory pension schemes (see highlight 2 for a policy discussion on introducing old-age social pensions and the special considerations that inform their design). Among those, some have mature contributory schemes but insufficient coverage (for example, Chile and Mexico), while others have immature contributory schemes for significant aging population trends (for example, Hong Kong SAR, China; the Republic of Korea; and Thailand).

Old-age social pensions reflect the economy context and take one of two forms: universal or means-tested. Universal pensions provide flat-rate benefits to all elderly people, generally those who reach a certain age and fulfill citizenship or residency criteria. Old-age social pensions can be considered a type of unconditional cash transfer.[4] Means-tested or targeted programs provide benefits to the poor, who tend not to be covered by other (contributory) elements of the pension system. Means-tested benefits have the potential to be a main source of income for elderly people, and thus have the capacity to be pension-tested (that is, the capacity to exclude beneficiaries of other pension schemes).[5] Figure 4.4 presents, for each region, the share of economies that had a social pension by 2014, the type of social pension, and the average total cost to GDP by region. Nearly 90 percent of Organisation for Economic Co-operation and Development (OECD) economies, 70 percent of Latin America and the Caribbean economies, and nearly 65 percent of Europe and Central Asian economies have old-age social pensions (panel a). Means-tested pensions are most common among all regions, except for Europe and Central Asia, where pension-tested schemes dominate (panel b).

The design of each program in terms of the eligibility age is independent of the type of

FIGURE 4.4 Distribution of Old-Age Pension Programs

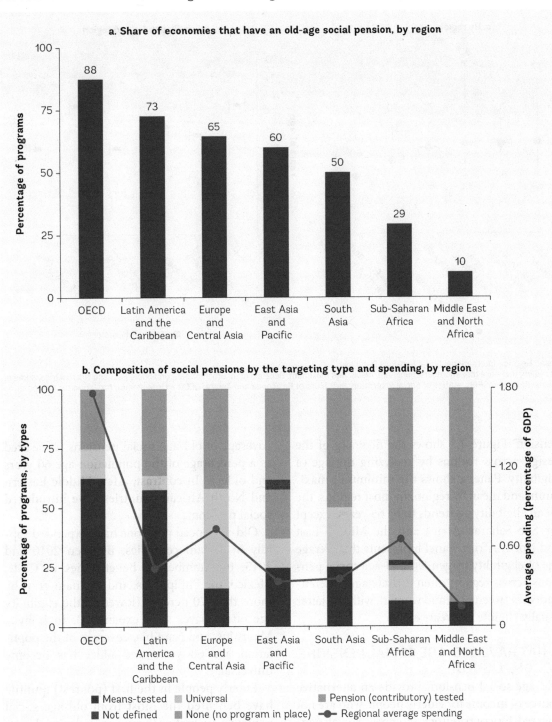

a. Share of economies that have an old-age social pension, by region

b. Composition of social pensions by the targeting type and spending, by region

Legend:
- Means-tested
- Universal
- Pension (contributory) tested
- Not defined
- None (no program in place)
- Regional average spending

Source: Calculations based on HelpAge International Social Pensions.
Note: Data are as of 2014. GDP = gross domestic product; OECD = Organisation for Economic Co-operation and Development.

FIGURE 4.5 Age of Eligibility for Pension Programs

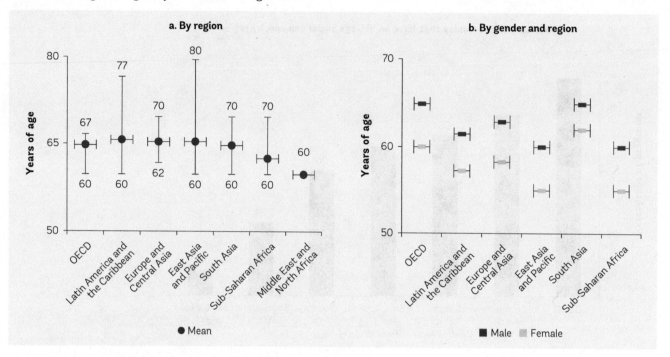

Sources: ASPIRE team, using HelpAge International Social Pensions Database.
Note: In panel a, for each region, there are three numbers: minimum, mean, and maximum. Because of insufficient data on Middle East and North Africa, some of the indicators could not be estimated. ASPIRE = Atlas of Social Protection: Indicators of Resilience and Equity; OECD = Organisation for Economic Co-operation and Development.

pension. Figure 4.5 shows the diversity of the design across regions by analyzing the age of eligibility. Panel a shows the minimum, maximum, and mean by region. In most regions, the mean eligibility age tends to be 65 years, except for Sub-Saharan Africa and the Middle East and North Africa. Panel b presents the average age of eligibility by gender. Old-age social pensions across regions often include age differentiation between men and women, with the latter usually eligible five years earlier.

WHAT HAVE OLD-AGE SOCIAL PENSIONS ACCOMPLISHED?

Old-age social pensions provide an alternative source of income for elderly people who are not covered by contributory schemes. Social pensions cover close to 35 percent of the population age 60 years and older in Organisation for Economic Co-operation and Development countries and in the Europe and Central Asia, East Asia and Pacific, Latin America and the Caribbean, and South Asia regions, according to estimations from HelpAge International data (figure 4.6). The Africa region has the largest

coverage of old-age social pensions (measured as a percentage of the population age 60 years and older).[6] In contrast, a few Middle Eastern and North African countries have introduced social pensions.

Old-age social pensions have expanded rapidly in certain countries. Between 2010 and 2015, the number of beneficiaries in Chile, Mexico, the Philippines, and Vietnam grew by more than 70 percent (lowering the eligibility age often drives such expansion). In Bolivia, Mauritius, and Namibia, coverage of the population age 60 years and older has become universal.[7]

Elderly people in the first (poorest) quintile have benefited the most from old-age social pensions, no matter the program design. Using household survey data from the Atlas of Social Protection: Indicators of Resilience and Equity (ASPIRE) database, the distribution of beneficiaries (or beneficiary incidence) of old-age social pension programs was estimated.[8] Figure 4.7 presents the distribution of old-age social pension beneficiaries by quintile of per capita pretransfer welfare and by type of

FIGURE 4.6 Old-Age Pension Coverage of Population Age 60 Years and Older, by Region

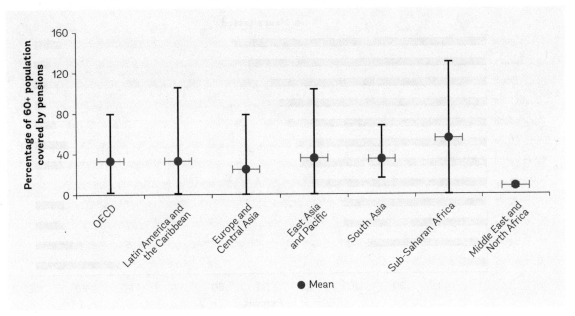

● Mean

Sources: ASPIRE database, using data from HelpAge International.
Note: For each region, there are three numbers: minimum, mean, and maximum. ASPIRE = Atlas of Social Protection: Indicators of Resilience and Equity; OECD = Organisation for Economic Co-operation and Development.

targeting method, based on available data. In Bulgaria, Latvia, Lithuania, and Turkey, more than 50 percent of the old-age social pension beneficiaries are in the poorest quintile, while in Swaziland and Guatemala, more than 50 percent of the beneficiaries of social pensions are in the wealthiest (fourth and fifth) quintiles.

Old-age social pensions provide income security and dignity in old age. To analyze the relative importance of the old-age social pension, Figure 4.8 presents the level of pension benefits as a share of beneficiary welfare for the poorest and second-poorest quintiles. In Brazil, Mauritius, and South Africa, old-age social pensions represent more than 50 percent of the total welfare for elderly people (and their households as indirect beneficiaries) in the poorest quintile.

Old-age social pensions have helped beneficiaries reduce or altogether escape poverty. In a sample of 18 countries (see figure 4.9), the effect of old-age social pensions on the poverty headcount and poverty gap reduction is significant (10–40 percent) in only three (Mauritius, South Africa, and Thailand). In the other 16 countries, the poverty impact is much less pronounced.

Furthermore, the effect of old-age social pensions on inequality (as a reduction in the Gini coefficient for the overall population) is less than 10 percent (see figure 4.9), except for the same three countries (where coverage and benefit levels are high).

In some African and Latin American countries, elderly people are not necessarily among the poorest, so the benefit's impact on poverty alleviation might be marginal. While Mali, Mauritius, and Namibia have large shares of elderly people in the poorest households (32 percent, 38 percent, and 43 percent, respectively), they have even larger shares of children who live there (92 percent, 64 percent, and 95 percent, respectively), Guven and Leite (2016) note. However, in Argentina, Brazil, and Chile, mandatory schemes and social pensions have contributed to lowering poverty among elderly people; they also had a larger overall poverty reduction impact than programs targeted at children (Acosta, Leite, and Rigolini 2011). Böger et al. (forthcoming) find that more than 50 percent of countries worldwide with old-age social pensions have raised elderly people above the international poverty line but not above national poverty lines.

FIGURE 4.7 Distribution of Old-Age Social Pension Beneficiaries, by Income Quintile

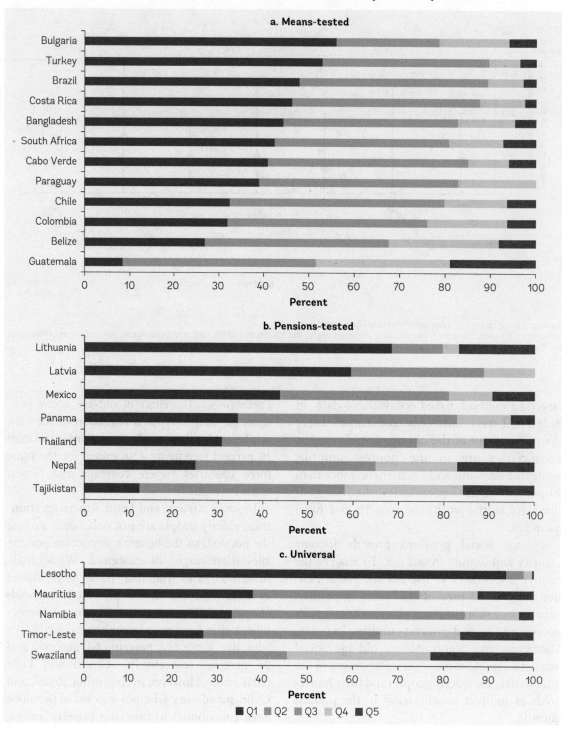

Sources: ASPIRE database; selected surveys.
Note: Countries were selected based on the availability of reliable household survey data (ASPIRE). Beneficiaries' incidence is determined as follows: (number of direct and indirect beneficiaries [people who live in a household where at least one member receives the transfer] in a given quintile)/(total number of direct and indirect beneficiaries). The sum of percentages across quintiles per given instrument equals 100 percent. Quintiles are calculated using per capita pretransfer welfare (income or consumption). ASPIRE = Atlas of Social Protection: Indicators of Resilience and Equity; Q = quintile.

FIGURE 4.8 Old-Age Social Pensions as a Share of Beneficiaries' Welfare, Poorest and Second-Poorest Quintiles

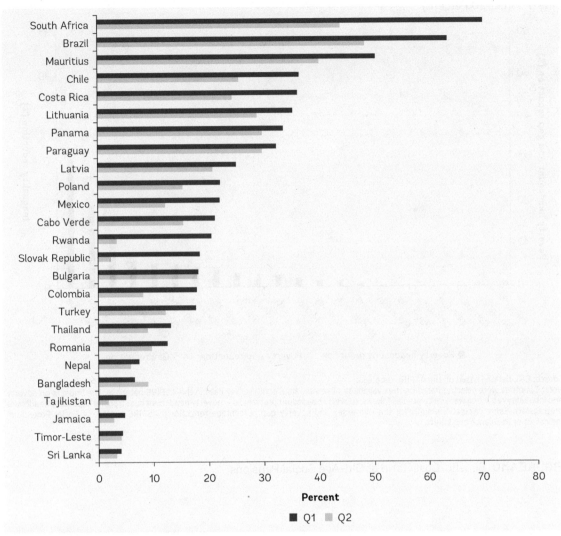

Sources: ASPIRE database; selected surveys.
Note: Countries are selected based on the availability of reliable household survey data (ASPIRE). Pensions as a share of beneficiary welfare is defined as the ratio of the pension size to the average household per capita consumption or income of the respective welfare quintile (Q1: bottom 20 percent; Q2: bottom 21–40 percent). The poorest first and second quintiles are calculated using per capita posttransfer welfare (income or consumption). ASPIRE = Atlas of Social Protection: Indicators of Resilience and Equity; Q = quintile.

Old-age social pensions have mixed results in reducing poverty, as seen in the benefit–cost ratio, measured as the reduction in the poverty gap obtained for each US$1 spent.[9] On average, among the social pensions and countries included in this analysis, the benefit–cost ratio is 0.32, meaning that every US$1 spent on old-age social pensions reduces the poverty gap by 32 cents. Only Latvia and Lithuania have a ratio above 0.5. The design of the old-age social pension (universal or means-tested) likely affects this indicator, but more evidence is needed to better understand the potential link.

FIGURE 4.9 Impact of Old-Age Social Pensions on Poverty Headcount, Poverty Gap, and Gini Inequality Index Reduction, as a Share of Pretransfer Indicator Levels, Using Relative Poverty Line (Poorest 20 Percent)

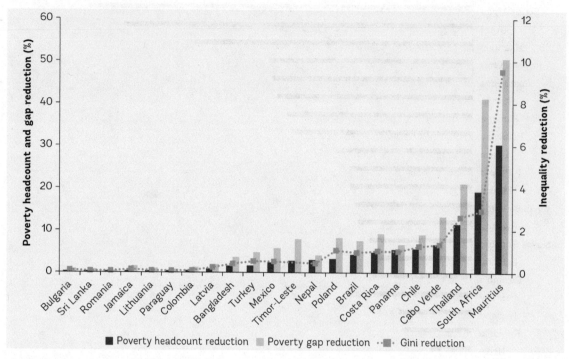

Source: Calculations based on the ASPIRE database.
Note: Countries were selected based on the availability of reliable household survey data in the ASPIRE database. The impacts on poverty and inequality reduction were calculated as follows: (poverty headcount pretransfer – poverty headcount post transfer)/(poverty headcount pretransfer). Same calculations apply for the Gini index and poverty gap percentage reductions. ASPIRE = Atlas of Social Protection: Indicators of Resilience and Equity.

FIGURE 4.10 Benefit–Cost Ratio of Old-Age Social Pensions

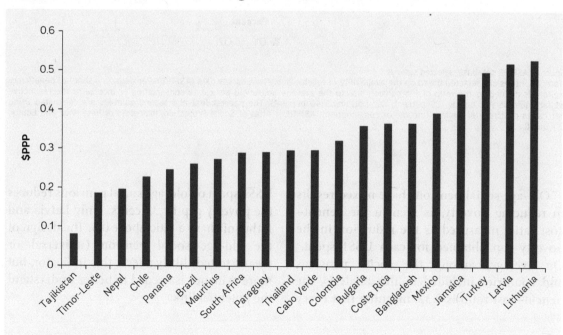

Source: Calculations based on the ASPIRE database.
Note: Countries were selected based on the availability of reliable household survey data in the ASPIRE database. The benefit–cost ratio is the poverty gap reduction in US$ for each unity (US$1) spent in the social program. ASPIRE = Atlas of Social Protection: Indicators of Resilience and Equity; PPP = purchasing power parity.

NOTES

1. In this book, *old-age social pensions* and *social pensions* are defined differently. Social pensions (discussed in part I) are defined using the ASPIRE database and include old-age social pensions, noncontributory disability benefits, noncontributory benefits to war victims or war veterans, and noncontributory survivorship benefits.

2. The 1938 Social Security Act lowered the age for the means-tested pension to 60 and introduced a universal (not means-tested) superannuation from age 65 years (https://en.wikipedia.org/wiki/Welfare_in_New_Zealand).

3. HelpAge's Social Pensions Database (http://www.pension-watch.net/about-social-pensions/about-social-pensions/social-pensions-database). For 20 of these 101 countries, there is no information on when the social pension was established.

4. More specifically, they are conditional only on an age threshold.

5. Countries like South Africa include an income test and an asset test. Beneficiaries cannot have assets worth more than R1,056,000 (US$77,728) if single or R2,112,000 (US$155,456) if married.

6. Coverage in Africa ranges from universal programs in Southern Africa to no programs in many countries across the continent. Hence, a measure of "average" coverage could be misleading.

7. Coverage rates above 100 percent are possible. Beneficiaries under universal old-age social pensions might outnumber the potential population of recipients because of identification issues (such as weak death registration systems) or fraud.

8. Beneficiary incidence is the percentage of program beneficiaries belonging to each quintile of the welfare distribution.

9. More precisely, the benefit–cost ratio is estimated as the poverty gap before the transfer minus the poverty gap divided by the total amount spent in the program.

REFERENCES

Acosta, P., P. Leite, and J. Rigolini. 2011. "Should Cash Transfers Be Confined to the Poor? Implications for Poverty and Inequality in Latin America." Policy Research Working Paper 5875, World Bank, Washington, DC.

ASPIRE (Atlas of Social Protection: Indicators of Resilience and Equity). 2017. "Data Sources and Methodology." Database, World Bank, Washington, DC. http://datatopics.worldbank.org/aspire/~/documentation/.

Böger, T., and L. Leisering. Forthcoming. "Social Citizenship for Older Persons? Measuring the Social Quality of Social Pensions in the Global South and Explaining Their Spread." World Bank Social Protection Working Paper, World Bank, Washington, DC.

Guven, M., and P. Leite. 2016. *Benefits and Costs of Social Pensions in Sub-Saharan Africa.* Washington, DC: World Bank.

Palacios, R., and C. Knox-Vydmanov. 2014. "The Growing Role of Social Pensions: History, Taxonomy, and Key Performance Indicators." *Public Administration and Development* 34 (4): 251–64.

Pallares-Miralles, M., C. Romero, and E. Whitehouse. 2012. "International Patterns of Pension Provision II: A Worldwide Overview of Facts and Figures." Social Protection and Labor Discussion Paper 1211, World Bank, Washington, DC.

United Nations Population Research Council. 2017. *World Population Prospects: The 2017 Revision.* New York: United Nations. https://www.un.org/development/desa/publications/world-population-prospects-the-2017-revision.html.

Most pension systems are mandatory, earnings-related, contributory programs. The first and second pillars of the pension system are mandatory (based on the World Bank's typology), either publicly or privately managed, and linked to workers' length of service or previous contributions (Pallares-Miralles, Romero, and Whitehouse 2012). These schemes tend to cover public sector employees, the military, occupational schemes, and, in some cases, the private sector, as well as facilitating the participation of the self-employed. In the Middle East and North Africa region and in many countries in Asia, most mandatory schemes cover only public sector employees and occupational schemes. Coverage as a percentage of the labor force of the working-age population and coverage of those age 60 years and older or 65 years and older (relative to the size of the population group) have decreased over time.

Different reasons have prevented mandatory schemes from reaching full coverage. Even though these schemes (first and second pillars) have been in place in low- and middle-income countries for decades, the labor force share (mainly in the formal sector) eligible to participate in them is low and has remained almost constant over time. The Latin America and the Caribbean region, for example, has high levels of informality as pensions systems are largely designed for salaried workers (Bosch, Melguizo, and Pagés 2013). In many Sub-Saharan African countries, pension schemes do not cover employees in the private sector and the combination of high contribution rates for social insurance, low wages, and high informality restrict coverage (Dorfman 2015). The rural poor are very unlikely to be able to participate in earnings-related pension schemes, Guven and Leite (2016) find. In addition, many civil servants and occupational schemes tend to be unfunded while providing high benefit levels. This limits the financial capacity of governments to introduce and implement other programs targeted at elderly people and the poor.

To this end, old-age social pensions are fast becoming a tool to meet the urgent needs of expanding coverage and alleviating poverty (Palacios and Knox-Vydmanov 2014). In Africa, full coverage of elderly people is (nearly) attained only in countries that have old-age social pensions (see figure H2.1). These high coverage rates are

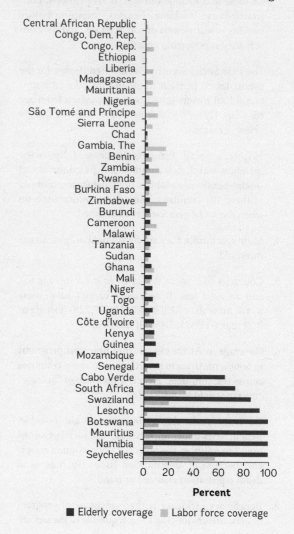

FIGURE H2.1 Elderly and Labor Force Coverage

■ Elderly coverage ■ Labor force coverage

Source: Dorfman 2015.

simply not possible through social insurance or mandatory pension schemes.

The short- and long-term fiscal implications of old-age social pensions need to be considered carefully. Guven and Leite (2016) find that certain Sub-Saharan African countries expend most of the social protection budget on old-age programs; 29–61 percent of total social assistance spending goes to old-age social pension programs. Bosch, Melguizo, and Pagés (2013) describe how, in Latin America, universal old-age social pensions provide coverage for elderly people but require considerable resources; in some cases, governments transfer resources from infrastructure, health, and/or education budgets to meet pension obligations.

Analyzing the long-term costs of old-age programs, given either slow or fast demographic changes, is imperative. In several regions, the population age 65 years and older as a percentage of the total population will double by 2050, jeopardizing the fiscal sustainability of old-age social pensions. Understanding the relationship between demographic trends, macroeconomic and labor market conditions, and key program parameters is necessary to maintain the fiscal sustainability of programs not only now but also in the medium and long terms.

Introducing old-age social pensions should take into consideration factors beyond closing the coverage gap. Key elements of program design and impact should be carefully analyzed before implementing such programs. This analysis should also take into consideration the overall social assistance programs in place in a country to avoid an overlap of benefits and to ensure an efficient use of limited resources.

From a design perspective, universal and means-tested programs have clear trade-offs in efficiency, cost, and effectiveness of implementation. In addition, parameters such as age of eligibility, benefit levels, and benefit indexations can all affect people's behavior during their working life, creating incentives or disincentives to participate or not in the pension system and/or in the labor force. Although a universal program might be perceived as easier to implement (that is, it leverages existing administrative capacities and reduces potential errors of inclusion and/or exclusion), it can be more expensive. Dorfman (2015) shows that despite the challenges of implementing an old-age social pension system targeted exclusively at the elderly poor, the policy has been found to reduce national poverty at almost twice the rate of a universal approach. In addition, targeting those age 65 years and older, rather than 60 years and older, has a significantly greater impact.

Setting the eligibility age, the benefit level, and the benefit indexation are key elements in the design and performance of an old-age social pension program. For example, if the benefit level is high and the eligibility age is close to or the same as the main social insurance, an old-age social pension might discourage labor force participation. Bosch, Melguizo, and Pagés (2013) find that certain parameters of old-age

social pensions in Latin America and the Caribbean, particularly when they exist in parallel with contributory pension systems, can affect labor market dynamics and generate incentives for informal employment.

An analysis at the microeconomic level, such as household characteristics, is also necessary to inform the instrument design. The poverty gap of elderly people living alone can be misconstrued. Guven and Leite (2016) find that for a set of countries in Africa, the poverty headcount is significantly higher for households with children than for any other population group. Dorfman (2015) shows that many African countries have high co-residency levels and that elderly people rarely live alone. Thus, social assistance programs targeted at poor households can benefit elderly people as much as other members, including children.

The context for old-age social pension design and implementation matters. Old-age social pensions are both a form of social assistance/safety net for alleviating poverty and a potential component of pension systems for addressing coverage gaps. Considering the totality of existing social assistance programs, the priorities and needs of the overall population, and budget constraints when analyzing their introduction, are essential to designing an effective old-age social pension system.

REFERENCES

Bosch, M., Á. Melguizo, and C. Pagés. 2013. *Better Pensions Better Jobs: Towards Universal Coverage in Latin America and the Caribbean.* Washington, DC: Inter-American Development Bank.

Dorfman, M. 2015. "Pension Patterns in Sub-Saharan Africa." World Bank Social Protection and Labor Discussion Paper 1503, World Bank, Washington, DC.

Guven, M., and P. Leite. 2016. *Benefits and Costs of Social Pensions in Sub-Saharan Africa.* Washington, DC: World Bank.

Palacios, R., and C. Knox-Vydmanov. 2014. "The Growing Role of Social Pensions: History, Taxonomy, and Key Performance Indicators." *Public Administration and Development* 34 (4): 251–64.

Pallares-Miralles, M., C. Romero, and E. Whitehouse. 2012. "International Patterns of Pension Provision II: A Worldwide Overview of Facts and Figures." Social Protection & Labor Discussion Paper 1211, World Bank, Washington, DC.

CHAPTER 5

The Emergence of Adaptive Social Protection

WHY DOES THE WORLD NEED ADAPTIVE SOCIAL PROTECTION?

Today's global landscape is fraught with multiple, interconnected, and often devastating shocks. Between 1980 and 2012, the annual frequency of natural disasters increased by 250 percent and the number of people affected increased 140 percent (figure 5.1). Climate change is expected to exacerbate these trends and, without climate-informed development, to push an additional 100 million people into extreme poverty by 2030 (World Bank 2016b). Forced displacement also has hit record highs; on average, 20 persons were estimated to have fled their homes every 60 seconds in 2016 (UNHCR 2016). In total, more than 64 million people were displaced worldwide by the end of 2015 (figure 5.2). Furthermore, the worst economic and financial shock in recent history materialized less than a decade ago, and the 2014 Ebola outbreak reawakened the global community to the potential devastation of pandemics. Such shocks, their trends, and associated risks are deeply interconnected (see, for example, WEF 2017), creating an environment of heightened complexity for households, policy makers, and practitioners alike to navigate.

Never has the challenge been more acute for social safety nets (SSNs) to build household resilience and to respond to shocks across the life cycle. Significant progress has been made in the past decade in terms of introducing new SSN programs and scaling up existing programs to expand the coverage of the poorest, as this book details. As a result, safety nets are better positioned than ever to help households manage the risks associated with the multiplicity and complexity of shocks. Indeed, SSNs and the broader social protection suite of policies, programs, and instruments are widely recognized as successful tools for building the resilience of the poor and most vulnerable. Specifically, the World Bank Social Protection and Labor Strategy (2012b) emphasizes that social protection builds the resilience "of the vulnerable through insuring against the impact of drops in well-being from a range of shocks." Safety nets can provide cash, food, insurance, and other means to smooth income and consumption when shocks occur, increasing the resilience of households. When combined with complementary interventions, safety nets can enhance household resilience in the long term by promoting human capital development and income-generating activities (World Bank 2012b).

However, limitations in SSN coverage and design restrict the ability for safety nets to protect households that are vulnerable to shocks. Generally, the poor are particularly vulnerable to shocks for multiple reasons, which include a lack of savings and limited access to finance and formal insurance (see, for example, World Bank 2016a). To protect their short-term well-being and consumption after a shock, poorer households may instead turn to such "negative coping" strategies as removing children from school to work for extra household

FIGURE 5.1 Total Number of Disasters and Affected People, 1980–2012

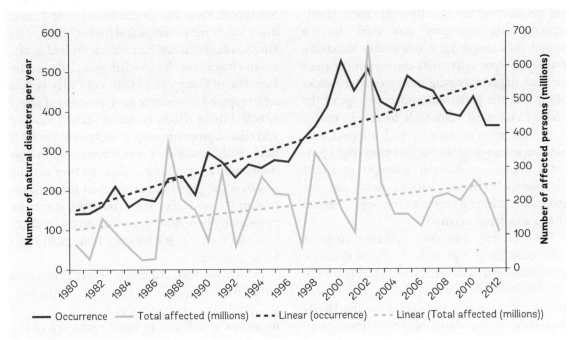

Source: EM-DAT database.

FIGURE 5.2 Total Number of Displaced People, 1951–2015

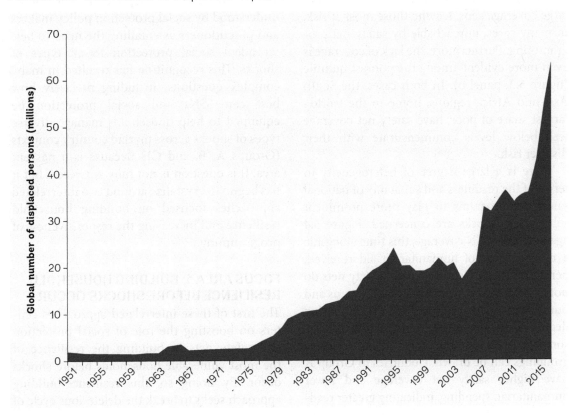

Source: United Nations High Commission on Refugees Population Statistics Database.

income, availing high-interest loans, and selling productive assets. However, such short-term coping strategies can work to the household's longer term detriment. Receiving assistance from safety nets can lessen the need for such negative coping strategies after shocks occur. But the persistent undercoverage of the poorest and most vulnerable to shocks means that those most in need of such support may have no access to SSNs. Furthermore, rigid program design can hamper attempts to adjust parameters to meet changed needs on the ground, reaching beyond a core SSN caseload after a shock has occurred.

For example, empirical evidence suggests that countries at high risk of natural disasters often have lower safety net coverage. Figure 5.3, panel a, measures the coverage of all SSN programs within a country (based on the latest-year data in the Atlas of Social Protection: Indicators of Resilience and Equity [ASPIRE] database) against a country's risk from natural disasters (as ranked by the 2016 *World Risk Report*). While there is a significant degree of variance, most disaster-prone countries have large coverage gaps, leaving those most at risk, in many cases, unreachable by safety net programming. Furthermore, the lack of coverage is even more evident among the poorest quintile (figure 5.3, panel b). In both cases, the South Asia and Africa regions, home to the world's largest share of poor, have safety net coverage well below levels commensurate with their disaster risk.

There is a large degree of heterogeneity in terms of the readiness and suitability of national safety net programs to play more prominent roles where shocks are concerned. Figure 5.4 again looks at SSN coverage, this time alongside a measurement of humanitarian aid received, per capita (from Gentilini 2016). Safety nets do not exist in a vacuum, and national systems and humanitarian programming coexist to varying degrees, depending on the context. The data are somewhat porous, but three broad country groupings can be drawn. Countries in Group A have higher safety net coverage and lower humanitarian spending, indicating greater readiness and suitability for their safety nets to address the risk of shocks; examples include the Philippines' Pantawid Conditional Cash Transfer

Program and Kenya's rapidly growing Hunger Safety Nets Program. Countries in Group C have lower safety net coverage and higher humanitarian spending—including countries mired in crises and fragility such as Afghanistan, Democratic Republic of Congo and Haiti—and may be less well prepared to institute government-led safety nets and more reliant on humanitarian funding and related programming. Countries in Group B have both low safety net coverage and low humanitarian spending, indicating they may be less beset by persistent crises than those countries in Group C. For such countries, it may be particularly beneficial to further invest in safety nets and their use for building household resilience to shocks.

In this context, Adaptive Social Protection (ASP) has emerged in recent years. At the outset, ASP was conceptualized as "a series of measures which aim to build resilience of the poorest and most vulnerable people to climate change by combining elements of social protection, disaster risk reduction and climate change" (Arnall et al. 2010; see also IDS 2012). Since then, the term "adaptive" has come to be understood by social protection policy makers and practitioners as entailing the need to better adapt social protection to all types of shocks. This recognition has resulted in many complex questions, including precisely how best can SSNs and social protection be equipped to help households manage diverse types of shocks across myriad country contexts (Groups A, B, and C)? Because is a nascent area, this question is not fully answered; but it has begun to crystalize around two interrelated approaches focused on building household resilience and increasing the responsiveness of programming.

FOCUS AREA 1: BUILDING HOUSEHOLD RESILIENCE BEFORE SHOCKS OCCUR

The first of these interrelated approaches centers on boosting the role of social protection and safety nets in building the resilience of the most vulnerable households before shocks occur. By doing so, this resilience-building approach seeks to break the deleterious cycle of poverty and vulnerability that may otherwise occur. In short, a more resilient household will be better able to withstand shocks if household

FIGURE 5.3 Ranking of Natural Disasters and Safety Net Coverage

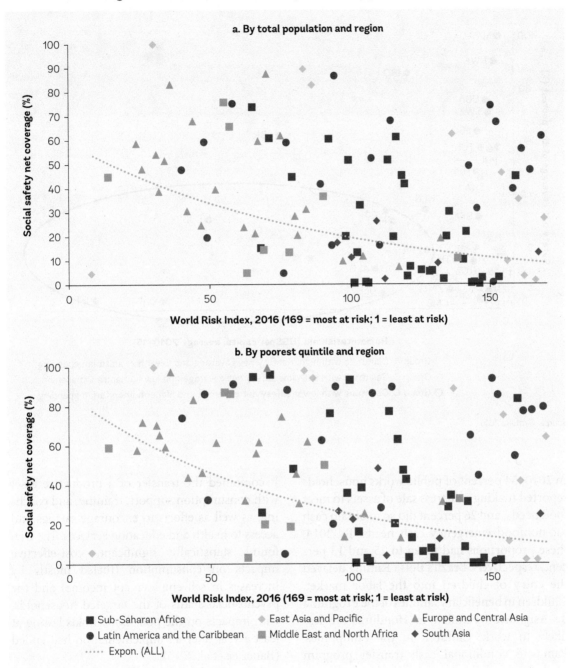

Sources: Garschagen et al. 2016; and ASPIRE database.
Note: Social safety net coverage is based on the latest year for the ASPIRE database (all programs). ASPIRE = Atlas of Social Protection: Indicators of Resilience and Equity.

members have more human capital and are able to access job opportunities, accumulate physical capital, and diversify their livelihoods.

Significant evidence confirms that SSNs, adaptive or otherwise, help improve resilience at the household level. Impact evaluations indicate that beneficiaries of cash transfer programs are more likely to save, as seen in Ghana's

Livelihood Empowerment Against Poverty (LEAP), Kenya's Hunger Safety Net Program, and Zambia's Child Grant Program (World Bank 2016c). For example, Hoddinott et al. (2015) examined distress sales of livestock between 2010 and 2014 among beneficiaries of Ethiopia's Productive Safety Net Program (PSNP), compared with a control group.

FIGURE 5.4 Social Safety Net Coverage of the Poor and Humanitarian Spending, 2010–15

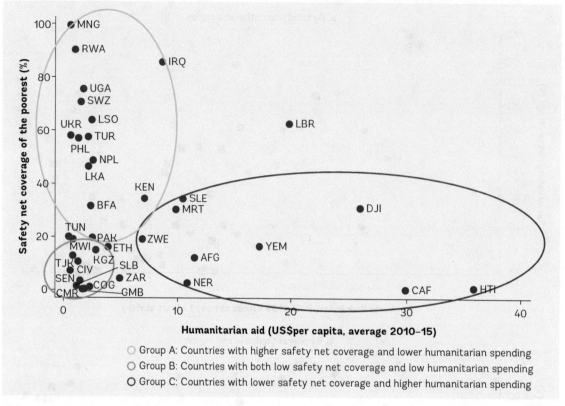

Source: Gentilini 2016.

In 2010, 54 percent of public works households reported making a distress sale of assets to meet food needs, and 26 percent did so to obtain cash for nonfood emergency cash needs. By 2014, these proportions had fallen to 25 and 13 percent, respectively. Brazil's Bolsa Família delayed the entry of children into the labor market. Children in beneficiary families of the Programa de Asignacion Familiar in Honduras are less likely to work. Children in the Philippines' Pantawid conditional cash transfer program work six fewer days per month than a control group (World Bank 2016c). These are selected examples from a proliferating body of evidence reporting similar findings.

The evidence base for the impact of productive inclusion interventions ("graduation models") that support sustainable exits from poverty—and by extension, resilience-building—is also growing. A primary example of this comes from a randomized control trial for a similar "integrated approach" in six countries (Ethiopia, Ghana, Honduras, India, Pakistan, and Peru).

It combined the transfer of a productive asset with consumption support, training, and coaching, as well as efforts to encourage savings and access to health and education services. The trial found statistically significant, cost-effective impacts on consumption (fueled mostly by increases in self-employment income) and the psychosocial status of the targeted households, with impacts on the poor households lasting at least a year after all implementation had ended (Banerjee et al. 2015).

This productive, inclusive approach is being implemented in many countries across West and East Africa, where similar ASP-focused initiatives look to boost household resilience in the face of repeated and chronic drought, along with other shocks. A recent World Bank publication, *Social Protection Programs for Africa's Drylands* (Del Ninno and Coll-Black 2016), describes resilience building as a process of "improving households' or communities' economic and social stability by addressing their structural vulnerabilities and increasing their access to services while helping them prepare against future crises.... This is achieved at the household level, for instance, through the regular distribution of cash transfers accompanied by training activities to help diversify livelihoods away from climate-dependent activities." In this context, resilience may be the product of (i) diversified livelihood strategies and access to markets; (ii) access to financial, social, human, physical, and natural capital; (iii) access to quality basic social services; (iv) access to social protection programs, including safety nets, particularly in difficult periods; (v) access to the information and skills needed to adapt to shocks; and (vi) local and national institutions able to adapt to changing realities.

In the form of public works, ASP programs can reduce the sources of risk from a shock in rural areas, as has been done in Ethiopia, Rwanda, and across the Sahel. A well-known example is the public works component of Ethiopia's PSNP. It helps increase household and community resilience to droughts by creating community assets that reverse the severe degradation of watersheds and provide a more reliable water supply under different climatic conditions. Similarly, the Rwanda Vision 2020 Umurenge Program targets public works for creating anti-erosive ditches and terracing hillsides, improving soil productivity, and expanding the area of cultivable land (IDS 2012).

FOCUS AREA 2: INCREASING THE CAPABILITY OF SAFETY NETS TO RESPOND TO SHOCKS AFTER THEY OCCUR

The second interrelated approach to ASP focuses on increasing the capability of safety nets to respond to shocks after they occur by introducing greater flexibility and scalability in program design. Such design features enable faster adjustment to postshock needs. Conceptually, a program becomes capable of "scaling out" to nonregular social protection beneficiaries that have been affected by a shock and/or "scaling up" to increase benefit amounts at an acute time of need to existing social protection beneficiaries (see figure 5.5). This process is also referred to as "horizontal"

and "vertical" expansion (Oxford Policy Management 2015). A commonly cited example of an SSN with these capabilities is Ethiopia's PSNP, as witnessed by its response to the 2011 drought (see box 5.1).

Increasing grant amounts to existing SSN beneficiaries following shocks (vertical expansion) is a pragmatic and increasingly common safety net response. Leveraged in this way, existing programs such as cash transfers and public works can can be used as conduits to rapidly inject assistance to pretargeted and enrolled poor households in affected areas. Recently, this approach reached existing beneficiaries that were affected by disasters in Fiji and the Philippines (see box 5.2). Preparedness measures for SSNs can be advanced even further through additional investments to make programs more flexible and capable of expanding horizontally to reach additional households, as in the case of the PSNP.

Specifially, horizontal expansion can be achieved by investing in more dynamic delivery systems. Safety nets designed to address chronic poverty in times of relative calm and stability adopt methodologies and supply-driven approaches to delivery for a fixed period. These may include time-bound approaches to targeting (that is, a "census sweep" approach, repeated again only after several years have passed) and fixed, centralized lists of beneficiaries. This approach is typically easier to administer, but its rigidity often produces unintended effects (for example, household exclusion errors), which are magnified under the influence of shocks when needs, poverty status, well-being, and vulnerability can change rapidly. In this sense, these delivery systems are static; they are unable to administratively respond to changes in household needs. The hallmark of an adaptive safety net is dynamic delivery systems that enable the required flexibility and scalability to achieve horizontal and/or vertical expansion, depending on postshock needs.

In addition, information systems tied to understanding risks and vulnerabilities, along with pre-positioned risk financing, can imbue safety net programs with the capability to horizontally expand and to reach more affected households. Early warning and related risk

FIGURE 5.5 Program Scalability to Enable Responsiveness to Shocks

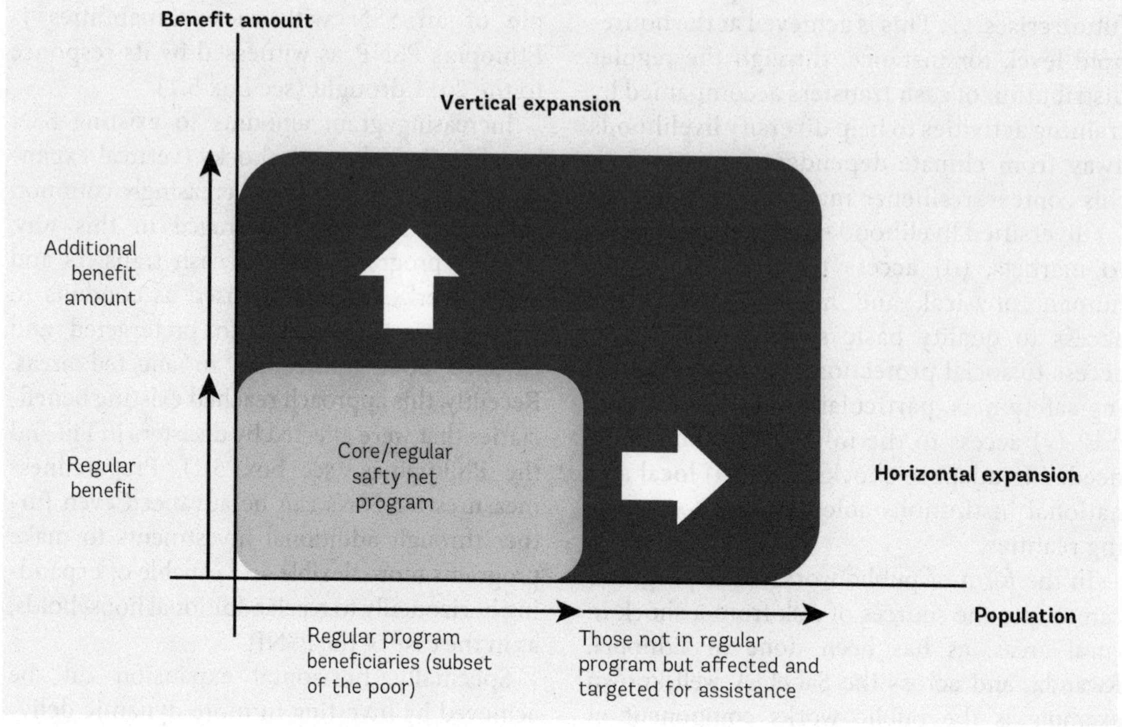

Source: World Bank 2017.

BOX 5.1 Horizontal and Vertical Expansions through Ethiopia's Productive Safety Net Program

Ethiopia's Productive Safety Net Program (PSNP) is a large, national SSN program. It is designed to respond to the impacts of chronic drought, food insecurity, and climate change on Ethiopia's poorest households. To do so, the PSNP incorporates public works activities that improve climate resilience and promote community-level adaptation; provide a federal contingency budget to help poor households and communities better cope with transitory shocks when they occur; and target methods to identify those communities most vulnerable to shocks and climate change. These investments in more dynamic targeting for the PSNP and other preparedness measures enabled the program to extend the duration of its regular support for 6.5 million existing beneficiaries, providing an extra three months of assistance (vertical expansion), while also extending programming to an additional 3.1 million people who were not in the core PSNP caseload (horizontal expansion) in response to the droughts of 2011 (White and Ellis 2012).

information (e.g., hazard mapping, market monitoring, meteorological monitoring, conflict mapping, climate variance mapping, and geospatial data), along with information on household composition and characteristics, can provide vital information about the nature, location, and depth of a shock as well as the appropriateness and type of responses. However, where they exist, these information systems often work in silos without coordination, integration, and direct linkages to social safety net programming. The Dominican Republic, Kenya, and the Republic of Yemen have all developed innovative and integrated information systems, looking to overcome these limitations (see box 5.3). Alongside these information systems, pre-positioned financing is of critical importance for more

BOX 5.2 Responding Rapidly to Disasters through Vertical Expansions in Fiji and the Philippines

In response to Typhoon Yolanda in 2013, the government of the Philippines released the equivalent of US$12.5 million between November 2013 and February 2014–three months after the disaster struck–in unconditional cash transfers to existing beneficiaries of the national conditional cash transfer program, Pantawid. In addition, the existing Pantawid cash delivery platform and national targeting systems helped the World Food Programme and the United Nations Children's Fund (UNICEF) provide top-up benefit amounts to Pantawid households in affected areas. Emergency support was provided for two months and included the activation of

previously agreed-on legislation to remove the conditionalities of the regular program during states of emergency (Bowen 2015).

In Fiji, following Tropical Cyclone Winston in 2016, the government disbursed F$19.9 million (US$39.6 million) in the form of top-up grants to beneficiaries of existing safety net programs, in order to reach vulnerable groups and inject much-needed liquidity into the economy. A recent impact evaluation found that the transfers were received in a timely fashion and that those receiving the transfers recovered faster than those who did not (Mansur, Doyle, and Ivaschenko 2017).

BOX 5.3 Investing in Risk and Vulnerability Information and Tying It to Safety Net Programming in the Dominican Republic, Kenya, and the Republic of Yemen

Kenya's Hunger Safety Nets Program is an unconditional, poverty-targeted cash transfer program that can expand horizontally and vertically, acting as an emergency cash transfer in times of drought. In response to drought events specifically, the scaling up is determined by objective triggers and thresholds in terms of environmental deterioration, measured by a Vegetation Condition Index. The predetermined triggers are used to set the benefit level and the eligibility of households (NDMA 2016).

The Dominican Republic's safety net systems use a single beneficiary system called SIUBEN, which contains socioeconomic and demographic information on poor populations. The information corresponds to a quality-of-life index that determines beneficiary eligibility for safety net programming. Recently, innovative steps have integrated vulnerability with climate change into SIUBEN. The integrated approach estimates the probability of a household being vulnerable to hurricanes, storms, and flooding, given its socioeconomic characteristics; this

helps predict and map potential vulnerable areas and coordinate disaster responses.

The Republic of Yemen used an adaptive approach to respond to a humanitarian crisis due to armed conflict. There, existing SSN and social protection programs were reoriented to help manage food insecurity, address the lack of critical basic services, and deal with losses of employment and livelihoods. The approach introduced a conflict-sensitive monitoring arrangement that uses GPS technology, real-time data flows, and third-party monitoring. Targeting also complemented a poverty approach with measures to identify conflict-related vulnerabilities, such as internally displaced people and their host communities, female-headed households, and youth. In addition, the allocation of assistance adopted a conflict-sensitive approach, ensuring predefined objectives as well as transparent and data-based criteria that could translate into a "distress index" and be used in a fund-allocation formula.

predictable and timely responses (see, for example, Decron and Clarke 2016). With direct linkages to safety nets, risk financing can mobilize funds quickly in support of the rapid scaling up of social protection programs

in response to shocks, based on predefined triggers for dispersal.

In summary, ASP is an emerging agenda in the field of social protection. Given the sheer degree of complexity associated with the issues that ASP seeks to address—multiple risks and shocks, vulnerability, uncertainty, and their interconnectedness—a neat and comprehensive framing of all elements of the growing ASP agenda is somewhat elusive. However, it is clear in the current global context that social protection and SSN practitioners and policy makers must begin to factor such issues into their thinking more fully and undertake greater preparedness for shocks. ASP is a recognition of this necessity. The approach outlined in this chapter—building the resilience of the most vulnerable before shocks occur, and increasing the preparedness of SSNs to respond to the shocks of the future—will likely serve to make social protection more adaptive in the long run, and enable it to more effectively protect the well-being of the most vulnerable against the impacts of all manner of shocks.

REFERENCES

Arnall, A., K. Oswald, M. Davies, T. Mitchell, and C. Coirolo. 2010. "Adaptive Social Protection: Mapping the Evidence and Policy Context in the Agriculture Sector in South Asia." Working Paper No. 345, Institute of Development Studies, Brighton, UK. http://www.ids.ac.uk/files/dmfile/Wp345.pdf.

ASPIRE (Atlas of Social Protection: Indicators of Resilience and Equity). 2017. Database, Washington, DC: World Bank. http://datatopics.worldbank.org/aspire/.

Banerjee, A., E. Duflo, N. Goldberg, D. Karlan, R. Osei, W. Pariente, J. Shapiro, B. Thuysbaert, and C. Udry. 2015. "A Multifaceted Program Uses Lasting Progress for the Very Poor: Evidence from Six Countries." *Science* 348 (6236): 1260799. http://www.econ.yale.edu/~cru2/pdf/Science-2015-TUP.pdf.

Bowen, T. 2015. "Social Protection and Disaster Risk Management in the Philippines: The Case of Typhoon Yolanda (Haiyan)." Policy Research Working Paper 7482, World Bank, Washington, DC.

Del Ninno, C., and S. Coll-Black. 2016. *Social Protection Programs for Africa's Drylands*. Washington, DC: World Bank.

Dercon, S., and D. Clarke. 2016. *Dull Disasters? How Planning Ahead Will Make a Difference*. Oxford, UK: Oxford University Press.

EM-DAT (Emergency Events Database). Database, Centre for Research on the Epidemiology of Disasters, School of Public Health, Universite Catholique de Louvain, Brussels, Belgium. http://www.emdat.be/database/.

Garschagen, M., M. Hagenlocher, M. Comes, R. Sabelfeld, Y. J. Lee, L. Grunewald, M. Lanzendörfer, P. Mucke, O. Neuschäfer, S. Pott, J. Post, S. Schramm, D. Schumann-Bölsche, B. Vandemeulebroecke, T. Welle, and J. Birkmann. 2016. *World Risk Report 2016: The Importance of Infrastructure*. Bonn: Bündnis Entwicklung Hilft and UNU-EHS. http://collections.unu.edu/eserv/UNU:5763/WorldRiskReport2016_small.pdf.

Gentilini, U. 2016. "Sorting through the Hype: Exploring the Interface between Humanitarian Assistance and Safety Nets." Social Protection and Labor Policy Note 19, World Bank, Washington, DC.

Hoddinott, J., J. Lind, G. Berhne, K. Hirvonen, N. Kumar, B. Biniyam, R. Sabates-Wheler, A. Strickland, A. Taffesse, M. Tefera, and Y. Yahanns. 2015. "PSNP-HABP Final Report, 2014". http://essp.ifpri.info/files/2017/07/PSNP-HABP_Final_Report_2014.pdf.

IDS (Institute for Development Studies). 2012. "Realising the Potential of Adaptive Social Protection." IDS in Focus Policy Briefing Note 28. http://www.ids.ac.uk/files/dmfile/IF28.pdf.

Mansur, A., J. Doyle, and O. Ivaschenko. 2017. "Social Protection and Humanitarian Assistance Nexus for Disaster Response: Lessons Learnt from Fiji's Tropical Cyclone Winston." Social Protection and Labor Discussion Paper 1701, World Bank, Washington, DC.

NDMA (National Disaster Management Authority of Kenya). 2016. "Hunger Safety Net Program Scalability Guidelines: Standard Operating Procedures for Scaling-Up HSNP Payments." http://www.hsnp.or.ke/index.php/news/current-news/12-current-news/112-new-hsnp-scalability-guidelines.

Oxford Policy Management. 2015. "Conceptualizing Shock-Responsive Social Protection." https://www.irishaid.ie/media/irishaid/allwebsitemedia/20newsandpublications/publicationpdfsenglish/s-2947/IA-Social-Protection-Strategy-2017.pdf.

UNHCR (United Nations High Commission on Refugees). 2016. *Global Trends: Forced Displacement in 2016*. http://www.unhcr.org/globaltrends2016/.

WEF (World Economic Forum). 2017. *The Global Risks Report, 2017*. Geneva: WEF. http://www3.weforum.org/docs/GRR17_Report_web.pdf.

White, P., and F. Ellis. 2012. "Ethiopia's Productive Safety Net Program, 2010–2014: A Value for Money Assessment." DFID/International Development UEA.

World Bank. 2012a. "An Evaluation of World Bank Support, 2000–2010." Independent Evaluation Group, World Bank, Washington, DC.

———. 2012b. "World Bank 2012–2022 Social Protection and Labor Strategy: Resilience, Equity, and Opportunity." World Bank, Washington, DC.

———. 2016a. "Closing the Gap: Building Resilience to Natural Disasters and Man-Made Shocks through Social Safety Nets." Brief, World Bank, Washington, DC.

———. 2016b. *Shock Waves: Managing the Impacts of Climate Change on Poverty*. Washington, DC: World Bank.

———. 2016c. *Unbreakable: Building the Resilience of the Poor in the Face of Natural Disasters*. Washington, DC: World Bank.

Methodological Framework, Definitions, and Data Sources

The Atlas of Social Protection: Indicators of Resilience and Equity (ASPIRE) database of the World Bank Group is the primary source of this book. This appendix provides ASPIRE's definitions, methodology, and data sources for generating public expenditure and performance indicators. Further information is available in Data Sources and Methodology of the ASPIRE website.[1]

SOCIAL PROTECTION AND LABOR PROGRAMS CLASSIFICATION

As discussed in Chapter 1, social protection and labor (SPL) generally fall into three main categories:

1. *Social safety net (SSN)/social assistance (SA) programs* are noncontributory interventions that are designed to help individuals and households cope with chronic poverty, destitution, and vulnerability. Potential beneficiaries are not required to pay a premium (contribute) to access benefits. SSN/SA programs target the poor and vulnerable.

2. *Social insurance* is a contributory intervention that is designed to help individuals manage sudden changes in income due to old age, sickness, disability, or natural disaster. Individuals pay insurance premiums to be eligible for coverage or contribute a percentage of their earnings to an insurance scheme to access benefits, which link to the total years and amount of contributions. Examples of social insurance programs include contributory old-age, survivor, and disability pensions; sick leave and maternity/paternity benefits; and health insurance coverage.

3. *Labor market programs* can be contributory or noncontributory and are designed to help protect individuals against loss of income from unemployment (passive labor market policies) or help individuals acquire skills and connect them to labor markets (active labor market policies). Unemployment insurance and early retirement incentives are examples of passive labor market policies, while training, employment intermediation services, and wage subsidies are examples of active policies.

For cross-country comparability, this book adheres to the ASPIRE harmonized classification of SPL programs. ASPIRE groups SPL programs into three program areas (social safety nets social assistance, social insurance, and labor markets) with 12 harmonized categories based on program objectives. While Chapter 1 discusses the SSN/SA classification, the information in this appendix is more extensive.

This standardization is applied to each country in the ASPIRE database to generate comparable expenditure and performance indicators (see table A.1).

TABLE A.1 ASPIRE Social Protection and Labor Program Classification

Program category	Program subcategory
Social safety net/social assistance	
Unconditional cash transfers	Poverty-targeted cash transfers and last-resort programs
	Family, children, and orphan allowances (including benefits for vulnerable children)
	Noncontributory funeral grants, burial allowances
	Emergency cash support (including support to refugees and returning migrants)
	Public charity, including *zakāt*
Conditional cash transfers	Conditional cash transfers
Social pensions (noncontributory)	Old-age social pensions
	Disability benefits, war victim noncontributory benefits
	Survivorship benefits
Food and in-kind transfers	Food stamps, rations, and vouchers
	Food distribution programs
	Nutritional programs (therapeutic, supplementary feeding, and people living with HIV)
	School supplies (free textbooks and uniforms)
	In-kind and nonfood emergency support
	Other in-kind transfers
School feeding	School feeding
Public works, workfare, and direct job creation	Cash for work
	Food for work (including food for training and for assets)
Fee waivers and targeted subsidies	Health insurance exemptions and reduced medical fees
	Education fee waivers
	Food subsidies
	Housing subsidies and allowances
	Utility and electricity subsidies and allowances
	Agricultural inputs subsidies
	Transportation benefits
Other social assistance	Scholarships, education benefits
	Social care services, transfers for caregivers (care for children, youth, family, disabled, and older persons)
	Tax exemptions
	Other
Social insurance	
Contributory pensions	Old-age pension (all schemes: national, civil servants, veterans, and other special categories)
	Survivors pension (all schemes: national, civil servants, veterans, and other special categories)
	Disability pension (all schemes: national, civil servants, veterans, and other special categories)
Other social insurance	Occupational injury benefits
	Paid sick leave
	Health
	Maternity and paternity benefits
	Contributory grants (insurance)
	Other social insurance

(Table continues next page)

TABLE A.1 ASPIRE Social Protection and Labor Program Classification *(Continued)*

Program category	Program subcategory
Labor market	
Labor market policy measures (active labor market programs)	Labor market services and intermediation through public employment services
	Training (vocational, life skills, and cash for training)
	Employment incentives and wage subsidies
	Employment measures for the disabled
	Entrepreneurship support and startup incentives (cash and in-kind grants, microcredit)
	Job rotation and job sharing
	Other active labor market programs
Labor market policy support (passive labor market programs)	Out-of-work income maintenance (contributory unemployment benefits)
	Out-of-work income maintenance (noncontributory employment benefits)
	Benefits for early retirement

Source: ASPIRE.
Note: ASPIRE = Atlas of Social Protection: Indicators of Resilience and Equity.

DATA SOURCES

The ASPIRE dataset has two main sources of information: administrative data and household survey data. The ASPIRE administrative database sources include primary and secondary sources of data. Program-level administrative data are used to generate public expenditure indicators and the number of beneficiaries.

Household survey data for 96 countries are used to generate the performance indicators (see appendix B for a full list of the surveys). Those cover national representative surveys with information on income, consumption, and SPL programs, including the following: Household Income and Expenditure/Budget Surveys, Living Standard Measurement Surveys, Multiple Indicator Cluster Surveys, Surveys on Income and Living Conditions, and Welfare Monitoring Surveys. The book only uses the latest year for each country and only if the data are not older than 2008; under this criterion, 20 countries were excluded. In addition, countries were excluded where the surveys did not have social safety nets information.

As of October of 2017, the ASPIRE administrative database included information on the number of beneficiaries for 142 countries (appendix C) and program-level spending data for 124 countries (see appendix D).

DATA HARMONIZATION METHODOLOGY

Harmonization Methodology for Administrative Data

The book uses only the latest year data available for each country and only if the data are not older than 2010. For four countries (Bhutan, Jordan, Marshal Islands, and Vanuatu), the latest available year is 2009 and includes only total SSN spending. To ensure comparability and aggregation in spending across programs, the book first divides program-level spending by the corresponding year GDP for which the program data are available (only active/ongoing programs are used). Overall spending for SSN programs in the country is then approximated by summing up all program shares as a percentage of GDP. For each country, the book then provides the total SSN spending (as percentage of GDP), total spending without health fee waivers (as a percentage of GPD), and the spending (as a percentage of GDP) on the SSN/SA specific component (see appendix D).

To calculate program expenditures, the book considers all program spending no matter whether it is government- or donor-financed. When calculating averages (global or regional), all countries are assumed to have equal weight (in other words, simple averages are calculated). Country GDP is taken from the World Development Indicators database. Timor-Leste data on GDP is taken from the World Economic

Outlook database. Average spending on SSNs for member countries of the Organisation for Economic Co-operation and Development (OECD) (Hungary, Slovak Republic, and Slovenia) and for OECD averages are based on the OECD Social Expenditure Database (SOCX) by combining "family" and "other social policy functions" as the closest approximation to non-contributory safety nets, as defined in this book.

Harmonization Methodology for Household Survey Data

Household surveys are reviewed to identify SPL program information. Individual variables are generated for each SPL program that is captured in the survey; the individual variables are then grouped into the 12 SPL harmonized program categories. Performance indicators are generated using the harmonized program variables.

Household weights are used to expand the results to the total population of each country.

For cross-country comparability, all monetary variables are expressed in 2011 prices and daily purchasing power parity (PPP) in U.S. dollars. The consumption or income aggregates used to rank households by their welfare distribution are validated by the World Bank regional poverty teams.

The book uses two definitions of poverty: relative poverty (individuals in the poorest 20 percent of the welfare distribution), and absolute poverty (individuals living on less than $1.90 purchasing power parity a day). Pre-transfer welfare (income or consumption without the SPL transfer) is used to generate the indicators by quintile, except for the adequacy of benefits indicator; posttransfer welfare is used to generate the adequacy indicator.

APPENDIX B

Household Surveys Used in the Book

TABLE B.1 Household Surveys Used in the Book

Country/economy/territory	Year	Region	Survey name
Afghanistan	2011	SA	National Risk and Vulnerability Assessment (NRVA) 2011–2012, Living Conditions Survey
Albania	2012	ECA	Living Standards Measurement Survey
Argentina	2013	LAC	Encuesta Permanente de Hogares Continua
Armenia	2014	ECA	Integrated Living Conditions Survey
Bangladesh	2010	SA	Household Income and Expenditure Survey
Belarus	2013	ECA	Household Budget Survey
Belize	2009	LAC	Living Standards Measurement Survey (LSMS)
Bhutan	2012	SA	Bhutan Living Standards Survey
Bolivia	2012	LAC	Encuesta de Hogares
Botswana	2009	SSA	Core Welfare Indicators Survey
Brazil	2015	LAC	Pesquisa Nacional por Amostra de Domicílios Contínua
Burkina Faso	2014	SSA	Enquete Multisectorielle Continue
Cameroon	2014	SSA	Quatrième Enquête Camerounaise Auprès des Ménages 2014 (ECAM4)
Central African Republic	2008	SSA	Enquête Centrafricaine pour le Suivi-Evaluation du Bien-être
Chad	2011	SSA	Troisième Enquete Sur La Consommation et le Secteur Informel
China	2013	EAP	Chinese Household Income Project 2013–2014
Chile	2013	LAC	Encuesta de Caracterización Socioeconómica Nacional (CASEN)
Colombia	2014	LAC	Encuesta Nacional de Calidad de Vida (ENCV)
Congo, Dem. Rep.	2012	SSA	Troisieme Enquete Sur La Consommation et le Secteur Informel
Costa Rica	2014	LAC	Encuesta Nacional de Hogares (ENAHO)
Côte d'Ivoire	2014	SSA	Enquete sur le Niveau de Vie des Menages de Côte d'Ivoire 2014–2015
Croatia	2010	ECA	Household Budget Survey
Djibouti	2012	MENA	Enquete Djiboutienne Aupres des Menages (EDAM 3-IS)
Dominican Republic	2014	LAC	Encuesta Nacional de Fuerza de Trabajo
Ecuador	2016	LAC	Encuesta Nacional de Empleo Desempleo y Subempleo
Egypt, Arab Rep.	2008	MENA	Household Income, Expenditure, and Consumption Survey 2008–2009
El Salvador	2014	LAC	Encuesta de Hogares de Propósitos Múltiples
Ethiopia	2010	SSA	Household Income, Consumption and Expenditures
Fiji	2008	EAP	Household Income and Expenditure Survey
Gambia	2010	SSA	Integrated Household Survey 2010–2011

(Table continues next page)

TABLE B.1 Household Surveys Used in the Book *(Continued)*

Country/economy/territory	Year	Region	Survey name
Georgia	2011	ECA	Welfare Monitoring Survey
Ghana	2012	SSA	Living Standards Survey V 2012–2013
Guatemala	2014	LAC	Encuesta Nacional de Condiciones de Vida
Guinea	2012	SSA	Enquête Légère pour l'Evaluation de la Pauvreté
Haiti	2012	LAC	Enquête sur les Conditions de Vie des Ménages après Séisme 2012–2013
Honduras	2013	LAC	Encuesta Permanente de Hogares de Propósitos Múltiples
India	2011	SA	National Sample Survey 2011–2012 (68th round) - Schedule 10 - Employment and Unemployment
Indonesia	2015	EAP	Survei Sosial Ekonomi Nasional 2015, Maret (SUSENAS)
Iraq	2012	MENA	Household Socio Economic Survey
Jamaica	2010	LAC	Survey of Living Conditions
Jordan	2010	MENA	Household Income and Expenditure Survey
Kazakhstan	2010	ECA	Household Budget Survey
Kosovo	2013	ECA	Household Budget Survey
Kyrgyz Republic	2013	ECA	Kyrgyz Integrated Household Survey
Latvia	2009	ECA	Household Budget Survey
Liberia	2014	SSA	Household Income and Expenditure Survey 2014–2015
Lithuania	2008	ECA	Household Budget Survey
Madagascar	2010	SSA	Enquete Periodique Aupres Des Menages (EPM 2010)
Malawi	2013	SSA	Integrated Household Panel Survey 2013
Malaysia	2008	EAP	Household Income Survey
Maldives	2009	SA	Household Income and Expenditure Survey 2009–2010
Mauritania	2014	SSA	Enquête Permanente sur les Conditions de Vie des ménages 2014
Mauritius	2012	SSA	Household Budget Survey
Mexico	2012	LAC	Encuesta Nacional de Ingresos y Gastos de los Hogares
Moldova	2013	ECA	Household Budget Survey
Mongolia	2012	EAP	Household Socio-Economic Survey 2012
Montenegro	2014	ECA	Household Budget Survey
Morocco	2009	MENA	Household and Youth Survey
Mozambique	2008	SSA	Inquerito Sobre Orçamento Familiar 2008–2009
Namibia	2009	SSA	National Household Income and Expenditure Survey 2009–2010
Nepal	2010	SA	Living Standards Survey 2010–2011, Third Round
Nicaragua	2014	LAC	Encuesta Nacional de Hogares sobre Medición de Nivel de Vida
Niger	2014	SSA	Enquête Nationale sur les Conditions de Vie des Ménages et l'Agriculture
Nigeria	2015	SSA	General Household Survey Panel
Pakistan	2013	SA	Social and Living Standards Measurement (PSLM_HIES) 2013–2014
Panama	2014	LAC	Encuesta de Mercado Laboral
Papua New Guinea	2009	EAP	Household Income and Expenditure Survey 2009–2010
Paraguay	2011	LAC	Encuesta Permanente de Hogares

(Table continues next page)

TABLE B.1 Household Surveys Used in the Book *(Continued)*

Country/economy/territory	Year	Region	Survey name
Peru	2014	LAC	Encuesta Nacional de Hogares
Philippines	2015	EAP	Family Income and Expenditure Survey 2015–2016
Poland	2012	ECA	Household Budget Survey
Romania	2012	ECA	Household Budget Survey
Russian Federation	2016	ECA	Statistical Survey of Income and Participation in Social Programs
Rwanda	2013	SSA	Integrated Household Living Conditions Survey 2013–2014
Senegal	2011	SSA	Enquete de Suivi de la Pauvrete au Senegal 2011
Serbia	2013	ECA	Household Budget Survey
Sierra Leone	2011	SSA	Integrated Household Survey (SLIHS)–Main Survey
Slovak Republic	2009	ECA	Household Income and Living Conditions Survey
South Africa	2010	SSA	Income and Expenditure Survey
South Sudan	2009	SSA	National Baseline Household Survey 2009, First Round
Sri Lanka	2012	SA	Household Income and Expenditure Survey 2012–2013
Sudan	2009	SSA	National Baseline Household Survey 2009
Swaziland	2009	SSA	Household Income and Expenditure Survey 2009–2010
Tajikistan	2011	ECA	Panorama
Tanzania	2014	SSA	LSMS - National Panel Survey 2014–2015, Wave 4
Thailand	2013	EAP	Household Socio-Economic Survey
Timor-Leste	2011	EAP	Household Income and Expenditure Survey 2011–2012
Tunisia	2010	MENA	Enquete Nationale Sur le Budget la Consommation et le Niveau de Vie des Menage
Turkey	2014	ECA	Household Income and Consumption Expenditures Survey
Uganda	2012	SSA	National Household Survey 2012–2013
Ukraine	2013	ECA	Household Living Conditions Survey
Uruguay	2012	LAC	Encuesta Continua de Hogares
Vietnam	2014	EAP	Household Living Standard Survey
West Bank and Gaza	2009	MENA	Expenditure and Consumption Survey
Zambia	2010	SSA	Living Conditions Monitoring Survey VI (LCMS VI)
Zimbabwe	2011	SSA	Income, Consumption and Expenditure Survey 2011–2012

Source: ASPIRE.
Note: The total number of countries/economies/territories for this analysis is 96. ASPIRE = Atlas of Social Protection: Indicators for Resilience and Equity; EAP = East Asia and Pacific; ECA = Europe and Central Asia; LAC = Latin America and the Caribbean; MENA = Middle East and North Africa; SA = South Asia; SSA = Sub-Saharan Africa.

APPENDIX C
Global Program Inventory

Appendix C presents information available in the ASPIRE database on the largest programs (in terms of beneficiary numbers) existing in 142 countries/economies/territories by aggregate program categories. Countries/economies/territories differ significantly in their number of operating social safety net (SSN) programs. In some cases, the number of programs might be fewer than 10–15 (as in Bolivia, Croatia, and Timor-Leste), whereas in high-number cases there might be more than 50 programs (as in Chile and Burkina Faso). Thus, for some more program-fragmented countries/economies/territories, appendix C does not show the full picture of coverage or versatility of programs and should be treated with caution.

TABLE C.1 Conditional Cash Transfers and Unconditional Cash Transfers

Country/economy/territory	Conditional cash transfer					Unconditional cash transfer	
	Program name	Number of individual beneficiaries (unless specified otherwise)	Beneficiary unit is HH	Estimated number of beneficiaries (individuals)	Year	Program name	Number of individual beneficiaries (unless specified otherwise)
Albania	—	—	—	—	—	Ndihme Ekonomike	106,635
Algeria	—	—	—	—	—	—	—
Angola	—	—	—	—	—	Cartão Kikuia–Kikuia Card Cash Transfer Programme	200,000
Argentina	Asignación Universal por Hijo para la Protección Social	3,560,704	—	3,560,704	2015	—	—
Armenia	—	—	—	—	—	Family Poverty Benefit	104,131
Azerbaijan	—	—	—	—	—	Targeted Social Assistance	530,670
Bangladesh	Stipend for primary students	7,800,000	—	7,800,000	2013	Allowances for Widows, Deserted and Destitute Women	1,113,200
Belarus	—	—	—	—	—	Child care benefit, for children up to 3 years old	348,261
Belize	Building Opportunities for Our Social Transformation (BOOST)	8,600	—	8,600	2012	—	—
Benin	—	—	—	—	—	Decentralized Services Driven by Communities	13,000
Bhutan	—	—	—	—	—	—	—
Bolivia	Bono Juancito Pinto	2,228,000	—	2,228,000	2015	—	—
Bosnia and Herzegovina	—	—	—	—	—	Child Protection Allowance	105,844
Botswana	—	—	—	—	—	Destitute persons program	35,441
Brazil	Bolsa Familia	41,810,373	—	41,810,373	2015	—	—
Bulgaria	—	—	—	—	—	Family or child allowance	777,726
Burkina Faso	Social safety net project "Burkin-Nong-Saya"	88,500	—	88,500	2016	Unconditional cash distribution operations (supplement to cereal distribution)	27,000

Unconditional cash transfer			Social pension				
Beneficiary unit is HH	Estimated number of beneficiaries (individuals)	Year	Program name	Number of individual beneficiaries (unless specified otherwise)	Beneficiary unit is HH	Estimated number of beneficiaries (individuals)	Year
HH	415,877	2014	—	—	—	—	—
—	—	—	—	—	—	—	—
—	200,000	2015	Old-age, survivor and disability	—	—	—	—
—	—	—	Pensión no contributiva por discapacidad	1,068,959	—	1,068,959	2015
HH	374,872	2014	—	—	—	—	—
HH	2,600,283	2014	Old-age allowance (persons who are not entitled for pension)	13,833	—	13,833	2015
—	1,113,200	2015	Old-age allowance	3,000,000	—	3,000,000	2015
—	348,261	2015	Benefit for taking care of disabled category 1 or seniors above 80	42,575	—	42,575	2015
—	—	—	Social pension	3,711	—	3,711	2015
—	13,000	2015	—	—	—	—	—
—	—	—	—	—	—	—	—
—	—	—	Renta Dignidad	934,748	—	934,748	2015
HH	324,941	2010	—	—	—	—	—
—	35,441	2016	The Old-Age Pension (OAP)	105,754	—	105,754	2016
—	—	—	Old-age social pensions (Beneficio de Prestacao Continuada– Idosos)	2,323,808	—	2,323,808	2015
HH	1,710,997	2014	—	—	—	—	—
HH	135,000	2015	—	—	—	—	—

(Table continues next page)

TABLE C.1 Conditional Cash Transfers and Unconditional Cash Transfers (*Continued*)

Country/ economy/ territory	Conditional cash transfer					Unconditional cash transfer	
	Program name	Number of individual beneficiaries (unless specified otherwise)	Beneficiary unit is HH	Estimated number of beneficiaries (individuals)	Year	Program name	Number of individual beneficiaries (unless specified otherwise)
Burundi	—	—	—	—	—	Take a Step Forward (Terintambwe)	2,000
Cabo Verde	—	—	—	—	—	Support for orphans and other vulnerable children	550
Cambodia	MoEYS Scholarships for Primary and Secondary Education	150,655	—	150,655	2015	—	—
Cameroon	Social Safety Nets–Cash transfers	21,500	—	21,500	2016	Program 559: National Solidarity and Social Justice	118,710
Central African Republic	—	—	—	—	—	Emergency livelihood support to conflict-affected populations in southwestern Central African Republic	46,168
Chad	Projet ECHO6 - CARE	11,833	—	11,833	2016	Protection awaiting solutions of Sudanese refugees settled in eastern Chad	308,862
Chile	Subsidio unico familiar	2,015,393	—	2,015,393	2015	—	—
China	—	—	—	—	—	Dibao	69,040,000
Colombia	Mas Familias en Accion	13,672,125	—	13,672,125	2015	—	—
Comoros	—	—	—	—	—	Cash transfers	2,537
Congo, Dem. Rep.	—	—	—	—	—	Alternative Responses for Communities in Crisis cash transfer programme (ARCC2)	64,343
Congo, Rep.	FSA project	40,000	—	40,000	2015	—	—
Costa Rica	Avancemos	167,029	—	167,029	2015	—	—
Côte d'Ivoire	—	—	—	—	—	Programme National des Filets Sociaux Productifs	5,000
Croatia	—	—	—	—	—	Child and family benefits	216,013

Unconditional cash transfer			Social pension				
Beneficiary unit is HH	Estimated number of beneficiaries (individuals)	Year	Program name	Number of individual beneficiaries (unless specified otherwise)	Beneficiary unit is HH	Estimated number of beneficiaries (individuals)	Year
HH	10,000	2013	—	—	—	—	—
—	550	2010	Basic Pension	23,000	—	23,000	2011
—	—	—	MoSAVY Diability Grant Pilot Project (starting May 2016)	—	—	—	—
—	118,710	2016	—	—	—	—	—
—	46,168	2015	—	—	—	—	—
—	308,862	2016	—	—	—	—	—
—	—	—	Old-age solidarity pensions	399,049	—	399,049	2015
—	69,040,000	2015	Government programs for disabled persons	12,638,000	—	12,638,000	2009
—	—	—	Programa Colombia Mayor	1,473,690	—	1,473,690	2014
HH	13,700	2016	—	—	—	—	—
—	64,343	2015	—	—	—	—	—
—	—	—	—	—	—	—	—
—	—	—	Social pension	104,141	—	104,141	2015
—	23,000	2016	—	—	—	—	—
—	216,013	2011	—	—	—	—	—

(Table continues next page)

TABLE C.1 Conditional Cash Transfers and Unconditional Cash Transfers (*Continued*)

| Country/ economy/ territory | Conditional cash transfer | | | | | Unconditional cash transfer | |
	Program name	Number of individual beneficiaries (unless specified otherwise)	Beneficiary unit is HH	Estimated number of beneficiaries (individuals)	Year	Program name	Number of individual beneficiaries (unless specified otherwise)
Czech Republic	—	—	—	—	—	Benefit in material need	71,153
Djibouti	Programme National de Solidarité Famille (PNSF)	16,344	HH	91,526	2015	Distribution de zakāt	6,740
Dominica	—	—	—	—	—	—	—
Dominican Republic	Progresando con Solidaridad (PROSOLI)	2,542,384	—	2,542,384	2015	—	—
Ecuador	Bono de Desarollo Humano	444,562	HH	1,640,434	2014	—	—
Egypt, Arab Rep.	Takāful and Karama	1,964,895	HH	8,347,320	2017	—	—
El Salvador	Comunidades Solidarias Rurales	75,000	HH	324,000	2014	—	—
Estonia	—	—	—	—	—	Child Allowance	251,075
Ethiopia	—	—	—	—	—	Pilot social cash transfer – Tigray	17,705
Fiji	iTaukei	3,500	—	3,500	2010	Family Assistance Program (FAP)	22,826
Gabon	—	—	—	—	—	National Social Action Fund (HIF)	—
Gambia, The	—	—	—	—	—	Cash transfers	—
Georgia	—	—	—	—	—	Targeted social assistance	428,492
Ghana	—	—	—	—	—	Livelihood Empowerment Against Poverty (LEAP)	213,414
Grenada	Support for Education, Empowerment & Development (SEED)	7,368	—	7,368	2015	Child assistance (Carriacou)	68
Guatemala	Mi Bono Seguro – Bono Seguro Escolar	1,021,959	HH	5,150,673	2013	—	—
Guinea	Cash transfer for nutrition and for girl's education	10,000	—	10,000	2012	—	—
Guinea-Bissau	—	—	—	—	—	Cash transfer program	200,000
Haiti	Ti Manman Cheri	86,234	—	86,234	2014	—	—

Unconditional cash transfer			Social pension				
Beneficiary unit is HH	Estimated number of beneficiaries (individuals)	Year	Program name	Number of individual beneficiaries (unless specified otherwise)	Beneficiary unit is HH	Estimated number of beneficiaries (individuals)	Year
HH	142,306	2008	—	—	—	—	—
—	6,740	2015	—	—	—	—	—
—	—	—	—	—	—	—	—
—	—	—	Suplemento Alimenticio del Programa de Protección a la Vejez en Extrema Pobreza	111,389	—	111,389	2015
—	—	—	Bono matrícula para la eliminación del aporte voluntario	3,015,199	—	3,015,199	2010
—	—	—	Social solidarity pension	7,000,000	—	7,000,000	2014
—	—	—	Universal basic pension for the elderly	28,200	—	28,200	2013
HH	502,150	2014	National pensions	6,516	—	6,516	2014
—	17,705	2014	—	—	—	—	—
HH	107,282	2015	Social Pension Scheme (SPS)	22,073	—	22,073	2015
—	—	—	—	—	—	—	—
—	—	—	—	—	—	—	—
—	428,492	2013	Old-age pension	684,301	—	684,301	2013
HH	939,022	2016	—	—	—	—	—
HH	202	2015	Public assistance	206	—	206	2015
—	—	—	Social Pension program for elderly	108,664	—	108,664	2013
—	—	—	—	—	—	—	—
—	200,000	2015	Program for the handicapped	800	—	800	2015
—	—	—	—	—	—	—	—

(Table continues next page)

TABLE C.1 Conditional Cash Transfers and Unconditional Cash Transfers *(Continued)*

Country/ economy/ territory	Conditional cash transfer					Unconditional cash transfer	
	Program name	Number of individual beneficiaries (unless specified otherwise)	Beneficiary unit is HH	Estimated number of beneficiaries (individuals)	Year	Program name	Number of individual beneficiaries (unless specified otherwise)
Honduras	Bono Vida Mejor	259,879	—	259,879	2015	—	—
Hungary	For the Road	26,000	—	26,000	2008	Regular social assistance	269,000
India	Janani Suraksha Yojana	1,946,858	—	1,946,858	2016	National Family Benefit Scheme (NFBS)	—
Indonesia	Program Keluarga Harapan	6,000,000	HH	23,400,000	2016	Bantuan Langsung Sementara Masyrakat (BLSM)	15,800,000
Iran, Islamic Rep.	—	—	—	—	—	Compensatory cash transfer	6,100,000
Iraq	—	—	—	—	—	Social Protection Network	877,520
Jordan	—	—	—	—	—	National Aid Fund	250,000
Kazakhstan	BOTA foundation CCT	135,000	—	135,000	2010	State payment to families with children under 18 years	562,614
Kenya	Cash transfer for Orphans and vulnerable children (OVC)	365,232	HH	1,765,000	2016	Hunger Safety net program (HSNP)	101,630
Kiribati	—	—	—	—	—	—	—
Kosovo	—	—	—	—	—	Social Assistance Scheme (Ndihma I and II)	29,506
Kuwait	Families with students grant	—	—	—	—	Physical Disability Grant	—
Kyrgyz Republic	—	—	—	—	—	Monthly Benefit for Poor Families with Children (MBPF)	361,500
Lao	—	—	—	—	—	—	—
Latvia	—	—	—	—	—	Family State Benefit	306,300
Lebanon	—	—	—	—	—	Family and education allowance	—
Lesotho	—	—	—	—	—	Child Grants Program (CGP)	24,500
Liberia	—	—	—	—	—	Social cash transfer program – income transfer plus	8,000
Lithuania	—	—	—	—	—	Social benefit	87,898

Unconditional cash transfer			Social pension				
Beneficiary unit is HH	Estimated number of beneficiaries (individuals)	Year	Program name	Number of individual beneficiaries (unless specified otherwise)	Beneficiary unit is HH	Estimated number of beneficiaries (individuals)	Year
—	—	—	Bono Tercera Edad	36,919	—	36,919	2012
—	269,000	2009	—	—	—	—	—
—	—	—	Indira Gandhi National Old-Age Pension Scheme (IGNOAPS)	24,243,753	—	24,243,753	2016
HH	61,620,000	2015	Elderly Social Security Programme (Pilot)	26,500	—	26,500	2014
—	6,100,000	2009	—	—	—	—	—
—	877,520	2013	—	—	—	—	—
—	250,000	2011	—	—	—	—	—
—	562,614	2014	Base Pension (Pillar Zero)	1,848,469	—	1,848,469	2014
HH	507,190	2016	Older Persons Cash Transfer (OPCT)	320,636	—	320,636	2016
—	—	—	Elderly Pension	2,090	—	2,090	2010
—	29,506	2014	Basic pension	125,883	—	125,883	2014
—	—	—	—	—	—	—	—
—	1,662,900	2012	—	—	—	—	—
—	—	—	Cash and in-kind transfer for veterans and elderly (Decree 343/PM)	—	—	—	—
—	306,300	2014	—	—	—	—	—
—	—	—	—	—	—	—	—
HH	117,600	2015	Old-age pension	85,087	—	85,087	2015
HH	41,086	2016	—	—	—	—	—
—	87,898	2016	Social pension	—	—	—	—

(Table continues next page)

TABLE C.1 Conditional Cash Transfers and Unconditional Cash Transfers *(Continued)*

| Country/ economy/ territory | Conditional cash transfer | | | | | Unconditional cash transfer | |
	Program name	Number of individual beneficiaries (unless specified otherwise)	Beneficiary unit is HH	Estimated number of beneficiaries (individuals)	Year	Program name	Number of individual beneficiaries (unless specified otherwise)
Macedonia, FYR	CCT – increased child allowance	7,679	—	7,679	2014	Social financial assistance	31,085
Madagascar	Filets Sociaux de Sécurité (FSS) TMDH	26,500	HH	127,272	2016	Travaux HIMO	6,660
Malawi	—	—	—	—	—	Social Cash Transfer Scheme (SCTS)	782,561
Malaysia	—	—	—	—	—	Bantuan Rakyat 1 Malaysia (BR1M) scheme	15,300,000
Maldives	—	—	—	—	—	Single Parents' Allowance	—
Mali	—	—	—	—	—	Jigisemejiri	60,715
Marshall Islands	—	—	—	—	—	—	—
Mauritania	Tekavou – conditional cash transfers	7,100	HH	31,110	2016	—	—
Mauritius	—	—	—	—	—	Basic Widow's Pension	19,619
Mexico	Prospera	6,168,900	HH	23,441,820	2015	—	—
Moldova	—	—	—	—	—	Ajutor Social	53,605
Mongolia	—	—	—	—	—	The Child Money Programme	960,300
Montenegro	—	—	—	—	—	Family material support and benefits based on social care	12,830
Morocco	—	—	—	—	—	INJAZ	22,627
Mozambique	—	—	—	—	—	Basic Social Subsidy Programme	379,850
Myanmar	Stipends Program (Ministry of Education)	37,000	—	37,000	2014	Cash and in-kind support to internally displaced people	318,157
Namibia	—	—	—	—	—	Provision of Social Assistance	175,659
Nepal	Basic Education for Dalits	1,075,260	—	1,075,260	2013	Basic education for girls	1,985,657
Nicaragua	Mi Beca familiar	—	—	—	—	—	—
Niger	Projet de Filets Sociaux – Cash transfer with disaster risk management component	68,737	—	309,317	2016	Family allowance	—

Unconditional cash transfer			Social pension				
Beneficiary unit is HH	Estimated number of beneficiaries (individuals)	Year	Program name	Number of individual beneficiaries (unless specified otherwise)	Beneficiary unit is HH	Estimated number of beneficiaries (individuals)	Year
—	31,085	2014	—	—	—	—	—
—	6,660	2016	—	—	—	—	—
—	782,561	2016	—	—	—	—	—
—	15,300,000	2014	Senior citizen aid	140,000	—	140,000	2013
—	—	—	Old-age Pension Scheme	—	—	—	—
HH	321,790	2016	—	—	—	—	—
—	—	—	—	—	—	—	—
—	—	—	—	—	—	—	—
—	19,619	2016	Basic Retirement Pension (BRP) zero pillar retirement only	195,591	—	195,591	2016
—	—	—	Pension para adultos mayores	5,701,662	—	5,701,662	2015
HH	160,815	2015	Social Pension ("for elderly")	6,222	—	6,222	2015
—	960,300	2013	Social Welfare Pension	63,423	—	63,423	2013
HH	42,339	2008	—	—	—	—	—
—	22,627	2013	—	—	—	—	—
HH	1,671,340	2015	—	—	—	—	—
—	318,157	2014	—	—	—	—	—
—	175,659	2013	Provision of Social Assistance – Old-Age Grant	146,482	—	146,482	2013
—	1,985,657	2013	Old-age pension scheme	922,741	—	922,741	2014
—	—	—	Defensa Civil	403,016	—	403,016	2013
—	—	—	—	—	—	—	—

(Table continues next page)

TABLE C.1 Conditional Cash Transfers and Unconditional Cash Transfers *(Continued)*

| Country/economy/territory | Conditional cash transfer | | | | | Unconditional cash transfer | |
	Program name	Number of individual beneficiaries (unless specified otherwise)	Beneficiary unit is HH	Estimated number of beneficiaries (individuals)	Year	Program name	Number of individual beneficiaries (unless specified otherwise)
Nigeria	Kano Conditional Cash Transfer for Girls' Education	16,271	—	16,271	2014	Eradication of Extreme Poverty and Hunger/cash transfer	47,746
Pakistan	Benazir Income Support Program (BISP), CCT component	51,000	—	51,000	2014	Benazir Income Support Program (BISP)	5,042,032
Panama	Red de Oportunidades	67,385	HH	222,371	2015	—	—
Papua New Guinea	—	—	—	—	—	—	—
Paraguay	Tekoporâ	722,377	—	722,377	2015	—	—
Peru	Juntos	771,970	HH	2,933,486	2015	—	—
Philippines	Pantawid Pamilyang Pilipino Program (4Ps)	4,400,000	HH	20,240,000	2015	National Comission of Indigenous Peoples (NCIP) cash program	—
Poland	—	—	—	—	—	Child allowance 500+	3,820,000
Qatar	—	—	—	—	—	—	—
Romania	Money for High School	79,810	—	79,810	2014	Universal Child Allowance (UCA)	3,727,859
Russian Federation	—	—	—	—	—	Child allowances	8,423,000
Rwanda	—	—	—	—	—	Vision 2020 Umurenge (VUP)	86,772
Samoa	—	—	—	—	—	—	—
São Tomé and Príncipe	Needy Mothers	1,224	HH	5,018	2017		
Saudi Arabia	Support assistance for school bags and uniforms	428,028	—	428,028	2012	Regular assistance: divorced/widowed women	370,846
Senegal	National cash transfer programme	300,000	HH	2,400,000	2016	Cash transfer nutritional programs	—
Serbia	—	—	—	—	—	Child allowances	394,557
Seychelles	—	—	—	—	—	Social Welfare Assistance	2,978
Sierra Leone	Social Safety Nets Program	136,768	—	136,768	2016	The National Commission for Social Action (NaCSA)	—
Slovak Republic	Motivation allowance	31,000	—	31,000	2011	Material need benefit	111,000
Slovenia	—	—	—	—	—	Child benefits	371,000

Unconditional cash transfer			Social pension				
Beneficiary unit is HH	Estimated number of beneficiaries (individuals)	Year	Program name	Number of individual beneficiaries (unless specified otherwise)	Beneficiary unit is HH	Estimated number of beneficiaries (individuals)	Year
—	47,746	2013	Ekiti State Social Security Scheme	—	—	—	2013
HH	31,260,598	2015	—	—	—	—	—
—	—	—	120-65	117,940	—	117,940	2015
—	—	—	—	—	—	—	—
—	—	—	Old-age social pensions	100,272	—	100,272	2015
—	—	—	Pension 65	501,681	—	501,681	2015
—	—	—	Social Pension/Value-Added-Tax-Assisted Cash Subsidy to grandparents	939,606	—	939,606	2015
—	3,820,000	2016	—	—	—	—	—
—	—	—	—	—	—	—	—
HH	10,065,219	2014	Social indemnity for pensioners	495,005	HH	1,336,514	2014
—	8,423,000	2013	Social pension	—	—	—	—
HH	246,009	2015	Direct support for disabled former combatants	2,821	—	2,821	2015
—	—	—	Senior citizens benefit	8,700	—	8,700	2010
—	—	—	Social pension –subsidy to the unknown	2,024	—	2,024	2014
—	370,846	2012	—	—	—	—	—
—	—	—	—	—	—	—	—
HH	1,144,215	2013	—	—	—	—	—
HH	11,019	2015	Retirement pension	9,496	—	9,496	2015
—	—	—	—	—	—	—	—
—	111,000	2011	—	—	—	—	—
—	371,000	2007	Social pension	—	—	—	—

(Table continues next page)

TABLE C.1 Conditional Cash Transfers and Unconditional Cash Transfers (*Continued*)

Country/ economy/ territory	Conditional cash transfer					Unconditional cash transfer	
	Program name	Number of individual beneficiaries (unless specified otherwise)	Beneficiary unit is HH	Estimated number of beneficiaries (individuals)	Year	Program name	Number of individual beneficiaries (unless specified otherwise)
Solomon Islands	—	—	—	—	—	—	—
Somalia	Building Resilience through Social Safety Nets in Somalia	15,000	HH	87,000	2016	Short-Term Humanitarian Transfers – Unconditional Cash Transfers	5,925
South Africa	—	—	—	—	—	Child Support Grant	11,703,165
South Sudan	—	—	—	—	—	Juba urban poor cash response pilot	42,000
Sri Lanka	Free scholarship programs for school children –Grade 5	85,000	—	85,000	2012	Divineguma Subsidy Program (ex Samurdhi)	1,400,000
St. Kitts and Nevis	—	—	—	—	—	—	—
St. Lucia	—	—	—	—	—	Public assistance program	2,396
St. Vincent and the Grenadines	—	—	—	—	—	Public assistance relief	6,000
Sudan	National Student Welfare Fund	200,000	—	200,000	2016	*Zakāt*	15,327,539
Suriname	—	—	—	—	—	—	—
Swaziland	—	—	—	—	—	Public assistance	5,075
Syrian Arab Republic	—	—	—	—	—	Social Welfare Fund	—
Tajikistan	Conditional cash payments, allowances to large families and children	—	—	—	—	Targeted social assistance (pilot)	11,184
Tanzania	Productive Social Safety Net (PSSN) – conditional cash transfer	1,098,856	HH	5,164,623	2016	—	—
Thailand	—	—	—	—	—	Baan Mankong Program	—
Timor-Leste	Bolsa da Mae	54,488	HH	316,030	2012	Benefits for veterans and survivor families	31,852
Togo	CCT with conditions on nutrition	12,079	HH	50,732	2015	Prise en charge des enfants victimes de la traite	—

Unconditional cash transfer			Social pension				
Beneficiary unit is HH	Estimated number of beneficiaries (individuals)	Year	Program name	Number of individual beneficiaries (unless specified otherwise)	Beneficiary unit is HH	Estimated number of beneficiaries (individuals)	Year
—	—	—	—	—	—	—	—
HH	34,365	2016	—	—	—	—	—
—	11,703,165	2015	Old-age grant	3,086,851	—	3,086,851	2015
—	42,000	2016	—	—	—	—	—
HH	5,880,000	2016	Public Assistance Monthly Allowance (PAMA)	580,720	—	580,720	2015
—	—	—	Assistance pensions	1,000	—	1,000	2008
HH	6,685	2014	—	—	—	—	—
—	6,000	2009	—	—	—	—	—
—	15,327,539	2016	—	—	—	—	—
—	—	—	Old-age social pensions	44,739	—	44,739	2015
—	5,075	2011	Old Age Grant (OAG)	63,500	—	63,500	2014
—	—	—	—	—	—	—	—
HH	26,842	2012	Social pension	—	—	—	—
—	—	—	—	—	—	—	—
—	—	—	Old-age allowance	5,698,414	—	5,698,414	2011
—	31,852	2015	Transfers for the elderly	84,569	—	84,569	2012
—	—	—	—	—	—	—	—

(Table continues next page)

TABLE C.1 Conditional Cash Transfers and Unconditional Cash Transfers *(Continued)*

Country/ economy/ territory	Conditional cash transfer					Unconditional cash transfer	
	Program name	Number of individual beneficiaries (unless specified otherwise)	Beneficiary unit is HH	Estimated number of beneficiaries (individuals)	Year	Program name	Number of individual beneficiaries (unless specified otherwise)
Tonga	—	—	—	—	—	—	—
Tunisia	Programme d'allocations scolaires du PNAFN	89 626	—	89 626	2017	Programme National d'Aide aux Familles Nécessiteuses (PNAFN) – cash transfers	242,000
Turkey	CCT education	1,965,633	HH	7,076,279	2013	Socio-economic Support for the Children of Needy Families	62,256
Uganda	Compassion International Child Development Programme	94,457	—	94,457	2016	Nothern Uganda Social Action Fund (II) – Household Income Support Programme	108,540
Ukraine	Social assistance for low-income families	564,062	HH	1,410,155	2014	Child birth benefit	500,700
Uruguay	Asignaciones Familiares	375,734	—	375,734	2015	—	—
Uzbekistan	—	—	—	—	—	Social assistance to poor families	600,000
Vanuatu	—	—	—	—	—	Family Assistance Support Program	38,493
Venezuela, RB	—	—	—	—	—	—	—
Vietnam	—	—	—	—	—	Subsidies for Tet holiday expenditures for poor households	808,581
West Bank and Gaza	—	—	—	—	—	Cash Transfer Program (CTP)	115,951
Yemen, Rep.	Basic Education Support for Girls CCT	39,791	—	39,791	2014	Social Welfare Fund (SWF)	1,500,000
Zambia	—	—	—	—	—	Social Cash Transfer Scheme	240,000
Zimbabwe	—	—	—	—	—	Harmonised Cash Transfer	52,000

Source: ASPIRE database.
Note: ASPIRE = Atlas of Social Protection: Indicators of Resilience and Equity; CCT = conditional cash transfer; HH = household.

Unconditional cash transfer			Social pension			
Beneficiary unit is HH	Estimated number of beneficiaries (individuals)	Year	Program name	Number of individual beneficiaries (unless specified otherwise)	Beneficiary unit is HH	Estimated number of beneficiaries (individuals)	Year
—	—	—	Social Welfare Scheme for the Elderly	—	—	—	—
HH	992,200	2017	—	—	—	—	—
—	62,256	2013	2022 Sayili Kanun Kapsaminda Yapilan (old-age social pension)	632,407	—	632,407	2013
HH	510,138	2016	Social Assistance Grants for Empowerment – Senior Citizens Grant	91,843	—	91,843	2013
—	500,700	2014	Social pension	65,569	—	65,569	2014
—	—	—	Noncontributory pensions for old age and disability	86,939	—	86,939	2015
—	600,000	2011	—	—	—	—	—
—	38,493	2009	—	—	—	—	—
—	—	—	Old-age social pensions	531,546	—	531,546	2015
HH	3,056,436	2014	Monthly subsidy for elderly according to Decree 136	1,500,844	—	1,500,844	2015
HH	695,706	2014	The Disabled Rehabilitation Fund/ Economic Empowerment program (DEEP)	2,813	—	2,813	2014
HH	7,500,000	2017	Disability Fund	361,514	—	361,514	2014
HH	1,248,000	2016	Disability Benefits (ZAPD, NTFPD)	—	—	—	—
HH	218,400	2015	National Heroes dependants assistance	582	HH	2,444	2015

TABLE C.2 Food and In Kind and School Feeding

| Country/ economy/ territory | | Food and in-kind | | | |
	Program name	Number of individual beneficiaries (unless specified otherwise)	Beneficiary unit is HH	Estimated number of beneficiaries (individuals)	Year
Albania	—	—	—	—	—
Algeria	—	—	—	—	—
Angola	Programa de Apoio Social	600,000	—	600,000	2011
Argentina	Plan Nacional de Seguridad Alimentaria	3,302,235	—	3,302,235	2014
Armenia	—	—	—	—	—
Azerbaijan	—	—	—	—	—
Bangladesh	Vulnerable Group Feeding	9,960,101	HH	48,306,490	2014
Belarus	—	—	—	—	—
Belize	Women's Iron and Folic Acid Distribution Program	9,000	—	9,000	2009
Benin	—	—	—	—	—
Bhutan	—	—	—	—	—
Bolivia	Assistance to drought-affected populations in Bolivia	893,696	—	893,696	2015
Bosnia and Herzegovina	—	—	—	—	—
Botswana	Vulnerable Group Feeding Program	383,392	—	383,392	2013
Brazil	Cestas de Alimentos	827,109	—	827,109	2015
Bulgaria	Assistance for pupils and students	47,096	HH	103,611	2014
Burkina Faso	Treatment of Acute Malnutrition Moderate	153,499	—	153,499	2016
Burundi	WFP food distribution (all programs)	111,301	—	111,301	2013
Cabo Verde	Nutritional support to vulnerable groups and people living with HIV	1,900	—	1,900	2011
Cambodia	—	—	—	—	—
Cameroon	Programme PAM/Cameroun (stock cereal) – Nutrition (treatment of moderate acute malnutrition)	—	—	—	—
Central African Republic	Distribution de vivres et protection de semences	80,000	—	80,000	2015
Chad	Food aid to vulnerable/ food-insecure households	422,457	—	422,457	2016
Chile	Programa nacional de alimentación complementaria	689,984	—	689,984	2015
China	Wubao	5,300,000	—	5,300,000	2014
Colombia	Raciones Alimentarias de emergencia del ICBF	481,362	—	481,362	2012
Comoros	—	—	—	—	—
Congo, Dem. Rep.	WFP food distribution (WFP's PPRO 200832)	3,233,000	—	3,233,000	2016
Congo, Rep.	—	—	—	—	—
Costa Rica	Cen-cinai	31,184	—	31,184	2013

	School feeding			
Program name	Number of individual beneficiaries (unless specified otherwise)	Beneficiary unit is HH	Estimated number of beneficiaries (individuals)	Year
School feeding	—	—	—	—
School feeding	31,000	—	31,000	2011
School feeding program	418,733	—	418,733	2011
Comedores Escolares	1,687,785	—	1,687,785	2015
School feeding	38,000	—	38,000	2011
—	—	—	—	—
School Feeding Programme in poverty-prone areas	3,003,124	—	3,003,124	2015
School feeding	—	—	—	—
School feeding	—	—	—	—
School feeding	103,440	—	103,440	2009
School feeding	30,345	—	30,345	2014
School feeding	2,162,921	—	2,162,921	2012
School feeding	—	—	—	—
School feeding	430,690	—	430,690	2013
National School Feeding Program	42,236,234	—	42,236,234	2014
School feeding	—	—	—	—
Government school feeding program (primary education)	2,906,000	—	2,906,000	2016
School feeding	316,315	—	316,315	2013
School lunch	3,168	—	3,168	2015
School feeding by WFP	296,007	—	296,007	2015
Programme PAM/Cameroun (stock cereal) – school feeding	55,000	—	55,000	2016
—	—	—	—	—
School meals – WFP	126,000	—	126,000	2016
Programa Nacional de Alimentacion Escolar	1,828,556	—	1,828,556	2015
School feeding	26,000,000	—	26,000,000	2011
Programa de Alimentación Escolar	4,000,000	—	4,000,000	2010
—	—	—	—	—
—	—	—	—	—
—	—	—	—	—
Programa de alimentacion y nutricion escolar (Comedores escolares) – MEP	691,294	—	691,294	2014

(Table continues next page)

TABLE C.2 Food and In Kind and School Feeding *(Continued)*

Country/ economy/ territory	Program name	Food and in-kind			
		Number of individual beneficiaries (unless specified otherwise)	Beneficiary unit is HH	Estimated number of beneficiaries (individuals)	Year
Côte d'Ivoire	—	—	—	—	—
Croatia	Child care (both cash and in-kind)	391,836	HH	1,097,141	2011
Czech Republic	—	—	—	—	—
Djibouti	Programme de distribution de vivres au camp de réfugiés	13,000	HH	72,800	2015
Dominica	—	—	—	—	—
Dominican Republic	Provisión Alimentaria – Comedores Económicos	10,999,125	—	10,999,125	2015
Ecuador	Alimentate Ecuador	935,061	—	935,061	2010
Egypt, Arab Rep.	Ration cards	—	—	—	—
El Salvador	Programa de Agricultura Familiar	570,000	HH	2,462,400	2014
Estonia	—	—	—	—	—
Ethiopia	Emergency Food Aid	2,550,579	—	2,550,579	2013
Fiji	Food Voucher Program (FVP)	26,394	—	26,394	2015
Gabon	Maternity grant in kind	—	—	—	—
Gambia, The	Emergency support to vulnerable people affected by floods (WFP)	50,100	—	50,100	2015
Georgia	—	—	—	—	—
Ghana	Targeted supplementary feeding for malnourished children	—	—	—	—
Grenada	Uniform and Transportation	4,532	—	4,532	2015
Guatemala	Mi Bolsa Segura (MIDES)	196,341	—	196,341	2013
Guinea	—	—	—	—	—
Guinea-Bissau	—	—	—	—	—
Haiti	Unconditional food transfer relief assistance	300,000	—	300,000	2014
Honduras	Comedores Solidarios	39,000	—	39,000	2011
Hungary	—	—	—	—	—
India	Public Distribution System (PDS)	152,074,000	—	152,074,000	2014
Indonesia	Rastra (ex. Raskin)	—	—	—	—
Iran, Islamic Rep.	—	—	—	—	—
Iraq	Food rations from Public Distribution System (PDS)	—	—	—	—
Jordan	Urban Targeted Food Assistance	115,000	—	115,000	2011
Kazakhstan	—	—	—	—	—
Kenya	WFP Kenya Rural Resilience		—	333,000	2016
Kiribati	—	—	—	—	—
Kosovo	—	—	—	—	—
Kuwait	—	—	—	—	—

| Program name | School feeding | | | |
	Number of individual beneficiaries (unless specified otherwise)	Beneficiary unit is HH	Estimated number of beneficiaries (individuals)	Year
Programme Intégré de Pérennisation des Cantines Scolaires (PIPCS)	1,086,721	—	1,086,721	2016
School feeding	152,000	—	152,000	2011
—	—	—	—	—
School feeding	16,814	—	16,814	2014
—	—	—	—	—
Programa de Alimentacion Escolar/ Desayuno Escolar	1,710,620	—	1,710,620	2015
Programa de Alimentación Escolar	293,303	—	293,303	2014
School feeding	13,500,000	—	13,500,000	2016
Programa de Alimentacion Escolar	1,453,118	—	1,453,118	2013
School feeding	—	—	—	—
Food for Education	681,195	—	681,195	2014
—	—	—	—	—
—	—	—	—	—
The School Feeding Program and take-home rations (WFP)	100,000	—	100,000	2016
—	—	—	—	—
Ghana School Feeding Programme	1,700,000	—	1,700,000	2014
School feeding	7,051	—	7,051	2012
School feeding	3,052,000	—	3,052,000	2011
—	—	—	—	—
School feeding program	145,000	—	145,000	2014
School feeding (cantines scolaire) – nombre d'élève	818,828	—	818,828	2013
Programa Escuela Saludables	1,460,000	—	1,460,000	2011
School feeding	—	—	—	—
School feeding	104,500,000	—	104,500,000	2014
School feeding (PMTAS)	1,400,000	—	1,400,000	2011
School feeding	3,000	—	3,000	2011
School feeding	555,000	—	555,000	2011
School nutrition	115,000	—	115,000	2011
School feeding	—	—	—	—
Home Grown School Meals (HGSM)	907,659	—	907,659	2016
—	—	—	—	—
—	—	—	—	—
School feeding	—	—	—	—

(Table continues next page)

TABLE C.2 Food and In Kind and School Feeding *(Continued)*

Country/ economy/ territory	Program name	Food and in-kind			
		Number of individual beneficiaries (unless specified otherwise)	Beneficiary unit is HH	Estimated number of beneficiaries (individuals)	Year
Kyrgyz Republic	Wheelchairs, assistive appliances for persons with disabilities	800	—	800	2012
Lao	Community-based social proteciton: Livelihood Opportunities and Nutritional Gains	—	—	—	—
Latvia	—	—	—	—	—
Lebanon	—	—	—	—	—
Lesotho	Targeted Supplementary Feeding	134,000	—	134,000	2011
Liberia	Libera Safety Nets Emergency Support refugees/returning migrants	30,000	—	30,000	2015
Lithuania	—	—	—	—	—
Macedonia, FYR	—	—	—	—	—
Madagascar	Réponse aux chocs et protection contre les risques sociaux – Prévention et gestion de sinistres	21,359	HH	115,339	2016
Malawi	WFP – Food Aid Program	—		—	—
Malaysia	Milk program	—	—	—	—
Maldives			—		
Mali	EMOP (opération d'urgence) et PRRO: intervention de secours prolongée et de redressement (lutte contre la malnutrition chez les enfants de 6–59 mois et les femmes enceintes ou allaitantes)	427,048	—	427,048	2016
Marshall Islands	—	—	—	—	—
Mauritania	Emergency Relief Program	50,000	HH	300,000	2015
Mauritius	Corrugated Iron Sheet Housing	3,000	—	3,000	2014
Mexico	Programa Social de Abasto de Leche a cargo de Liconsa	6,432,853	—	6,432,853	2015
Moldova		—		—	—
Mongolia	Free school textbooks	343,700	—	343,700	2013
Montenegro	—	—	—	—	—
Morocco	Un million de cartables	3,906,948	—	3,906,948	2014
Mozambique	Direct Social Assistance (Apoio Social Directo)	258,940	—	258,940	2015
Myanmar	Provision of food and micronutrient supplements for pregnant and lactating mothers, fortified food for children	40,399	—	40,399	2013

| Program name | School feeding | | | |
	Number of individual beneficiaries (unless specified otherwise)	Beneficiary unit is HH	Estimated number of beneficiaries (individuals)	Year
School feeding	400,000	—	400,000	2012
School feeding	179,297	—	179,297	2013
School feeding	—	—	—	—
School feeding	—	—	—	—
School feeding program	389,000	—	389,000	2014
WFP school feeding	648,000	—	648,000	2011
School meal	635,500	—	635,500	2016
—	—	—	—	—
School feeding – WFP	237,000	—	237,000	2011
World Food Program – Malawi Government School Meals Programme (SMP)	2,230,000	—	2,230,000	2016
School feeding	—	—	—	—
Programe cantine scolaires (CNCS)	479,465	—	479,465	2016
School feeding	—	—	—	—
School feeding	346,164	—	346,164	2016
School feeding program	75,000	—	75,000	2011
School feeding	5,164,000	—	5,164,000	2011
School feeding	—	—	—	—
School feeding	280,400	—	280,400	2009
—	—	—	—	—
School feeding program (various programs)	1,267,109	—	1,267,109	2014
School Feeding (Alimentação Escolar)	427,000	—	427,000	2011
School feeding	583,271	—	583,271	2014

(Table continues next page)

TABLE C.2 Food and In Kind and School Feeding *(Continued)*

Country/economy/territory	Program name	Food and in-kind			
		Number of individual beneficiaries (unless specified otherwise)	Beneficiary unit is HH	Estimated number of beneficiaries (individuals)	Year
Namibia	—	—	—	—	—
Nepal	Fortified flour distribution	—	—	—	—
Nicaragua	Programa de Seguridad Alimentaria Nutricional	54,217	—	54,217	2013
Niger	PAM Récupération Nutritionnelle	1,178,830	—	1,178,830	2016
Nigeria	Save the Children	7,000	—	7,000	2012
Pakistan	—	—	—	—	—
Panama	Bono Familiar para la compra de alimentos	9,200	HH	30,360	2009
Papua New Guinea	—	—	—	—	—
Paraguay	Programme to Progressively Decrease Child Work in the Streets: Food and Health Services	7,700	—	7,700	2015
Peru	Vaso de Leche	1,768,049	—	1,768,049	2010
Philippines	Supplemental Feeding Program	—	—	—	—
Poland	Food benefit (in-kind and cash)	554,400	—	554,400	2013
Qatar	—	—	—	—	—
Romania	School supplies for pupils	680,260	—	680,260	2014
Russian Federation	—	—	—	—	—
Rwanda	Girinka: MINAGRI's One Cow One Family	203,000	HH	872,900	2015
Samoa	—	—	—	—	—
São Tomé and Príncipe	Cantine for elderly poor	280	—	280	2014
Saudi Arabia	—	—	—	—	—
Senegal	Food insecurity ripost (CSA)	927,416	—	927,416	2015
Serbia	—	—	—	—	—
Seychelles	—	—	—	—	—
Sierra Leone	Caregiver and Supplementary Feeding (government and WFP)	110,000	—	110,000	2012
Slovak Republic	—	—	—	—	—
Slovenia	—	—	—	—	—
Solomon Islands	—	—	—	—	—
Somalia	Short-Term Humanitarian Transfers – Food Voucher	4,122	HH	24,732	2016
South Africa	Social Relief of Distress	—	—	—	—
South Sudan	Emergency Operation EMOP 200859 for IDPs and returnees	2,208,005	—	2,208,005	2016

| Program name | School feeding | | | |
	Number of individual beneficiaries (unless specified otherwise)	Beneficiary unit is HH	Estimated number of beneficiaries (individuals)	Year
National School Feeding Programme to Orphans and Vulnerable Children	300,000	—	300,000	2013
School feeding (various programs)	666,378	—	666,378	2014
Programa Integral de Nutrición Escolar	1,050,000	—	1,050,000	2013
School feeding (different programs): Cantine scolaire	168,000	—	168,000	2011
School feeding	155,000	—	155,000	2011
—	—	—	—	—
School feeding	461,000	—	461,000	2011
—	—	—	—	—
School feeding	10,000	—	10,000	2011
Qali Warma	2,398,480	—	2,398,480	2015
Breakfast feeding program	562,000	—	562,000	2013
School feeding	730,000	—	730,000	2011
School feeding	—	—	—	—
School feeding	—	—	—	—
School feeding	2,647,000	—	2,647,000	2011
School feeding	25,000	—	25,000	2014
—	—	—	—	—
School feeding	41,000	—	41,000	2014
School feeding	—	—	—	—
School Lunch Program School Feeding (government)	344,706	—	344,706	2015
School feeding	—	—	—	—
—	—	—	—	—
School feeding (different programs)	125,000	—	125,000	2012
School feeding	—	—	—	—
School feeding	—	—	—	—
—	—	—	—	—
—	—	—	—	—
National School Nutrition Programme	9,200,000	—	9,200,000	2013
	—			

(Table continues next page)

TABLE C.2 Food and In Kind and School Feeding *(Continued)*

| Country/ economy/ territory | Food and in-kind | | | |
	Program name	Number of individual beneficiaries (unless specified otherwise)	Beneficiary unit is HH	Estimated number of beneficiaries (individuals)	Year
Sri Lanka	Free school uniform material program	3,973,909	—	3,973,909	2013
St. Kitts and Nevis	Uniforms and shoes	2,000	—	2,000	2008
St. Lucia	—	—	—	—	—
St. Vincent and the Grenadines	Nutrition Support Program	1,000	—	1,000	2009
Sudan	General food distribution program	2,095,568	—	2,095,568	2015
Suriname	—	—	—	—	—
Swaziland	Food distribution	88,511	—	88,511	2010
Syrian Arab Republic	—	—	—	—	—
Tajikistan	Food for tuberculosis patients	45,000	—	45,000	2011
Tanzania	Disaster relief food response	910,653	—	910,653	2016
Thailand	—	—	—	—	—
Timor-Leste	Ad hoc in-kind support	—	—	—	—
Togo	Nutrition program by UNICEF	25,914	—	25,914	2011
Tonga	—	—	—	—	—
Tunisia	—	—	—	—	—
Turkey	Food assistance (GIDA YARDIMI)	2,442,599	HH	8,793,356	2013
Uganda	Intergrated Management of Acute Malnutrition	55,000	—	55,000	2015
Ukraine	—	—	—	—	—
Uruguay	Tarjeta Uruguay social	69,162	—	69,162	2013
Uzbekistan	Support for breastfeeding	475,000	—	475,000	2008
Vanuatu	—	—	—	—	—
Venezuela, RB	—	—	—	—	—
Vietnam	Food subsidy for hunger according to Decree 136	2,092,170	—	2,092,170	2015
West Bank and Gaza	Food rations, in-kind assistance	876,497	—	876,497	2015
Yemen, Rep.	Emergency Food and Nutrition Support to Food Insecure and Conflict-Affected People.	4,313,631	—	4,313,631	2013
Zambia	Food Security Pack	30,100	HH	156,520	2015
Zimbabwe	Amalima – Response to Humanitarian Situation	266,277	HH	1,118,363	2015

Source: ASPIRE database.
Note: ASPIRE = Atlas of Social Protection: Indicators of Resilience and Equity; OVC = Orphans and Vulnerable children; CCT = conditional cash transfer; DFID = U.K. Department for International Development; HH = household; IPD = internally displaced persons; UNICEF = United Nations Children's Fund; WFP = World Food Programme.

| Program name | School feeding | | | |
	Number of individual beneficiaries (unless specified otherwise)	Beneficiary unit is HH	Estimated number of beneficiaries (individuals)	Year
School Meal Program – Mid-day Meal Program	890,404	—	890,404	2014
School feeding	—	—	—	—
School feeding	7,500	—	7,500	2014
School feeding	—	—	—	—
School Feeding Programme	974,099	—	974,099	2016
—	—	—	—	—
National school meal program	328,000	—	328,000	2011
School feeding	46,000	—	46,000	2011
School feeding	330,000	—	330,000	2011
Fee-free Basic Education – School meal susidy	127,118	—	127,118	2016
School feeding	1,677,000	—	1,677,000	2011
School feeding program	288,000	—	288,000	2011
School feeding (different programs)	40,000	—	40,000	2011
School feeding	—	—	—	—
School feeding	240,000	—	240,000	2011
School Milk Project	6,182,368	—	6,182,368	2013
—	—	—	—	—
School feeding	—	—	—	—
School feeding program	256,000	—	256,000	2011
School feeding	—	—	—	—
—	—	—	—	—
School feeding	4,031,000	—	4,031,000	2011
School feeding	—	—	—	—
School feeding	65,000	—	65,000	2014
School feeding	65,000	—	65,000	2011
School feeding program	1,052,760	—	1,052,760	2016
—	—	—	—	—

TABLE C.3 Public Works and Fee Waivers

Country/ economy/ territory	Program name	Public works			
		Number of individual beneficiaries (unless specified otherwise)	Beneficiary unit is HH	Estimated number of beneficiaries (individuals)	Year
Albania	Employment program	834	—	834	2013
Algeria	—	—	—	—	—
Angola	—	—	—	—	—
Argentina	Plan de Empleo Comunitario (PEC)	187,282	—	187,282	2015
Armenia	Partial wage subsidy/Relocation Allowances/Work practice for unemployed and disabled/Public Work	4,161	HH	14,980	2014
Azerbaijan	Public works	1,605	—	1,605	2014
Bangladesh	Employment Generation Program for the Poorest (EGPP)	1,400,000	—	1,400,000	2014
Belarus	Public works	55,300	—	55,300	2015
Belize	—	—	—	—	—
Benin	Community works	12,000	—	12,000	2015
Bhutan	—	—	—	—	—
Bolivia	Empleo Digno e Intensivo de Mano de Obra	—	—	—	—
Bosnia and Herzegovina	—	—	—	—	—
Botswana	Ipelegeng (self-reliance)	65,000	—	65,000	2014
Brazil	Economia Solidaria – Programa Economia Solidaria em Desemvolvimento	534,053	—	534,053	2012
Bulgaria	Direct job creation	44,222	—	44,222	2013
Burkina Faso	Cash for work	25,619	HH	128,095	2016
Burundi	WFP different PW (excluding the ones through IFAD)	91,480	—	91,480	2013
Cabo Verde	Project insertion female heads of families and disabled in the job market	—	—	—	—
Cambodia	Productive Assets and Livelihoods Support (food for work component)	28,680	HH	131,928	2015
Cameroon	Social Safety Nets – labor-intensive public works (THIMO)	5,000	—	5,000	2016
Central African Republic	Support to the stabilisation and early recovery of communities at risk in CAR (SIRIRI) Phase 2	60,000	—	60,000	2015
Chad	Food Assistance for Assets (Volunteer cooks) – WFP	10,000	—	10,000	2016
Chile	Programa de Apoyo al Empleo Sistema Chile Solidario (part of PROEMPLEO programs)	1,913	—	1,913	2015
China	Food-for-Work Program of Poverty Alleviation Fund	—	—	—	—
Colombia	Programa de Empleo Temporal	6,049	—	6,049	2015
Comoros	Productive safety net	24,756	—	24,756	2016

| Program name | Fee waivers | | | |
	Number of individual beneficiaries (unless specified otherwise)	Beneficiary unit is HH	Estimated number of beneficiaries (individuals)	Year
Energy benefit	45,833	HH	178,749	2014
—	—	—	—	—
—	—	—	—	—
PROGRESARE	708,029	—	708,029	2015
Health benefits and reduced medical fees for vulnerable groups	38,951	—	38,951	2013
—	—	—	—	—
Construction of Houses for Landless and Insolvent Freedom Fighters	—	—	—	—
Subsidies for housing and utilities	1,490,000	—	1,490,000	2011
—	—	—	—	—
Health fund for the poor	10,932	—	10,932	2008
—	—	—	—	—
—	—	—	—	—
—	—	—	—	—
—	—	—	—	—
—	—	—	—	—
Energy benefit	254,012	—	254,012	2014
Additional subsidy of emergency obstetric and neonatal care for indigent women	702,083	—	702,083	2014
Fee waivers for indigents	7,846	—	7,846	2015
Medical assistance	153,326	—	153,326	2010
Health Equity Fund	2,956,305	—	2,956,305	2015
Centre Pasteur Case Management	46,449	—	46,449	2016
Shelter and Food Security in Ouham Province	50,000	—	50,000	2015
—	—	—	—	—
Subsidio para la Prueba de Seleccion Universitaria	187,619	—	187,619	2015
Medical assistance	91,190,000	—	91,190,000	2014
—	—	—	—	—
—	—	—	—	—

(Table continues next page)

TABLE C.3 Public Works and Fee Waivers (Continued)

Country/ economy/ territory	Program name	Public works			
		Number of individual beneficiaries (unless specified otherwise)	Beneficiary unit is HH	Estimated number of beneficiaries (individuals)	Year
Congo, Dem. Rep.	World Bank – Eastern Recovery Project	588,359	—	588,359	2016
Congo, Rep.	—	—	—	—	—
Costa Rica	Programa Nacional de Empleo – MTSS	9,225	—	9,225	2014
Côte d'Ivoire	—	—	—	—	—
Croatia	—	—	—	—	—
Czech Republic	—	—	—	—	—
Djibouti	Social Safety Net Project	6,740	HH	37,744	2015
Dominica	—	—	—	—	—
Dominican Republic	—	—	—	—	—
Ecuador	Mi Primer Empleo	1,222	—	1,222	2013
Egypt, Arab Rep.	Labor-Intensive Investment Project for Egypt	38,308	—	38,308	2014
El Salvador	Temporary Income Support Program – Urban	5,500	—	5,500	2014
Estonia	Public works, workfare, and direct job creation, including community development programs	143	—	143	2013
Ethiopia	Productive Safety Net (PSNP)	7,997,218	—	7,997,218	2016
Fiji	—	—	—	—	—
Gabon	—	—	—	—	—
Gambia, The	—	—	—	—	—
Georgia	—	—	—	—	—
Ghana	Labour-Intensive Public Works (LIPW) programme	164,785	—	164,785	2016
Grenada	Debushing Program	33,392	—	33,392	2015
Guatemala	—	—	—	—	—
Guinea	Labor-intensive public works program with a focus on women and youth, and life skills development – urban areas	24,005	—	24,005	2013
Guinea-Bissau	—	—	—	—	—
Haiti	National Project of Community Participation Development (PRODEP, in French)	450,000	—	450,000	2009
Honduras	Public works	13,000	—	13,000	2011
Hungary	Public work	329,000	—	329,000	2015
India	Mahatma Gandhi National Rural Employment Guarantee (MGNREG)	75,287,000	—	75,287,000	2016
Indonesia	Cash for work/disaster risk reduction program	106,810	HH	416,559	2013

Program name	Fee waivers			
	Number of individual beneficiaries (unless specified otherwise)	Beneficiary unit is HH	Estimated number of beneficiaries (individuals)	Year
UNICEF – Projet d'Appui a la Mise en Oeuvre des Mesures de Protection Sociales pour la Scolarisation des Eleves Vulnerables	47,580	—	47,580	2016
—	—	—	—	—
Education scholarships (from El Fondo Nacional de Becas)	135,895	—	135,895	2015
—	—	—	—	—
—	—	—	—	—
—	—	—	—	—
Educational program for poor children/ orphans	600	—	600	2015
—	—	—	—	—
Seguro Familiar de Salud – Regimen Subsidiado	—	—	—	—
Programa Textos Escolares	6,206,416	—	6,206,416	2015
—	—	—	—	—
Becas Escolares para Estudiantes de Educación Media	181,171	—	181,171	2013
Subsistence benefit to cover expenses for standard allotted living space	56,948	—	56,948	2014
—	—	—	—	—
Poverty Alleviation Scheme	5,877	HH	27,622	2010
Health insurance plan for economically weak Gabonese	483,000	—	483,000	2014
—	—	—	—	—
Domestic subsidies (household allowance)	59,741	HH	203,119	2013
National Health Insurance Scheme (NHIS) indigent exemptions	6,700,000	—	6,700,000	2014
—	—	—	—	—
—	—	—	—	—
Health grants	—	—	—	—
Fee waivers and scholarships	—	—	—	—
Fee waiver for primary education	1,399,173	—	1,399,173	2013
—	—	—	—	—
—	—	—	—	—
Rashtriya Swasthya Bima Yoja (RSBY)		—		
PBI-JKN (Penerima Bantuan Luran – Jaminan Kesehatan Nasional)	92,000,000	—	92,000,000	2016

(Table continues next page)

TABLE C.3 Public Works and Fee Waivers (Continued)

Country/ economy/ territory	Program name	Public works			
		Number of individual beneficiaries (unless specified otherwise)	Beneficiary unit is HH	Estimated number of beneficiaries (individuals)	Year
Iran, Islamic Rep.	—	—	—	—	—
Iraq	—	—	—	—	—
Jordan	Rural Food for Assets	42,000	—	42,000	2011
Kazakhstan	"Road Map" program	94,500	—	94,500	2014
Kenya	WFP cash for assets CFA	60,000	HH	300,000	2016
Kiribati	—	—	—	—	—
Kosovo	—	—	—	—	—
Kuwait	—	—	—	—	—
Kyrgyz Republic	Public works	—	—	—	—
Lao	Poverty Reduction Fund	—	—	—	—
Latvia	Public works	7,223	—	7,223	2011
Lebanon	—	—	—	—	—
Lesotho	Integrated Watershed Management Public Works Program	115,000	—	115,000	2012
Liberia	Youth, Employment, Skills (YES)	58,581	—	58,581	2016
Lithuania	Direct job creation	3,076	—	3,076	2015
Macedonia, FYR	—	—	—	—	—
Madagascar	PUPIRV et PURSAPS	69,848	HH	377,179	2013
Malawi	Public Works Program – conditional cash transfer	2,623,702	—	2,623,702	2014
Malaysia	—	—	—	—	—
Maldives		—			
Mali	Assistance Alimentaire pour la création d'actifs (3A)	91,038	—	91,038	2016
Marshall Islands	—	—	—	—	—
Mauritania	National integration program and support for microenterprises	—			
Mauritius	Workfare Programme	1,107	—	1,107	2009
Mexico	Programa de Empleo Temporal Ampliado	1,440,640	—	1,440,640	2014
Moldova	Moldova Social Investment Fund	112,000	—	112,000	2009
Mongolia	—	—	—	—	—
Montenegro	—	—	—	—	—
Morocco	Promotion Nationale	50,000	—	50,000	2009
Mozambique	Productive Social Action Program	12,498	HH	282,480	2015
Myanmar	Asset Creation Program food and cash for work (WFP only)	225,511	—	225,511	2014
Namibia	—	—	—	—	—
Nepal	Karnali Employment Program	323,600	—	323,600	2014
Nicaragua	—	—	—	—	—

Program name	Fee waivers			
	Number of individual beneficiaries (unless specified otherwise)	Beneficiary unit is HH	Estimated number of beneficiaries (individuals)	Year
—	—	—	—	—
—	—	—	—	—
Housing for the Poor	—	—	—	—
—	—	—	—	—
Health Insurance Subsidy Programme (HISP)	186,462	HH	932,310	2016
—	—	—	—	—
—	—	—	—	—
Housing Conditions Grant (permanent to temporary)	—	—	—	—
Electricity compensation	532,300	HH	2,448,580	2012
Health Equity Funds	626,180	—	626,180	2014
Housing benefit	185,146	HH	444,350	2012
—	—	—	—	—
OVC Bursaries	13,000	—	13,000	2014
Basic Package of Health and Social Welfare Services (BPHS)	—	—	—	—
Utility allowance (compensation for heating expenses)	111,000	—	111,000	2009
Fee waivers for health insurance	5,653	—	5,653	2014
Subvention aux écoles	—	—	—	—
—	—	—	—	—
Rental assistance	—	—	—	—
Welfare Assistance for Medical Services within Maldives and Abroad		—		
		—		
—	—	—	—	—
Indigent Health Coverage	603	—	603	2015
Preprimary school project	517	—	517	2009
Programa Atencion a la Demanda de Educacion para Adultos	2,984,153	—	2,984,153	2015
Heating allowance	123,375	—	123,375	2015
Free public transportation	103,000	—	103,000	2013
Electricity bill subsidy	20,829	HH	68,736	2007
Villes Sans Bidonvilles	324,000	HH	1,684,800	2010
—	—	—	—	—
Support to compulsory primary education	5,200,000	—	5,200,000	2013
—	—	—	—	—
Healthcare subsidies – free medicine, free surgery, food supplements	—	—	—	—
Paquetes educativos soldarios	300,000	—	300,000	2013

(Table continues next page)

TABLE C.3 Public Works and Fee Waivers *(Continued)*

Country/ economy/ territory	Program name	Number of individual beneficiaries (unless specified otherwise)	Beneficiary unit is HH	Estimated number of beneficiaries (individuals)	Year
		Public works			
Niger	Projet de Filets Sociaux – Public Works	14,510	—	14,510	2016
Nigeria	Inputs For Work Programme (FADAMA)	720,000	—	720,000	2015
Pakistan	PPAF: CPI (Community Physical Infrastructure) + WECC (Water, Energy and Climate Change)	502,976	HH	3,118,451	2016
Panama	Public works, training programs	110,095	—	110,095	2011
Papua New Guinea	Public works program	—	—	—	—
Paraguay	—	—	—	—	—
Peru	Programa para la Generación de Empleo Social Inclusivo "Trabaja Perú"	46,936	—	46,936	2014
Philippines	Cash for Work	—	—	—	—
Poland	Direct job creation	9,070	—	9,070	2013
Qatar	—	—	—	—	—
Romania	Solidarity contracts for young people with difficulties and at risk of professional exclusion	2,812	—	2,812	2012
Russian Federation	Organization of temporary employment	811,900	—	811,900	2013
Rwanda	Vision 2020 Umurenge (VUP)	106,041	HH	296,915	2015
Samoa	—	—	—	—	—
São Tomé and Príncipe	—	—	—	—	—
Saudi Arabia	—	—	—	—	—
Senegal	—	—	—	—	—
Serbia	Public works	6,127	—	6,127	2012
Seychelles	—	—	—	—	—
Sierra Leone	—	—	—	—	—
Slovak Republic	—	—	—	—	—
Slovenia	—	—	—	—	—
Solomon Islands	Rapid Employment Program	—	—	—	—
Somalia	Resilience Building	880	HH	5,104	2016
South Africa	Extended Public Works Programme (EPWP)	350,068	—	350,068	2013
South Sudan	Safety Nets and Skills Development Project – public works	4,864	HH	29,184	2015
Sri Lanka	Emergency Northern Recovery Project (ENReP)	—	—	—	—
St. Kitts and Nevis	—	—	—	—	—
St. Lucia	Short-term Employment Programme	9,487	—	9,487	2013

Program name	Fee waivers			
	Number of individual beneficiaries (unless specified otherwise)	Beneficiary unit is HH	Estimated number of beneficiaries (individuals)	Year
—	—	—	—	—
—	—	—	—	—
Child Domestic Labor Basic Education Enabling Programme	—	—	—	—
Beca universal	554,953	—	554,953	2015
—	—	—	—	—
—	—	—	—	—
—	—	—	—	—
Philhealth-sponsored program	38,640,000	—	38,640,000	2013
Health premium for caregivers	188,650	—	188,650	2013
—	—	—	—	—
Heating allowance	3,592,213	—	3,592,213	2009
Housing and heating subsidies	9,076,000	—	9,076,000	2009
—	—	—	—	—
—	—	—	—	—
—	—	—	—	—
—	—	—	—	—
Universal health coverage	792,985	—	792,985	2015
—	—	—	—	—
—	—	—	—	—
School fees subsidy	—	—	—	—
Parent fees for full time care in preschool institutions	314	HH	848	2013
Housing subsidy	4,500	—	4,500	2007
—	—	—	—	—
—	—	—	—	—
—	—	—	—	—
Kerosene oil stamp	977,463	HH	4,105,345	2007
—	—	—	—	—
Education assistance	3,000	—	3,000	2008

(Table continues next page)

TABLE C.3 Public Works and Fee Waivers *(Continued)*

Country/economy/territory	Program name	Public works			
		Number of individual beneficiaries (unless specified otherwise)	Beneficiary unit is HH	Estimated number of beneficiaries (individuals)	Year
St. Vincent and the Grenadines	Road Cleaning Program	3,000	—	3,000	2009
Sudan	Food for assets	108,362	—	108,362	2015
Suriname	—	—	—	—	—
Swaziland	Pilot food for work	—	—	—	—
Syrian Arab Republic	Public works program	—	—	—	—
Tajikistan	Direct job creation	—	—	—	—
Tanzania	Productive Social Safety Net (PSSN) –Public Works	298,970	HH	1,405,159	2016
Thailand	Income-generation activities	—	—	—	—
Timor-Leste	Cash-for-Work	55,000	—	55,000	2008
Togo	Public Works with High Labor Instensity	25,000	—	25,000	2011
Tonga	—	—	—	—	—
Tunisia	—	—	—	—	—
Turkey	Community Services Program (TYCP)	197,182	—	197,182	2013
Uganda	Northern Uganda Social Action Fund II Karamoja/Karamoja Productive Assets Programme (KPAP)	33,085	—	33,085	2015
Ukraine	Direct job creation	45,500	—	45,500	2012
Uruguay	Uruguay Trabaja	3,081	—	3,081	2015
Uzbekistan	Public Works Employment Program	100	HH	560	2009
Vanuatu	—	—	—	—	—
Venezuela, RB	—	—	—	—	—
Vietnam	Public Works Program for Poor Unemployed or Underemployed Labourers	—	—	—	—
West Bank and Gaza	Cash for Work Program	20,550	HH	123,300	2014
Yemen, Rep.	Labor-intensive works by Social Fund for Development (SFD)	400,000	—	400,000	2017
Zambia	Public Works Programs in Rural Area	—	—	—	—
Zimbabwe	Food deficit mitigation program	180,000	HH	756,000	2015

Source: ASPIRE.
Note: ASPIRE = Atlas of Social Protection: Indicators of Resilience and Equity; CCT = conditional cash transfer; HH = household; OVC = Orphans and vulnerable children; WFP = World Food Progamme. – = not available.

| Program name | Fee waivers | | | |
	Number of individual beneficiaries (unless specified otherwise)	Beneficiary unit is HH	Estimated number of beneficiaries (individuals)	Year
—	—	—	—	—
Heath insurance	15,725,537	—	15,725,537	2016
—	—	—	—	—
Fee waivers for health care	—	—	—	—
—	—	—	—	—
—	—	—	—	—
Fee-free basic education – transport benefits	48,717	—	48,717	2016
The Universal Coverage Scheme (UCS)	48,142,994	—	48,142,994	2011
Food Security Fund	—	—	—	—
—	—	—	—	—
—	—	—	—	—
—	—	—	—	—
Genel Sağlik Sigortasi Prim Ödemeleri (green card project)	9,403,251	HH	33,851,704	2013
—	—	—	—	—
Housing and utility allowances	1,845,300	HH	4,613,250	2012
Programa Maestros Comunitarios (PMC)	14,875	—	14,875	2015
—	—	—	—	—
—	—	—	—	—
—	—	—	—	—
Support production land, housing and clean water according to Decision 134	43,000	HH	162,540	2013
Waivers on school fees	250,000	HH	1,500,000	2014
—	—	—	—	—
OVC Bursary Program	20,676	—	20,676	2013
Basic Education Assistance Module (BEAM) primary	118,408	—	118,408	2015

APPENDIX D

Spending on Social Safety Net Programs

TABLE D.1 Spending on Social Safety Net Programs

| Country/Economy/Territory | Region | Year | Annual spending as a percentage of GDP | | | | |
			Total	CCT	UCT	Social pension	School feeding
Albania	ECA	2014	1.57	–	0.46	1.03	–
Angola	SSA	2015	2.30	–	1.96	0.32	0.03
Argentina	LAC	2015	2.05	0.98	0.02	0.78	0.01
Armenia	ECA	2014	1.37	–	1.03	0.25	–
Azerbaijan	ECA	2014	0.84	–	0.39	0.45	–
Bangladesh	SA	2015	0.73	0.10	0.05	0.17	0.03
Belarus	ECA	2015	3.06	–	2.10	0.66	–
Benin	SSA	2014	2.95	–	2.90	..	0.04
Bhutan	SA	2009	0.33	–	–	–	–
Bolivia	LAC	2015	2.18	0.28	–	1.21	0.29
Bosnia and Herzegovina	ECA	2010, 2011	3.89	–	0.27	3.62	–
Botswana	SSA	2014–16	1.66	–	0.31	0.28	–
Brazil	LAC	2015	1.35	0.44	0.03	0.70	0.06
Bulgaria	ECA	2014	1.39	–	0.61	0.27	–
Burkina Faso	SSA	2016	1.99	0.03	0.25	–	0.38
Burundi	SSA	2015	2.28	–	0.31	0.04	0.06
Cabo Verde	SSA	2010	2.50	–	0.05	1.13	0.17
Cambodia	EAP	2015	0.90	0.06	–	–	0.04
Cameroon	SSA	2016	0.04	0.03	0.01	–	–
Central African Republic	SSA	2015	2.79	–	0.23	–	–
Chad	SSA	2014–16	0.69	–	0.03	–	–
Chile	LAC	2015	3.49	0.07	0.99	0.47	0.31
China	EAP	2014	0.76	–	0.26	–	–
Colombia	LAC	2015	3.01	0.29	0.10	0.15	0.09
Comoros	SSA	2016	0.67	–	0.01	–	–
Congo, Dem. Rep.	SSA	2016	0.72	–	–	–	–
Congo, Rep.	SSA	2015	0.05	0.05	–	–	–
Costa Rica	LAC	2013	0.74	–	–	–	–
Côte d'Ivoire	SSA	2016	0.01	–	..	–	0.01
Croatia	ECA	2014	3.38	–	1.74	1.63	–
Djibouti	MENA	2013–15	0.18	0.07	0.07	–	–
Dominican Republic	LAC	2015	1.18	0.06	0.15	–	0.33
Ecuador	LAC	2010, 2015	1.49	0.26	0.26	0.47	0.21
Egypt, Arab Rep.	MENA	2010	0.17	–	0.17	–	–
El Salvador	LAC	2014	0.81	0.07	0.09	0.01	0.10
Estonia	ECA	2014	2.60	–	1.46	0.35	–

Public works	In kind	All fee waivers	Other SA	Total excluding health fee waivers	Annual absolute spending per capita (2011 $PPP)	
					Total	Total excluding health fee waivers
0.01	–	0.03	0.04	1.57	163	163
–	..	–	–	2.30	117	117
0.10	0.03	0.12	–	2.05	278	278
–	–	0.09	..	1.28	105	98
..	–	–	–	0.84	144	144
0.28	0.09	..	0.01	0.73	23	23
..	–	0.10	0.20	2.96	472	456
–	–	0.01	..	2.94	58	58
–	–	–	–	0.33	20	20
–	0.40	–	–	2.18	129	129
–	–	–	–	3.89	371	371
0.47	0.58	–	0.01	1.66	232	232
–	..	0.08	0.03	1.35	204	204
0.15	0.02	0.11	0.23	1.39	239	239
0.30	0.96	0.06	0.01	1.94	31	30
0.97	0.65	0.21	0.04	2.07	17	15
..	0.06	0.63	0.45	1.88	154	115
0.01	–	0.10	0.69	0.80	28	25
..	..	..	..	0.04	1	1
1.05	1.02	–	0.48	2.79	11	11
0.02	0.56	0.08	–	0.62	10	9
..	0.17	0.75	0.74	3.49	771	770
–	0.03	0.48	–	0.72	96	91
0.02	0.12	1.86	0.37	1.19	378	149
0.66	–	–	–	0.67	11	11
0.04	0.69	–	–	0.72	6	6
–	–	–	..	0.05	2	2
–	–	–	–	0.46	102	63
–	–	–	..	0.01	0	0
–	–	–	–	3.38	661	661
..	0.04	..	–	0.18	6	6
–	0.30	0.23	0.11	0.97	156	129
..	0.09	0.07	0.13	1.46	151	148
–	–	–	–	0.17	17	17
0.05	0.14	0.31	0.05	0.81	66	66
..	0.33	–	0.46	2.60	716	716

(Table continues next page)

TABLE D.1 Spending on Social Safety Net Programs *(Continued)*

| Country/Economy/Territory | Region | Year | Annual spending as a percentage of GDP | | | | |
			Total	CCT	UCT	Social pension	School feeding
Ethiopia	SSA	2013–16	0.97	–	..	–	0.03
Fiji	EAP	2015	1.14	0.02	0.65	0.09	–
Gabon	SSA	2014	0.20	–	0.06	–	–
Georgia	ECA	2013	6.99	–	1.14	4.59	–
Ghana	SSA	2014–16	0.58	–	0.29	–	0.15
Grenada	LAC	2015	1.98	0.40	0.49	–	0.12
Guatemala	LAC	2013	0.19	0.13	0.01	–	–
Guinea	SSA	2015	1.55	0.08	–	–	–
Guinea-Bissau	SSA	2015	0.02	–	–	–	0.01
Honduras	LAC	2014	0.77	0.65	0.07	0.01	0.04
Hungary	ECA	2013	3.06	–	–	–	–
India	SA	2016	1.52	–	..	0.06	0.06
Indonesia	EAP	2013–15	0.84	0.17	0.14	..	..
Iraq	MENA	2012–13	2.56	–	0.36	–	–
Jordan	MENA	2009	0.68	–	–	–	–
Kazakhstan	ECA	2014	1.62	0.03	0.46	0.98	–
Kenya	SSA	2016	0.37	0.12	0.07	0.11	0.02
Kiribati	EAP	2012	0.69	–	–	0.69	–
Kosovo	ECA	2014	2.84	–	0.48	2.32	–
Kuwait	MENA	2010	0.80	0.02	0.19	0.18	–
Kyrgyz Republic	ECA	2014	3.08	–	2.53	0.37	0.15
Lao PDR	EAP	2011	0.16	–	–	0.06	–
Latvia	ECA	2012–14	0.77	–	0.50	0.13	–
Lebanon	MENA	2013	1.04	–	0.40	0.04	–
Lesotho	SSA	2010, 2013	7.09	–	2.62	2.03	1.37
Liberia	SSA	2010, 2016	2.64	–	0.15	–	0.98
Lithuania	ECA	2016	0.45	–	0.37	–	0.04
Macedonia, FYR	ECA	2014	1.22	0.55	0.03	0.64	–
Madagascar	SSA	2016	0.16	0.07	..	–	0.04
Malawi	SSA	2015–16	1.50	–	–	–	1.09
Malaysia	EAP	2013	0.72	–	0.51	0.06	0.11
Maldives	SA	2010–11	1.21	–	0.02	1.02	–
Mali	SSA	2016	0.60	–	0.11	–	0.05
Marshall Islands	EAP	2009	1.05	–	–	–	–
Mauritania	SSA	2015–16	2.49	1.65	–	–	0.08
Mauritius	SSA	2014–15	3.46	–	0.25	3.19	–
Mexico	LAC	2015	1.67	0.39	0.34	0.22	–
Moldova	ECA	2015	1.25	–	0.83	0.42	–
Mongolia	EAP	2010–13	2.00	–	1.60	0.28	–
Montenegro	ECA	2013	1.76	–	1.04	0.57	–
Morocco	MENA	2014–16	1.09	0.10	0.01	–	0.10
Mozambique	SSA	2010, 2015	1.27	–	0.55	–	0.09
Myanmar	EAP	2013–15	0.27	..	–	–	–
Namibia	SSA	2014	3.19	–	0.29	2.82	0.08
Nepal	SA	2010, 2014	1.32	–	0.85	0.28	0.16
Nicaragua	LAC	2013	2.22	–	0.19	–	0.20

| | Annual spending as a percentage of GDP | | | | Annual absolute spending per capita (2011 $PPP) | |
Public works	In kind	All fee waivers	Other SA	Total excluding health fee waivers	Total	Total excluding health fee waivers
0.65	0.30	–	–	0.97	16	16
–	0.02	0.34	0.02	1.05	104	96
–	–	0.14	–	0.06	31	9
–	–	1.24	0.02	5.75	588	483
0.01	–	0.11	0.03	0.54	26	24
0.77	..	..	0.21	1.98	275	275
–	0.05	–	–	0.19	13	13
0.29	–	1.18	–	1.49	16	15
–	–	0.01	–	0.01	0	0
–	..	–	..	0.77	34	34
–	–	–	–	3.06	698	698
0.25	1.03	0.06	0.06	1.51	77	77
..	–	0.51	0.01	0.65	83	64
–	2.20	–	..	2.56	368	368
–	–	–	–	0.68	68	68
0.04	–	–	0.10	1.62	390	390
0.03	0.01	0.02	–	0.35	11	10
–	–	–	–	0.69	12	12
–	–	–	0.04	2.84	255	255
–	–	0.41	–	0.80	525	525
0.01	0.02	–	–	3.08	101	101
0.05	0.03	–	0.01	0.16	7	7
0.07	0.01	0.06	..	0.77	178	177
–	–	0.61	–	0.44	157	66
0.63	0.27	0.18	–	7.09	188	188
1.00	0.50	–	–	2.64	23	23
0.05	–	–	–	0.45	124	124
–	–	..	0.01	1.22	152	151
0.03	0.01	–	..	0.16	2	2
0.41	–	–	–	1.50	16	16
–	0.03	–	–	0.72	164	164
–	–	0.10	0.07	1.11	135	124
0.07	0.31	–	0.06	0.60	11	11
–	–	–	–	1.05	33	33
–	0.70	0.07	–	2.43	28	28
–	0.02	–	–	3.46	626	626
0.01	0.07	0.62	0.02	1.13	269	181
–	–	–	–	1.25	62	62
–	–	–	0.12	2.00	202	202
–	0.07	–	0.09	1.76	246	246
–	0.02	0.14	0.72	0.95	80	70
0.13	0.44	0.04	0.02	1.27	15	15
–	–	0.27	..	0.03	12	1
–	–	–	–	3.19	334	334
–	–	–	0.03	1.32	29	29
–	..	1.70	0.14	1.03	98	46

(Table continues next page)

TABLE D.1 Spending on Social Safety Net Programs *(Continued)*

Country/Economy/Territory	Region	Year	Annual spending as a percentage of GDP				
			Total	CCT	UCT	Social pension	School feeding
Niger	SSA	2016	0.67	0.11	–	–	0.02
Nigeria	SSA	2014–16	0.28	–	–	..	–
Pakistan	SA	2011, 2016	0.58	..	0.43	–	–
Panama	LAC	2014–15	1.52	0.08	0.57	0.33	0.05
Papua New Guinea	EAP	2015	0.01	–	–	0.01	–
Peru	LAC	2015	1.43	0.49	–	0.13	0.20
Philippines	EAP	2013–14	0.67	0.49	0.01	0.02	0.00
Poland	ECA	2013	1.98	–	1.48	0.22	–
Romania	ECA	2014	1.06	0.14	0.46	0.39	–
Russian Federation	ECA	2015	1.89	–	–	–	–
Rwanda	SSA	2015–16	1.50	–	1.21	0.09	–
Samoa	EAP	2014	0.76	–	–	0.76	–
São Tomé and Príncipe	SSA	2014	..	..	–	..	–
Saudi Arabia	MENA	2012	0.71	..	0.35	0.36	..
Senegal	SSA	2015	0.99	0.21	0.49	–	0.03
Serbia	ECA	2013	1.96	–	1.50	0.45	–
Seychelles	SSA	2015	2.57	–	0.45	2.06	–
Sierra Leone	SSA	2011, 2016	0.90	0.14	0.03	–	0.45
Slovak Republic	ECA	2013	2.43	–	–	–	–
Slovenia	ECA	2013	2.61	–	–	–	–
Somalia	SSA	2015–16	0.18	0.18	–	–	–
South Africa	SSA	2015	3.31	–	1.27	1.68	0.13
South Sudan	SSA	2016	10.10	–	–	–	–
Sri Lanka	SA	2013–15	0.66	0.01	0.39	0.04	0.04
St. Lucia	LAC	2013–14	0.48	–	0.20	–	0.03
Sudan	SSA	2016	1.02	0.02	0.50	–	0.01
Swaziland	SSA	2010–11	1.71	–	0.77	0.47	0.09
Tajikistan	ECA	2014	0.56	0.02	0.10	0.33	–
Tanzania	SSA	2016	0.46	0.25	–	–	0.13
Thailand	EAP	2010–11	0.47	–	–	0.30	0.07
Timor-Leste	EAP	2015	6.48	0.31	0.02	5.71	0.12
Togo	SSA	2010, 2015	0.18	–	..	–	0.04
Tunisia	MENA	2013–15	0.76	0.03	0.54	–	–
Turkey	ECA	2013	1.14	0.04	0.22	0.22	0.02
Uganda	SSA	2014–16	0.77	0.17	0.01	0.10	–
Ukraine	ECA	2014	4.36	0.39	2.32	0.44	–
Uruguay	LAC	2015	1.15	0.29	0.14	0.54	–
Vanuatu	EAP	2009	0.28	–	–	–	–
Vietnam	EAP	2015	1.02	..	0.87	..	0.03
West Bank and Gaza	MENA	2013–14	2.34	–	1.13	..	–
Zambia	SSA	2016	0.25	–	0.01	0.02	0.02
Zimbabwe	SSA	2015	0.43	–	0.11	..	–

Source: ASPIRE database, except for Hungary, Slovak Republic, and Slovenia, for which the data come from ESSPROS (European System of Integrated Social Protection Statistics).
Note: The total social safety net spending for the Russian Federation is provided by the Research Institute of Finance of the Ministry of Finance of the Russia Federation in collaboration with the ASPIRE team. ASPIRE = Atlas of Social Protection: Indicators of Reselience and Equity; CCT = conditional cash transfer; ECA = Europe and Central Asia; EAP = East Asia and Pacific; FW = fee waivers; IK = in-kind; LAC = Latin America and the Caribbean; MENA = Middle East and North Africa; PPP = purchasing power parity; PW = public works; Other SA = other social assistance; SA = South Asia; SSA = Sub-Saharan Africa; UCT = unconditional cash transfer. – = not available; .. = value was very close to zero (less than 0.001 percent).

	Annual spending as a percentage of GDP				Annual absolute spending per capita (2011 $PPP)	
Public works	In kind	All fee waivers	Other SA	Total excluding health fee waivers	Total	Total excluding health fee waivers
0.03	0.50	–	–	0.67	6	6
0.28	–	–	–	0.28	13	13
..	–	..	0.14	0.58	27	27
..	0.03	0.45	0.01	1.52	325	325
–	–	–	–	0.01	0	0
–	0.06	0.29	0.27	1.14	159	127
..	0.03	0.11	0.01	0.56	43	36
0.03	0.10	..	0.14	1.98	501	501
..	0.01	–	0.06	1.06	212	212
–	–	–	–	1.89	437	437
0.13	..	–	0.08	1.50	25	25
–	–	–	–	0.76	43	43
–	–	–	–	..	0	0
–	–	–	–	0.71	352	352
–	0.13	0.10	0.03	0.89	22	20
0.01	–	..	–	1.96	253	253
–	0.02	–	0.04	2.57	671	671
–	0.18	0.02	0.08	0.90	13	13
–	–	–	–	2.43	626	626
–	–	–	–	2.61	698	698
–	–	–	–	0.18	2	2
0.22	0.01	–	..	3.31	408	408
0.05	10.05	–	–	10.10	92	92
–	0.12	0.01	0.04	0.66	76	76
0.23	–	–	0.03	0.48	49	49
0.01	0.13	0.35	–	0.67	42	28
0.07	0.10	0.22	..	1.49	130	114
–	–	–	0.12	0.56	18	18
0.06	0.02	–	..	0.46	11	11
–	0.08	–	0.01	0.47	64	64
0.33	–	–	–	6.48	116	116
–	0.02	0.12	–	0.07	3	1
–	–	0.16	0.02	0.59	79	62
0.04	0.09	0.32	0.19	0.82	207	150
0.20	0.04	–	0.25	0.77	14	14
..	..	0.62	0.59	4.34	395	393
0.02	0.12	–	0.04	1.15	231	231
–	–	–	–	0.28	8	8
–	0.03	0.07	0.01	1.02	57	57
0.17	0.90	0.15	–	2.24	106	102
–	0.02	0.18	..	0.25	9	9
0.06	0.20	0.05	0.01	0.43	8	8

APPENDIX E
Monthly Benefit Level Per Household

TABLE E.1 Monthly Benefit Level Per Household for Selected Programs
$PPP 2011

Country	Year	Income group	Program name	Monthly transfer amount in $PPP 2011
Argentina	2016	UMIC	Asignación Universal por Hijo para la Protección Social	468
Ukraine	2014	LMIC	Social assistance for low-income families	362
Mauritius	2016	UMIC	Basic Widow's Pension	255
South Africa	2008	UMIC	Disability grant	226
Cambodia	2015	LMIC	MoEYS Scholarships for Primary and Secondary Education	141
China	2016	UMIC	Urban Dibao	129
Romania	2014	UMIC	Minimum guaranteed income	118
Peru	2013	UMIC	Juntos	112
Brazil	2016	UMIC	Bolsa Familia	101
Namibia	2014	UMIC	Provision of Social Assistance	95
Philippines	2016	LMIC	Pantawid Pamilyang Pilipino Program (4Ps)	66
Fiji	2016	UMIC	Poverty Benefit Scheme (PBS)	61
Cameroon	2016	LMIC	Pilot CCT with Productive Aspects	59
Mexico	2015	UMIC	Prospera	58
Malaysia	2014	UMIC	Bantuan Rakyat 1 Malaysia (BR1M) scheme	48
Pakistan	2015	LMIC	Benazir Income Support Program (BISP)	48
Angola	2015	LMIC	Cartão Kikuia—Kikuia Card Cash Transfer Programme	48
Indonesia	2017	LMIC	Program Keluarga Harapan (PKH)	44
Kenya	2016	LMIC	Cash transfer for OVC (CT-OVC)	43
Burkina Faso	2015	LIC	Social Safety net project "Burkin-Nong-Saya"	43
Niger	2011	LIC	Projet de Filets Sociaux	43
Lesotho	2016	LMIC	Child Grants Program (CGP)	40
Senegal	2015	LIC	National cash transfer programme	33
Ghana	2015	LMIC	Livelihood Empowerment Against Poverty (LEAP)	28
Mozambique	2015	LIC	Basic Social Subsidy Programme	26
Sierra Leone	2011	LIC	Social Safety Nets Program	25
Congo, Dem. Rep.	2016	LIC	UNICEF – Femme et Homme Progressons Ensemble	25
Mongolia	2015	LMIC	The Child Money programme	23
Malawi	2016	LIC	Social Cash Transfer Scheme (SCTS)	19
Kazakhstan	2014	UMIC	Conditional Targeted Social Assistance (CTSA)	19
Swaziland	2011	LMIC	Public assistance	15
Mauritania	2013	LMIC	Tekavou – conditional cash transfers	13
Bangladesh	2016	LMIC	Allowances for Widows, Deserted and Destitute Women	12
Timor-Leste	2011	LMIC	Bolsa da Mãe	11
Madagascar	2016	LIC	Filets Sociaux de Sécurité (FSS)	2
Zambia	2016	LMIC	Social Cash Transfer Scheme	0

Source: ASPIRE.
Note: ASPIRE = Atlas of Social Protection: Indicators of Resilience and Equity; LIC = low-income country; LMIC = lower-middle-income country; OVC = orphans and vulnerable children; PPP = purchasing power parity; UMIC = upper-middle-income country; UNICEF = United Nations Children's Fund.

APPENDIX F
Performance Indicators

TABLE F.1 Key Performance Indicators of Social Protection and Labor Programs

Percent

Country/economy/ territory	Year	Coverage		Benefit incidence	Beneficiary incidence	Transfer as a share of beneficiary welfare (adequacy)	
		Poorest quintile	Total	Poorest quintile	Poorest quintile	Poorest quintile	Total
Afghanistan	2011	12.47	8.82	–	28.27	–	–
Albania	2012	71.81	54.89	25.61	26.14	34.80	27.99
Argentina	2013	70.18	46.36	11.43	30.27	34.76	38.15
Armenia	2014	88.08	66.76	33.46	26.37	59.81	33.63
Bangladesh	2010	28.81	17.77	46.25	32.42	5.40	9.12
Belarus	2013	97.46	75.05	34.35	25.89	73.16	48.08
Belize	2009	47.02	39.39	51.04	23.79	53.07	23.35
Bhutan	2012	4.68	2.92	54.42	32.04	17.20	27.64
Bolivia	2012	91.55	76.75	17.66	23.85	41.14	13.50
Botswana	2009	94.93	73.77	32.76	25.71	22.53	9.53
Brazil	2015	78.84	53.81	9.24	29.30	36.09	44.76
Burkina Faso	2014	1.96	4.28	3.51	9.16	32.18	17.15
Cameroon	2014	1.17	5.01	7.11	4.67	2.91	3.13
Central African Republic	2008	0.87	1.39	11.28	12.54	27.87	4.82
Chad	2011	1.96	2.97	16.97	13.17	41.18	24.52
Chile	2013	97.34	88.54	18.68	21.98	20.29	18.76
China	2013	81.67	63.05	27.84	25.90	17.03	36.83
Colombia	2014	83.86	65.68	4.40	25.51	13.06	25.30
Congo, Dem. Rep.	2012	15.08	11.06	37.61	27.26	64.40	38.26
Costa Rica	2014	85.51	66.64	9.18	25.66	27.53	28.58
Croatia	2010	93.48	70.72	25.56	26.41	45.34	39.52
Côte d'Ivoire	2014	42.29	32.86	36.75	25.73	75.38	47.54
Djibouti	2012	40.05	20.94	51.77	38.23	28.90	28.95
Dominican Republic	2014	46.60	34.53	12.91	26.98	13.31	12.72
Ecuador	2016	88.99	72.70	12.02	24.47	34.04	32.67
Egypt, Arab Rep.	2008	67.96	55.45	19.77	24.51	14.96	21.03
El Salvador	2014	73.43	58.09	4.98	25.25	11.76	25.86
Ethiopia	2010	16.21	13.25	–	24.46	–	–
Fiji	2008	24.90	14.33	51.76	34.73	38.12	24.20
Gambia, The	2010	6.11	8.31	13.75	14.66	27.56	5.22
Georgia	2011	92.95	64.65	38.82	28.72	68.49	29.25
Ghana	2012	64.63	63.73	56.26	20.28	62.48	91.72
Guatemala	2014	72.27	63.25	1.54	22.84	25.20	22.32
Guinea	2012	2.07	3.89	7.59	10.64	29.46	10.27

(Table continues next page)

TABLE F.1 Key Performance Indicators of Social Protection and Labor Programs *(Continued)*

Country/economy/territory	Year	Coverage		Benefit incidence	Beneficiary incidence	Transfer as a share of beneficiary welfare (adequacy)	
		Poorest quintile	Total	Poorest quintile	Poorest quintile	Poorest quintile	Total
Haiti	2012	21.53	19.46	–	22.11	33.08	34.60
Honduras	2013	72.34	55.79	11.42	25.92	24.58	13.33
India	2011	30.45	29.71	–	20.49	–	–
Indonesia	2015	83.07	57.41	52.67	28.94	27.32	15.94
Iraq	2012	91.65	83.56	18.72	21.92	9.63	9.52
Jamaica	2010	76.67	58.26	25.32	26.20	11.02	11.59
Jordan	2010	89.02	73.19	22.52	24.32	20.78	18.49
Kazakhstan	2010	64.11	48.31	17.16	26.54	9.85	9.10
Kosovo	2013	67.06	44.53	27.44	30.06	26.37	17.81
Kyrgyz Republic	2013	81.45	57.86	37.01	28.15	57.57	42.16
Latvia	2009	96.51	80.30	32.45	24.02	59.08	32.37
Liberia	2014	9.66	7.33	28.35	26.31	16.88	9.49
Lithuania	2008	97.53	81.91	37.82	23.82	80.09	33.19
Madagascar	2010	1.25	5.90	96.40	4.23	2.63	39.07
Malawi	2013	43.19	42.46	21.47	17.64	1.83	1.92
Malaysia	2008	94.78	84.09	14.73	22.54	8.36	4.51
Maldives	2009	16.32	14.85	20.88	18.47	74.50	24.21
Mauritania	2014	47.46	45.22	–	20.98	–	–
Mauritius	2012	85.62	46.63	42.59	36.71	63.01	45.87
Mexico	2012	83.38	72.23	20.10	23.08	31.92	28.59
Moldova	2013	79.60	56.59	30.89	28.09	51.06	34.33
Mongolia	2012	99.83	99.90	25.69	19.97	40.99	20.71
Montenegro	2014	86.60	56.44	29.49	30.68	46.68	50.78
Morocco	2009	52.47	41.01	–	25.57	–	–
Mozambique	2008	9.81	6.98	29.90	28.03	188.17	43.10
Namibia	2009	26.52	16.15	–	32.85	–	–
Nepal	2010	54.27	43.49	21.86	24.96	3.78	5.95
Nicaragua	2014	77.04	68.15	4.96	22.60	42.30	17.14
Niger	2014	17.28	21.38	7.03	16.14	3.53	3.38
Nigeria	2015	6.06	6.41	20.11	18.88	7.40	18.37
Pakistan	2013	25.08	16.80	13.38	29.86	8.40	19.53
Panama	2014	86.52	63.39	9.11	27.28	20.63	19.72
Papua New Guinea	2009	2.10	4.24	4.47	9.87	1.28	0.46
Paraguay	2011	74.33	52.27	3.72	28.43	24.02	29.23
Peru	2014	88.68	64.85	6.53	27.34	13.46	17.83
Philippines	2015	67.56	40.62	15.32	33.26	9.08	7.75
Poland	2012	97.03	64.41	35.59	30.13	65.61	60.56
Romania	2012	98.47	83.69	31.98	23.52	45.78	49.18
Russian Federation	2016	94.18	77.88	19.18	24.19	30.29	25.58
Rwanda	2013	37.96	31.40	28.05	24.17	8.33	4.93
Senegal	2011	10.58	16.79	9.30	12.59	4.81	11.79
Serbia	2013	90.37	63.18	29.72	28.57	58.80	54.96
Sierra Leone	2011	34.57	30.20	15.05	22.89	0.00	0.00

(Table continues next page)

TABLE F.1 Key Performance Indicators of Social Protection and Labor Programs *(Continued)*

| Country/economy/territory | Year | Coverage | | Benefit incidence | Beneficiary incidence | Transfer as a share of beneficiary welfare (adequacy) | |
		Poorest quintile	Total	Poorest quintile	Poorest quintile	Poorest quintile	Total
Slovak Republic	2009	98.69	88.62	29.63	22.26	31.85	32.30
South Africa	2010	96.10	62.76	39.97	30.61	72.36	23.87
South Sudan	2009	3.42	6.24	8.67	10.96	3.85	1.53
Sri Lanka	2012	53.61	33.13	21.39	32.36	7.85	15.46
Sudan	2009	13.10	7.45	18.40	35.18	1.07	1.05
Swaziland	2009	77.28	51.65	44.84	29.90	21.71	15.70
Tajikistan	2011	50.92	39.29	21.99	25.83	10.86	7.60
Tanzania	2014	13.32	17.21	9.82	15.47	11.88	13.35
Thailand	2013	87.11	79.38	32.79	21.94	13.45	16.62
Timor-Leste	2011	41.71	35.33	7.55	23.58	16.75	20.62
Tunisia	2010	20.07	14.43	20.58	27.79	17.99	3.80
Turkey	2014	74.85	49.87	16.39	30.01	31.87	37.85
Uganda	2012	76.01	60.71	11.78	25.02	5.22	13.51
Ukraine	2013	96.92	71.71	36.12	27.03	67.70	51.16
Uruguay	2012	96.00	79.82	8.26	24.06	42.06	45.24
Vietnam	2014	58.29	34.86	16.13	33.44	7.70	22.52
West Bank and Gaza	2009	25.91	10.72	56.45	48.31	21.59	20.67
Zambia	2010	1.61	1.62	60.30	19.89	37.61	34.02
Zimbabwe	2011	38.53	29.55	12.93	26.07	25.08	21.26

Source: ASPIRE.
Note: The information presented is for 96 countries/economies/territories for which household survey data are available. The poorest quintile is calculated using per capita post transfer welfare (income or consumption) except for the indicator that expresses the social transfers as a share of total beneficiary welfare, which includes transfers. ASPIRE = Atlas of Social Protection: Indicators of Resilience and Equity; − = not available.

TABLE F.2 Key Performance Indicators of Social Safety Nets Programs

Percent

| Country/economy/territory | Year | Coverage | | Benefit incidence | Beneficiary incidence | Transfer as a share of beneficiary welfare (adequacy) | |
		Poorest quintile	Total	Poorest quintile	Poorest quintile	Poorest quintile	Total
Afghanistan	2011	12.47	8.82	−	28.27	−	−
Albania	2012	31.34	19.08	39.34	32.82	10.88	6.02
Argentina	2013	49.19	19.76	54.41	49.78	21.92	11.31
Armenia	2014	45.67	28.40	50.92	32.15	32.39	16.99
Bangladesh	2010	24.81	13.09	47.26	37.90	4.39	4.00
Belarus	2013	70.40	54.10	31.97	25.95	23.04	11.09
Belize	2009	20.12	16.28	32.63	24.63	23.43	8.62
Bhutan	2012	3.95	2.25	−	34.98	−	−
Bolivia	2012	91.33	75.18	30.12	24.29	40.70	7.76
Botswana	2009	94.93	73.77	32.76	25.71	22.53	9.53

(Table continues next page)

TABLE F.2 Key Performance Indicators of Social Safety Nets Programs (Continued)

Country/economy/territory	Year	Coverage		Benefit incidence	Beneficiary incidence	Transfer as a share of beneficiary welfare (adequacy)	
		Poorest quintile	Total	Poorest quintile	Poorest quintile	Poorest quintile	Total
Brazil	2015	64.15	23.72	57.02	54.10	24.52	17.27
Burkina Faso	2014	1.58	2.29	1.87	13.82	12.82	5.50
Cameroon	2014	0.12	0.87	32.02	2.79	–	2.61
Central African Republic	2008	0.39	0.57	–	13.77	–	–
Chad	2011	0.15	0.57	12.20	5.40	23.18	10.48
Chile	2013	93.40	74.69	38.09	25.00	14.12	7.66
China	2013	60.99	43.81	33.00	27.84	6.02	2.34
Colombia	2014	83.32	59.25	40.79	28.10	12.36	5.10
Congo, Dem. Rep.	2012	14.11	9.99	38.42	28.24	65.10	37.45
Costa Rica	2014	79.43	45.85	50.03	34.65	22.88	13.31
Croatia	2010	46.34	24.57	48.36	37.69	15.69	8.92
Côte d'Ivoire	2014	36.09	27.23	33.27	26.50	9.76	14.74
Djibouti	2012	32.71	9.53	71.33	68.65	20.92	11.91
Dominican Republic	2014	44.75	29.96	27.77	29.87	10.67	5.25
Ecuador	2016	87.48	67.19	50.21	26.03	29.49	13.73
Egypt, Arab Rep.	2008	59.09	44.88	28.87	26.33	5.00	3.56
El Salvador	2014	71.86	53.14	44.15	27.01	9.38	7.39
Ethiopia	2010	16.21	13.25	–	24.46	–	–
Fiji	2008	16.47	9.55	57.00	34.47	30.28	14.02
Gambia, The	2010	5.73	7.08	–	16.15	–	–
Georgia	2011	92.95	64.64	38.78	28.72	68.43	29.18
Ghana	2012	1.60	1.51	52.89	21.14	74.90	23.55
Guatemala	2014	71.48	59.08	–	24.19	–	–
Guinea	2012	1.29	1.71	–	14.99	–	–
Haiti	2012	21.53	19.13	–	22.49	–	–
Honduras	2013	72.05	54.22	31.60	26.56	23.80	5.65
India	2011	26.56	17.27	–	30.75	–	–
Indonesia	2015	82.05	48.74	52.67	33.67	27.32	15.94
Iraq	2012	87.15	75.77	34.26	22.98	3.45	2.75
Jamaica	2010	73.88	54.97	45.70	26.75	9.62	4.63
Jordan	2010	86.42	65.68	47.67	26.31	6.89	3.98
Kazakhstan	2010	43.99	30.58	25.49	28.77	5.23	3.34
Kosovo	2013	42.66	14.05	72.18	60.60	22.95	12.99
Kyrgyz Republic	2013	15.66	7.18	48.37	43.63	17.61	11.15
Latvia	2009	58.11	50.81	36.93	22.85	14.85	7.08
Liberia	2014	9.66	7.33	28.35	26.31	16.88	9.49
Lithuania	2008	57.80	58.67	33.07	19.70	18.59	6.50
Madagascar	2010	0.22	0.24	96.40	17.93	2.63	39.07
Malawi	2013	42.79	41.74	13.56	17.78	1.76	1.03
Malaysia	2008	94.25	82.81	25.54	22.76	6.49	1.75
Maldives	2009	15.40	13.49	22.21	19.19	75.63	24.76

(Table continues next page)

TABLE F.2 Key Performance Indicators of Social Safety Nets Programs *(Continued)*

Country/economy/territory	Year	Coverage		Benefit incidence	Beneficiary incidence	Transfer as a share of beneficiary welfare (adequacy)	
		Poorest quintile	Total	Poorest quintile	Poorest quintile	Poorest quintile	Total
Mauritania	2014	47.46	45.22	–	20.98	–	–
Mauritius	2012	83.52	44.85	45.59	37.23	54.90	28.76
Mexico	2012	75.38	37.05	46.43	40.69	30.10	10.21
Moldova	2013	32.09	23.79	36.39	26.94	21.93	9.04
Mongolia	2012	99.83	99.83	22.36	19.98	26.10	11.07
Montenegro	2014	24.81	8.08	55.47	61.45	27.98	22.09
Morocco	2009	50.11	36.59	–	27.37	–	–
Mozambique	2008	7.75	5.40	–	28.65	–	–
Namibia	2009	26.08	15.18	–	34.37	–	–
Nepal	2010	53.24	40.14	24.58	26.53	3.60	2.51
Nicaragua	2014	74.27	59.75	–	24.86	–	–
Niger	2014	17.27	20.11	16.97	17.15	3.53	1.63
Nigeria	2015	4.34	3.76	8.71	23.02	1.24	2.26
Pakistan	2013	22.45	11.20	31.61	40.10	6.09	7.91
Panama	2014	83.78	51.12	35.03	32.76	17.52	6.78
Papua New Guinea	2009	1.92	3.36	7.70	11.44	0.17	0.04
Paraguay	2011	74.07	47.75	60.65	31.01	19.64	13.45
Peru	2014	88.02	56.10	65.18	31.38	12.49	7.99
Philippines	2015	66.28	33.83	33.20	39.18	8.85	5.43
Poland	2012	65.49	38.75	52.03	33.80	27.46	10.24
Romania	2012	74.67	61.83	41.30	24.14	19.70	10.91
Russian Federation	2016	85.30	67.89	29.69	25.13	10.47	6.80
Rwanda	2013	23.00	20.09	35.09	22.90	9.94	4.59
Senegal	2011	6.06	8.24	18.37	14.69	6.96	7.22
Serbia	2013	27.00	11.72	52.91	46.00	27.17	19.00
Sierra Leone	2011	34.57	30.20	–	–	–	–
Slovak Republic	2009	97.49	83.20	40.81	23.42	14.45	4.37
South Africa	2010	96.10	60.81	39.97	31.60	72.36	23.87
South Sudan	2009	3.42	6.24	8.67	10.96	3.85	1.53
Sri Lanka	2012	48.29	26.19	46.02	36.88	5.83	3.65
Sudan	2009	13.10	7.45	18.40	35.18	1.07	1.05
Swaziland	2009	77.28	51.65	44.84	29.90	21.71	15.70
Tajikistan	2011	13.70	9.75	8.52	28.00	1.26	2.43
Tanzania	2014	9.22	10.94	42.95	16.85	5.82	3.69
Thailand	2013	83.75	59.32	35.01	28.23	13.08	6.21
Timor-Leste	2011	41.71	35.21	13.87	23.66	3.72	2.06
Tunisia	2010	20.07	14.43	20.58	27.79	17.99	3.80
Turkey	2014	44.50	17.68	45.56	50.35	7.78	5.77
Uganda	2012	75.93	60.47	16.95	25.10	3.66	9.46
Ukraine	2013	71.91	48.07	39.25	29.91	21.28	11.76
Uruguay	2012	86.28	59.21	–	29.14	–	–

(Table continues next page)

TABLE F.2 Key Performance Indicators of Social Safety Nets Programs *(Continued)*

Country/economy/territory	Year	Coverage		Benefit incidence	Beneficiary incidence	Transfer as a share of beneficiary welfare (adequacy)	
		Poorest quintile	Total	Poorest quintile	Poorest quintile	Poorest quintile	Total
Vietnam	2014	48.41	17.51	73.04	55.29	4.64	2.89
West Bank and Gaza	2009	25.91	10.72	56.45	48.31	21.59	20.67
Zambia	2010	1.02	0.57	–	35.78	–	–
Zimbabwe	2011	37.92	27.73	42.71	27.34	19.79	19.24

Source: ASPIRE.
Note: The information presented here is for 96 countries for which household survey data are available. ASPIRE = Atlas of Social Protection: Indicators of Resilience and Equity. The poorest quintile is calculated using per capita post-transfer welfare (income or consumption) except for the indicator that expresses the social transfers as a share of total beneficiary welfare, which includes transfers. – = not available.

TABLE F.3 Poverty and Inequality Reduction as a Result of Social Safety Nets Programs

Country/economy/territory	Year	Poverty headcount reduction (% population)		Poverty gap reduction (% population)		Gini inequality reduction (%)	Benefit-cost ratio ($PPP)	
		Poorest quintile	$1.90 poverty line	Poorest quintile	$1.90 poverty line	Total population	Poorest quintile	$1.90 poverty line
Afghanistan	2011	–	–	–	–	–	–	–
Albania	2012	4.62	38.20	10.97	65.63	1.62	0.33	0.03
Argentina	2013	6.46	60.09	16.69	79.12	2.13	0.52	0.04
Armenia	2014	11.79	49.02	28.69	67.50	4.24	0.43	0.13
Bangladesh	2010	3.21	4.11	6.26	8.17	0.71	0.34	0.26
Belarus	2013	24.19	100.00	43.37	100.00	9.78	0.38	0.01
Belize	2009	0.71	58.74	2.24	88.79	0.18	0.26	0.13
Bhutan	2012	–	–	–	–	–	–	–
Bolivia	2012	17.35	33.62	28.86	43.56	5.30	0.29	0.13
Botswana	2009	20.02	28.64	38.36	49.19	3.92	0.19	0.14
Brazil	2015	10.90	39.39	23.55	59.89	2.78	0.44	0.11
Burkina Faso	2014	0.00	0.12	0.10	0.06	−0.08	0.02	0.00
Cameroon	2014	0.12	0.10	0.35	0.29	0.02	0.17	0.20
Central African Republic	2008	–	–	–	–	–	–	–
Chad	2011	0.07	0.16	0.16	0.11	−0.01	0.05	0.13
Chile	2013	14.42	55.09	25.50	65.89	3.48	0.31	0.02
China	2013	5.03	16.60	10.03	24.83	1.09	0.29	0.07
Colombia	2014	6.54	15.74	10.63	20.17	0.95	0.38	0.11
Congo, Dem. Rep.	2012	8.89	1.98	18.55	4.40	0.50	0.10	0.40
Costa Rica	2014	8.92	38.82	16.88	49.04	1.90	0.42	0.04
Croatia	2010	9.00	100.00	24.04	100.00	3.87	0.49	0.01
Côte d'Ivoire	2014	0.21	0.18	0.34	0.29	0.01	0.10	0.12
Djibouti	2012	2.42	3.52	7.60	9.46	0.90	0.61	0.56
Dominican Republic	2014	6.10	20.50	10.25	19.40	1.32	0.26	0.01
Ecuador	2016	7.58	24.82	17.23	36.52	2.22	0.43	0.15
Egypt, Arab Rep.	2008	5.78	22.83	11.69	50.13	1.35	0.22	0.01
El Salvador	2014	1.90	7.40	3.14	13.60	0.36	0.36	0.07

(Table continues next page)

TABLE F.3 Poverty and Inequality Reduction as a Result of Social Safety Nets Programs
(Continued)

Country/economy/ territory	Year	Poverty headcount reduction (% population)		Poverty gap reduction (% population)		Gini inequality reduction (%)	Benefit-cost ratio ($PPP)	
		Poorest quintile	$1.90 poverty line	Poorest quintile	$1.90 poverty line	Total population	Poorest quintile	$1.90 poverty line
Ethiopia	2010	–	–	–	–	–	–	–
Fiji	2008	5.75	9.79	11.22	29.54	1.04	0.21	0.09
Gambia, The	2010	–	–	–	–	–	–	–
Georgia	2011	42.63	61.18	68.39	80.73	19.06	0.33	0.23
Ghana	2012	0.10	0.00	0.36	0.07	0.02	0.23	0.57
Guatemala	2014	–	–	–	–	–	–	–
Guinea	2012	–	–	–	–	–	–	–
Haiti	2012	–	–	–	–	–	–	–
Honduras	2013	5.93	7.35	11.10	11.56	1.19	0.27	0.25
India	2011	–	–	–	–	–	–	–
Indonesia	2015	16.87	45.02	38.17	67.97	4.62	0.47	0.22
Iraq	2012	7.88	81.18	14.77	96.63	1.55	0.21	0.02
Jamaica	2010	10.18	16.39	9.42	43.44	1.20	0.40	0.05
Jordan	2010	10.35	94.95	24.78	98.56	3.02	0.35	0.02
Kazakhstan	2010	5.48	32.49	8.93	42.89	1.11	0.24	0.00
Kosovo	2013	7.53	59.23	21.77	76.49	3.83	0.62	0.10
Kyrgyz Republic	2013	4.74	14.58	10.57	32.82	1.39	0.44	0.16
Latvia	2009	11.44	69.48	26.44	84.53	4.05	0.30	0.03
Liberia	2014	2.45	–	4.94	–	0.69	0.20	–
Lithuania	2008	14.64	100.00	29.83	100.00	4.45	0.30	0.00
Madagascar	2010	0.04	0.02	0.18	0.03	−0.11	0.02	0.08
Malawi	2013	0.55	0.23	1.03	0.58	0.13	0.14	0.41
Malaysia	2008	6.26	59.79	13.34	68.05	1.32	0.24	0.01
Maldives	2009	11.74	47.40	27.93	76.06	3.86	0.29	0.11
Mauritania	2014	–	–	–	–	–	–	–
Mauritius	2012	36.88	89.05	60.93	96.20	13.83	0.32	0.06
Mexico	2012	13.18	36.18	29.70	54.04	3.38	0.42	0.19
Moldova	2013	9.61	91.54	23.80	96.29	3.24	0.37	0.03
Mongolia	2012	34.75	90.11	52.85	95.26	10.28	0.24	0.01
Montenegro	2014	3.94	100.00	23.08	100.00	2.59	0.53	0.01
Morocco	2009	–	–	–	–	–	–	–
Mozambique	2008	–	–	–	–	–	–	–
Namibia	2009	–	–	–	–	–	–	–
Nepal	2010	4.79	6.26	7.16	8.73	0.72	0.20	0.13
Nicaragua	2014	–	–	–	–	–	–	–
Niger	2014	1.71	0.29	1.56	0.98	0.28	0.15	0.53
Nigeria	2015	0.26	0.06	0.26	0.16	0.02	0.08	0.32
Pakistan	2013	3.16	11.54	7.21	20.49	0.67	0.23	0.08
Panama	2014	12.33	41.87	20.45	52.37	2.77	0.31	0.05
Papua New Guinea	2009	0.00	0.00	0.00	0.04	0.00	0.08	0.03
Paraguay	2011	2.34	2.91	3.10	5.56	0.30	0.42	0.07

(Table continues next page)

TABLE F.3 Poverty and Inequality Reduction as a Result of Social Safety Nets Programs *(Continued)*

Country/economy/territory	Year	Poverty headcount reduction (% population)		Poverty gap reduction (% population)		Gini inequality reduction (%)	Benefit-cost ratio ($PPP)	
		Poorest quintile	$1.90 poverty line	Poorest quintile	$1.90 poverty line	Total population	Poorest quintile	$1.90 poverty line
Peru	2014	2.55	20.28	7.65	30.59	0.80	0.64	0.13
Philippines	2015	8.75	19.10	15.24	27.81	1.51	0.32	0.11
Poland	2012	17.03	98.76	41.58	99.76	7.25	0.53	0.03
Romania	2012	23.07	100.00	43.51	100.00	9.25	0.36	0.02
Russian Federation	2016	16.85	67.94	25.50	76.70	4.76	0.22	0.00
Rwanda	2013	3.99	0.58	8.12	2.12	0.61	0.21	0.51
Senegal	2011	0.91	0.67	1.63	1.00	−0.11	0.06	0.10
Serbia	2013	7.38	91.63	21.19	97.06	3.40	0.48	0.04
Sierra Leone	2011	–	–	–	–	–	–	–
Slovak Republic	2009	15.77	81.20	28.92	90.25	7.15	0.44	0.03
South Africa	2010	40.04	56.82	66.85	79.61	7.36	0.36	0.25
South Sudan	2009	0.06	0.00	0.09	0.07	0.00	0.06	0.17
Sri Lanka	2012	4.07	31.14	9.11	43.15	0.93	0.32	0.04
Sudan	2009	0.00	0.34	0.07	0.13	0.01	0.18	0.10
Swaziland	2009	11.72	6.12	27.75	14.34	2.79	0.20	0.35
Tajikistan	2011	0.35	1.83	0.67	2.05	−0.04	0.08	0.01
Tanzania	2014	0.90	0.01	0.38	0.27	0.05	0.24	0.54
Thailand	2013	11.55	87.79	21.14	96.55	2.62	0.30	0.00
Timor-Leste	2011	0.00	0.00	0.35	0.26	0.04	0.14	0.42
Tunisia	2010	0.27	–	1.73	–	0.14	0.20	–
Turkey	2014	4.18	77.62	8.49	84.94	0.97	0.43	0.01
Uganda	2012	0.35	0.23	0.54	0.44	−0.02	0.08	0.12
Ukraine	2013	23.29	99.49	44.57	99.99	9.39	0.39	0.02
Uruguay	2012	–	–	–	–	–	–	–
Vietnam	2014	0.90	15.86	4.19	31.32	0.43	0.68	0.19
West Bank and Gaza	2009	4.56	42.63	10.84	74.37	1.30	0.36	0.03
Zambia	2010	–	–	–	–	–	–	–
Zimbabwe	2011	0.93	–	1.89	–	0.15	0.18	–

Source: ASPIRE.
Note: The information presented here is for 96 countries for which household survey data are available. ASPIRE = Atlas of Social Protection: Indicators of Resilience and Equity. − = not available.

APPENDIX G
Old-Age Social Pensions

TABLE G.1 Old-Age Social Pensions around the World

Country/economy/territory	Region	Year	Name of scheme	Location
Algeria	MENA	2009–13	Allocation forfaitaire de solidarite	National
Antigua and Barbuda	LAC	2011	Old-Age Assistance Programme	National
Argentina	LAC	2011–13	Pensiones Asistenciales	National
Armenia	ECA	–	Old-Age Social Pension	National
Australia	OECD	2009–11	Age Pension	National
Azerbaijan	ECA	2008	Social Allowance (Old-Age)	National
Bangladesh	SA	2011–12	Old-Age Allowance	National
Barbados	LAC	2008–12	Noncontributory Old-Age Pension	National
Belarus	ECA	–	Social Pension	National
Belgium	OECD	2011–13	IGO/GRAPA (Income Guarantee for the Elderly)	National
Belize	LAC	2011	Non-Contributory Pension Programme (NCP)	National
Bolivia	LAC	2013–14	Renta Dignidad or Renta Universal de Vejez (previously Bonosol)	National
Botswana	SSA	2010	State old-age pension	National
Brazil	LAC	2011–13	Previdencia Rural (Rural Pension)	Regional/Rural
Brazil (2)	LAC	2012	Beneficio de Prestacao Continuada (BPC/Continuous Cash Benefit)	National
Brunei Darussalam	EAP	2009	Old-age pension	National
Bulgaria	ECA	–	Social Old-Age Pension	National
Cabo Verde	SSA	2011	Pensao Social Minima (Minimum Social Pension)	National
Canada	OECD	2011	Pension de la Securite Vieillesse (S.V.) (Old-Age Security Pension)	National
Chile	LAC	2012–14	Sistema de pensiones solidarias (vejez) –includes Pensión Básica Solidaria de Vejez (PBS-Vejez) and Aporte Previsional Solidario de Vejez (APS-Vejez)	National
China	EAP	2012	Rural social pension	National
Colombia	LAC	2012–14	Programa Colombia Mayor	National
Costa Rica	LAC	2009–10	Programa Regimen No Contributivo	National
Denmark	OECD	2012–13	Folkepension (national pension)	National
Ecuador	LAC	2012–13	Pension para Adultos Mayores (Pension for Older People)	National
El Salvador	LAC	2009–13	Pension Basica Universal (Universal Basic Pension)	National
Estonia	ECA	2012–13	National Pension	National
Fiji	EAP	2013–14	Social Pension Scheme (SPS)	National

Targeting	Age of eligibility (years)	Benefit level (% of GDP per capita)	Beneficiaries (% of population over eligible age)	Total cost (% of GDP)
Means-tested	60	21	14	0.06
Means-tested	77	8	–	0.02
Means-tested	70	25	1	0.04
Pensions-tested	65	8	–	–
Means-tested	65	26	71	2.23
Pensions-tested	Men: 67 Women: 62	10	–	–
Means-tested	Men: 65 Women: 62	5	35	0.08
Means-tested	65 and 6 months	23	30	0.74
Pensions-tested	Men: 60 Women: 55	5	–	–
Means-tested	65	35	5	0.30
Means-tested	Men: 67 Women: 65	12	30	0.13
Universal	60	15	155	1.08
Universal	65	4	133	0.27
Means-tested	Men: 60 Women: 55	31	42	0.98
Means-tested	65	33	12	0.26
Universal	60	6	143	0.02
Means-tested	70	11	–	–
Means-tested	60	17	84	0.93
Universal	65	12	96	1.45
Means-tested	65	12	55	0.05
	60	1	75	0.11
Means-tested	Men: 59 Women: 54	5	40	0.13
Means-tested	65	15	29	0.37
Means-tested	65	21	101	5.82
Means-tested	65	7	61	0.24
Means-tested	70	15	6	0.07
Pensions-tested	63	12	3	0.06
Pensions-tested	66	4	22	0.05

(Table continues next page)

TABLE G.1 Old-Age Social Pensions around the World (*Continued*)

Country/economy/territory	Region	Year	Name of scheme	Location
Finland	OECD	2010	Kansanelake (Old-Age Pension)	National
France	OECD	2007–12	Allocation de Solidarité aux Personnes Agées (ASPA)	National
Georgia	ECA	2010–12	Old-Age Pension	National
Germany	OECD	2012	Grundsicherung im Alter (Needs-Based Pension Supplement)	National
Greece	OECD	2008	Pension to uninsured elderly	National
Guatemala	LAC	2010–12	Programa de aporte economico o del Adulto Mayor (Economic Contribution Program for Older People)	National
Guyana	LAC	2014	Old-age Pension	National
Hong Kong SAR, China	EAP	2013	Normal/higher old-age allowance)	National
Hungary	ECA	2012	Idoskoruak jaradeka (Old-Age Allowance)	National
Iceland	OECD	2011	Lífeyristryggingar Almannatrygginga (National Basic Pension)	National
India	SA	2006–14	Indira Gandhi National Old-Age Pension Scheme	National
Indonesia	EAP	2010	Program Jaminan Sosial Lanjut Usia (JSLU) (Elderly Social Security Program) (pilot)	National
Ireland	OECD	2010	State Pension (noncontributory)	National
Israel	OECD	–	Special old-age benefit	National
Italy	OECD	–	Assegno sociale (Social Allowance)	National
Kazakhstan	ECA	–	State Basic Pension	National
Kenya	SSA	2011	Older Persons Cash Transfer	National
Kiribati	EAP	2010–12	Elderly fund	National
Korea, Rep. of	EAP	2009–11	Basic old-age pension	National
Kosovo	ECA	2011	Old-age "basic pension"	National
Kyrgyzstan	ECA	–	Social assistance allowance (old-age)	National
Latvia	ECA	–	State social security benefit	National
Lesotho	SSA	2009	Old-Age Pension	National
Lithuania	ECA	–	Old-age social assistance pension	National
Malaysia	EAP	2010	Bantuan Orang Tua (Elderly Assistance Scheme)	National
Maldives	SA	2011–12	Old-Age Basic Pension	National
Malta	MENA	2009	Age Pension	National
Mauritius	SSA	2011–14	Basic Retirement Pension	National
Mexico	LAC	2013	Pensión para Adultos Mayores	National
Moldova	ECA	2009	State Social Allocation for Aged Persons	National
Mongolia	EAP	2007	Social welfare pension	National
Mozambique	SSA	2013	Programa de Subsido Social Basico (PSSB) (Basic Social Subsidy Program)	National
Namibia	SSA	2007–10	Old-Age Pension (OAP)	National
Nepal	SA	2010	Old-Age Allowance	National
Netherlands	OECD	2011–13	Old-Age pension	National

Targeting	Age of eligibility (years)	Benefit level (% of GDP per capita)	Beneficiaries (% of population over eligible age)	Total cost (% of GDP)
Pensions-tested	65	20	53	0.90
Means-tested	65	29	6	0.25
Universal	Men: 65 Women: 60	18	106	2.96
Means-tested	65	12	3	–
Means-tested	60	24	3	0.18
Means-tested	65	18	16	0.13
Universal	65	18	151	1.06
Means-tested	65	4	61	0.38
Means-tested	62	9	0	0.01
Means-tested	67	6	66	0.60
Means-tested	60	2	25	0.03
Means-tested	70	9	0	–
Means-tested	66	33	18	0.60
Means-tested	Men: 65–67 Women: 60–64	13	–	–
Means-tested	65 and 3 months	21	–	–
Pensions-tested	Men: 63 Women: 58	5		–
Means-tested	65	24	5	0.02
Universal	67	36	56	0.74
Means-tested	65	4	70	0.30
Universal	65		91	1.19
Pensions-tested	Men: 63 Women: 58	17	–	–
Pensions-tested	67	6	–	–
Universal	70	39	93	1.31
Pensions-tested	Men: 62.5 Women: 60	2		–
Means-tested	60	10	9	0.04
Pensions-tested	65	21	91	1.03
Means-tested	60	30	8	0.24
Universal	60	14	159	2.18
Pensions-tested	65	5	63	0.20
Pensions-tested	Men: 62 Women: 57	4	1	0.12
Means-tested	Men: 60 Women: 55	6	3	0.02
Means-tested	Men: 60 Women: 55	13	32	0.19
Universal	60	12	200	0.56
Pensions-tested	70	12	47	0.32
Universal	65	34	110	6.49

(Table continues next page)

TABLE G.1 Old-Age Social Pensions around the World *(Continued)*

Country/economy/territory	Region	Year	Name of scheme	Location
New Zealand	OECD	2010	Superannuation	National
Nigeria	SSA	2013	Ekiti State Social Security Scheme	Regional/Rural
Nigeria (2)	SSA	2012	Osun Elderly Persons Scheme	Regional/Rural
Norway	OECD	2011	Grunnpensjon (Basic Pension)	National
Panama	LAC	2011	100 a los 70	National
Papua New Guinea	EAP	2009	Old-Age and Disabled Pension Scheme (New Ireland Province)	Regional/Rural
Paraguay	LAC	2014	Pensión Alimentaria para las Personas Adultas Mayores	National
Peru	LAC	2014	Pension 65	National
Philippines	EAP	2013–14	Social Pension	National
Portugal	OECD	2012	Pensao Social de Velhice (Old-Age Social Pension)	National
Samoa	EAP	2010–14	Senior Citizens Benefit	National
Seychelles	SSA	2006–12	Old-age pension (social security fund)	National
Slovenia	ECA	2010	State Pension	National
South Africa	SSA	2011–13	Older Persons Grant	National
Spain	OECD	2011–13	Pension no Contributiva de Jubilacion (Noncontributory Pension for Retirement)	National
St. Vincent and the Grenadines	LAC	2009–12	Elderly Assistance Benefit	National
Suriname	LAC	2012	Algemene Oudedags Voorzieningsfonds (AOV) (State Old-Age Pension)	National
Swaziland	SSA	2009	Old-Age Grant	National
Sweden	OECD	2011	Garantipension (Guaranteed Pension)	National
Switzerland	OECD	2012	Extraordinary pension	National
Tajikistan	ECA	2011	Old-age pension	National
Thailand	EAP	2011	Old-Age Allowance	National
Timor-Leste	EAP	2011–12	Support allowance for the elderly	National
Trinidad and Tobago	LAC	2012	Senior Citizens' Pension	National
Turkey	ECA	–	Means-Tested Old-Age Pension	National
Turkmenistan	ECA	–	Social Allowance	National
Uganda	SSA	2012–13	Senior Citizens Grant (pilot in 14 districts)	Regional/Rural
Ukraine	ECA	–	Social pension and social pension supplement	National
United Kingdom	OECD	2011–13	Pension credit (guarantee credit)	National
United States	OECD	2014	Old-Age Supplementary Security Income	National
Uruguay	LAC	2013–14	Programa de Pensiones No-Contributivas	National
Uzbekistan	ECA	2012	Social pension	National
Venezuela, RB	LAC	2012–13	Gran Mision Amor Mayor	National
Vietnam	EAP	2008–11	Social assistance benefit (category 1)	National
Zambia	SSA	2009	Social Cash Transfer Programme, Katete (pilot)	Regional/Rural

Source: HelpAge International and ASPIRE.
Note: ASPIRE = Atlas of Social Protection: Indicators of Resilience and Equity. EAC = Europe and Central Asia; EAP = East Asia and Pacific; LAC = Latin America and the Caribbean; MENA = Middle East and North Africa; OECD = Organisation of Economic Cooperation and Development; SA = South Asia; SSA = Sub-Saharan Africa; – = not available.

Targeting	Age of eligibility (years)	Benefit level (% of GDP per capita)	Beneficiaries (% of population over eligible age)	Total cost (% of GDP)
Universal	65	34	97	3.87
Pensions-tested	65	23	1	0.00
Means-tested	–	45	–	0.01
Means-tested	67	12	95	4.51
Pensions-tested	70	5	32	0.17
Universal	60	7	3	0.01
Means-tested	65	27	26	0.44
Means-tested	65	8	16	0.11
Means-tested	77	5	7	0.03
Means-tested	66	15	–	–
Universal	65	19	93	0.89
Universal	63	17	116	1.52
Means-tested	68	13	5	0.10
Means-tested	60	23	100	1.15
Means-tested	65	20	2	0.12
Means-tested	67	10	77	–
Universal	60	19	154	1.61
Universal	60	8	134	0.41
Pensions-tested	65	25	41	0.52
Pensions-tested	Men: 65 Women: 60	18	–	–
Pensions-tested	Men: 65 Women: 60	12	36	–
Pensions-tested	60	4	94	0.32
Universal	60	7	149	2.20
Means-tested	65	27	68	1.41
Means-tested	65	6	–	–
Pensions-tested	Men: 62 Women: 57	7	–	–
Not defined	65 (60 in Karamoja Region)	17	7	0.03
Means-tested	Men: 63 Women: 59	26	–	–
Means-tested	65	27	11	0.44
Means-tested	65	16	5	0.07
Means-tested	70	22	7	0.24
Pensions-tested	Men: 60 Women: 55	26	–	–
Means-tested	Men: 60 Women: 55	18	28	0.60
Pensions-tested	80	5	16	0.01
Not defined	60	10	0	–

TABLE G.2 Old-Age Social Pensions Captured in ASPIRE Household Surveys

Country	Year	Region	Program name
Bangladesh	2010	SA	Old-Age Allowance (MOSW)
Belize	2009	LAC	Noncontributory pension for women (SSB)
Brazil	2012	LAC	Beneficio de Prestacao Continuada (BPC)
Bulgaria	2007	ECA	Social pension
Cabo Verde	2007	SSA	Minimum social pension
Chile	2013	LAC	Pensión Básica Solidaria (PBS) de vejez
Colombia	2012	LAC	Programa de adultos mayores
Costa Rica	2012	LAC	Pensiones del Régimen no Contributivo
Guatemala	2011	LAC	Programa Adulto Mayor
Honduras	2011	LAC	Bono por tercera edad
Lithuania	2008	ECA	Social pension for persons after retirement age
Mauritius	2012	SSA	Old-age pension (Basic Retirement Pension)
Mexico	2012	LAC	Programa 70 y mas
Namibia	2009	SSA	State old-age pension
Nepal	2010	SA	Social pension
Panama	2012	LAC	100 a los 70
Paraguay	2011	LAC	Adulto Mayor
Poland	2012	ECA	Social pension
Romania	2012	ECA	Social assistance pension
Rwanda	2010	SSA	Old-age grant
Slovak Republic	2009	ECA	Other old-age repeated monetary allowances and benefits
South Africa	2010	SSA	Old-age pension
Sri Lanka	2012	SA	Elderly payment
Swaziland	2009	SSA	Pension
Tajikistan	2011	ECA	Social pension
Thailand	2013	EAP	Social pension for the elderly and disable
Timor-Leste	2011	EAP	Elderly pensions
Turkey	2012	ECA	Old-age benefits paid by Turkish Pension Fund to those individuals who are older than 65 years of age (Yasli)

Source: ASPIRE household surveys.
Note: ASPIRE = Atlas of Social Protection: Indicators of Resilience and Equity.
EAP = East Asia and Pacific; ECA = Europe and Central Asia; LAC = Latin America and the Caribbean; SA = South Asia; SSA = Sub-Saharan Africa.

APPENDIX H

Basic Characteristics of Countries Included in the Book

TABLE H.1 Basic Characteristics of Countries Included in the Book

Country/ economy/ territory	Code	Region	Income classification	GNI per capita, PPP	GDP per capita, PPP	Total population (million)
Afghanistan	AFG	SA	LIC	1,900	1,877	34.7
Albania	ALB	ECA	UMIC	11,929	11,880	2.9
Algeria	DZA	MENA	UMIC	15,075	14,720	40.6
Angola	AGO	SSA	LMIC	6,499	6,220	28.8
Argentina	ARG	LAC	UMIC	19,934	19,480	43.8
Armenia	ARM	ECA	LMIC	8,818	9,000	2.9
Azerbaijan	AZE	ECA	UMIC	17,253	16,130	9.8
Bangladesh	BGD	SA	LMIC	3,581	3,790	163.0
Belarus	BLR	ECA	UMIC	18,060	17,210	9.5
Belize	BLZ	LAC	UMIC	8,448	8,000	0.4
Benin	BEN	SSA	LIC	2,168	2,170	10.9
Bhutan	BTN	SA	LMIC	8,744	8,070	0.8
Bolivia	BOL	LAC	LMIC	7,236	7,090	10.9
Bosnia and Herzegovina	BIH	ECA	UMIC	12,075	12,140	3.5
Botswana	BWA	SSA	UMIC	16,735	16,380	2.3
Brazil	BRA	LAC	UMIC	15,128	14,810	207.7
Bulgaria	BGR	ECA	UMIC	19,199	19,020	7.1
Burkina Faso	BFA	SSA	LIC	1,720	1,680	18.6
Burundi	BDI	SSA	LIC	778	770	10.5
Cabo Verde	CPV	SSA	LMIC	6,553	6,220	0.5
Cambodia	KHM	EAP	LMIC	3,735	3,510	15.8
Cameroon	CMR	SSA	LMIC	3,286	3,250	23.4
Central African Republic	CAF	SSA	LIC	699	700	4.6
Chad	TCD	SSA	LIC	1,991	1,950	14.5
Chile	CHL	LAC	HIC	23,960	23,270	17.9
China	CHN	EAP	UMIC	15,535	15,500	1378.7
Colombia	COL	LAC	UMIC	14,158	13,910	48.7
Comoros	COM	SSA	LIC	1,522	1,520	0.8
Congo, Dem. Rep.	ZAR	SSA	LIC	801	730	78.7
Congo, Rep.	COG	SSA	LMIC	5,719	5,380	5.1

(Table continues next page)

TABLE H.1 Basic Characteristics of Countries Included in the Book (Continued)

Country/economy/territory	Code	Region	Income classification	GNI per capita, PPP	GDP per capita, PPP	Total population (million)
Costa Rica	CRI	LAC	UMIC	16,614	15,750	4.9
Croatia	HRV	ECA	UMIC	23,596	22,880	4.2
Czech Republic	CZE	ECA	HIC	34,711	32,710	10.6
Côte d'Ivoire	CIV	SSA	LMIC	3,720	3,610	23.7
Djibouti	DJI	MENA	LMIC	3,342	2,200	0.9
Dominica	DMA	LAC	UMIC	10,975	10,610	0.1
Dominican Republic	DOM	LAC	UMIC	15,209	14,480	10.6
Ecuador	ECU	LAC	UMIC	11,286	11,070	16.4
Egypt, Arab Rep.	EGY	MENA	LMIC	11,132	11,110	95.7
El Salvador	SLV	LAC	LMIC	8,619	8,220	6.3
Estonia	EST	ECA	HIC	29,365	28,920	1.3
Ethiopia	ETH	SSA	LIC	1,735	1,730	102.4
Fiji	FJI	EAP	UMIC	9,561	9,140	0.9
Gabon	GAB	SSA	UMIC	18,108	16,720	2.0
Gambia, The	GMB	SSA	LIC	1,689	1,640	2.0
Georgia	GEO	ECA	LMIC	9,997	9,450	3.7
Ghana	GHA	SSA	LMIC	4,294	4,150	28.2
Grenada	GRD	LAC	UMIC	13,928	13,440	0.1
Guatemala	GTM	LAC	LMIC	7,947	7,750	16.6
Guinea	GIN	SSA	LIC	1,311	1,200	12.4
Guinea-Bissau	GNB	SSA	LIC	1,582	1,580	1.8
Guyana	GUY	LAC	UMIC	7,819	7,860	0.8
Haiti	HTI	LAC	LIC	1,784	1,790	10.8
Honduras	HND	LAC	LMIC	4,738	4,410	9.1
Hungary	HUN	ECA	HIC	26,681	25,640	9.8
India	IND	SA	LMIC	6,572	6,490	1324.2
Indonesia	IDN	EAP	LMIC	11,612	11,220	261.1
Iran, Islamic Rep.	IRN	MENA	UMIC	17,046	17,370	80.3
Iraq	IRQ	MENA	UMIC	17,353	17,240	37.2
Jamaica	JAM	LAC	UMIC	8,835	8,500	2.9
Jordan	JOR	MENA	LMIC	9,050	8,980	9.5
Kazakhstan	KAZ	ECA	UMIC	25,264	22,910	17.8
Kenya	KEN	SSA	LMIC	3,156	3,130	48.5
Kiribati	KIR	EAP	LMIC	2,047	3,240	0.1
Kosovo	KSV	ECA	LMIC	10,066	10,200	1.8
Kuwait	KWT	MENA	HIC	73,817	83,420	4.1
Kyrgyz Republic	KGZ	ECA	LMIC	3,551	3,410	6.1
Lao PDR	LAO	EAP	LMIC	6,186	5,920	6.8
Latvia	LVA	ECA	HIC	26,031	26,090	2.0
Lebanon	LBN	MENA	UMIC	13,996	13,860	6.0
Lesotho	LSO	SSA	LMIC	3,029	3,390	2.2
Liberia	LBR	SSA	LIC	813	700	4.6
Lithuania	LTU	ECA	HIC	29,966	28,840	2.9

(Table continues next page)

TABLE H.1 Basic Characteristics of Countries Included in the Book *(Continued)*

Country/ economy/ territory	Code	Region	Income classification	GNI per capita, PPP	GDP per capita, PPP	Total population (million)
Macedonia, FYR	MKD	ECA	UMIC	15,121	14,480	2.1
Madagascar	MDG	SSA	LIC	1,506	1,440	24.9
Malawi	MWI	SSA	LIC	1,169	1,140	18.1
Malaysia	MYS	EAP	UMIC	27,681	26,900	31.2
Maldives	MDV	SA	UMIC	13,199	11,970	0.4
Mali	MLI	SSA	LIC	2,117	2,040	18.0
Marshall Islands	MHL	EAP	UMIC	4,072	5,280	0.1
Mauritania	MRT	SSA	LMIC	3,854	3,760	4.3
Mauritius	MUS	SSA	UMIC	21,088	20,980	1.3
Mexico	MEX	LAC	UMIC	17,862	17,740	127.5
Moldova	MDA	ECA	LMIC	5,334	5,670	3.6
Mongolia	MNG	EAP	LMIC	12,220	11,290	3.0
Montenegro	MNE	ECA	UMIC	16,854	17,090	0.6
Morocco	MAR	MENA	LMIC	7,838	7,700	35.3
Mozambique	MOZ	SSA	LIC	1,217	1,190	28.8
Myanmar	MMR	EAP	LMIC	5,773	5,070	52.9
Namibia	NAM	SSA	UMIC	10,585	10,550	2.5
Nepal	NPL	SA	LIC	2,468	2,520	29.0
Nicaragua	NIC	LAC	LMIC	5,541	5,390	6.1
Niger	NER	SSA	LIC	978	970	20.7
Nigeria	NGA	SSA	LMIC	5,867	5,740	186.0
Pakistan	PAK	SA	LMIC	5,249	5,580	193.2
Panama	PAN	LAC	UMIC	23,015	20,990	4.0
Papua New Guinea	PNG	EAP	LMIC	2,761	2,700	8.1
Paraguay	PRY	LAC	UMIC	9,577	9,060	6.7
Peru	PER	LAC	UMIC	13,022	12,480	31.8
Philippines	PHL	EAP	LMIC	7,806	9,400	103.3
Poland	POL	ECA	HIC	27,811	26,770	37.9
Qatar	QAT	MENA	HIC	127,523	124,740	2.6
Romania	ROM	ECA	UMIC	23,626	22,950	19.7
Russian Federation	RUS	ECA	UMIC	23,163	22,540	144.3
Rwanda	RWA	SSA	LIC	1,913	1,870	11.9
Samoa	WSM	EAP	UMIC	6,345	6,200	0.2
Saudi Arabia	SAU	MENA	HIC	54,431	55,760	32.3
Senegal	SEN	SSA	LIC	2,568	2,480	15.4
Serbia	SRB	ECA	UMIC	14,512	13,680	7.1
Seychelles	SYC	SSA	HIC	28,391	28,390	0.1
Sierra Leone	SLE	SSA	LIC	1,473	1,320	7.4
Slovak Republic	SVK	ECA	HIC	30,632	29,910	5.4
Slovenia	SVN	ECA	HIC	32,885	32,360	2.1
Solomon Islands	SLB	EAP	LMIC	2,236	2,150	0.6
Somalia	SOM	SSA	LIC	–	–	14.3

(Table continues next page)

TABLE H.1 Basic Characteristics of Countries Included in the Book (Continued)

Country/ economy/ territory	Code	Region	Income classification	GNI per capita, PPP	GDP per capita, PPP	Total population (million)
South Africa	ZAF	SSA	UMIC	13,225	12,860	55.9
South Sudan	SSD	SSA	LIC	1,925	1,700	12.2
Sri Lanka	LKA	SA	LMIC	12,316	11,970	21.2
St. Kitts and Nevis	KNA	LAC	HIC	26,686	25,940	0.1
St. Lucia	LCA	LAC	UMIC	11,546	11,370	0.2
St. Vincent and the Grenadines	VCT	LAC	UMIC	11,606	11,530	0.1
Sudan	SDN	SSA	LMIC	4,730	4,290	39.6
Suriname	SUR	LAC	UMIC	14,146	13,720	0.6
Swaziland	SWZ	SSA	LMIC	8,343	7,980	1.3
Syrian Arab Republic	SYR	MENA	LMIC	–	–	18.4
São Tomé and Príncipe	STP	SSA	LMIC	3,229	3,240	0.2
Tajikistan	TJK	ECA	LMIC	2,980	3,500	8.7
Tanzania	TZA	SSA	LIC	2,787	2,740	55.6
Thailand	THA	EAP	UMIC	16,916	16,070	68.9
Timor-Leste	TMP	EAP	LMIC	2,290	4,340	1.3
Togo	TGO	SSA	LIC	1,491	1,370	7.6
Tonga	TON	EAP	UMIC	5,752	5,760	0.1
Trinidad and Tobago	TTO	LAC	HIC	31,908	30,810	1.4
Tunisia	TUN	MENA	LMIC	11,599	11,150	11.4
Turkey	TUR	ECA	UMIC	24,244	23,990	79.5
Uganda	UGA	SSA	LIC	1,849	1,820	41.5
Ukraine	UKR	ECA	LMIC	8,272	8,190	45.0
Uruguay	URY	LAC	HIC	21,625	21,090	3.4
Uzbekistan	UZB	ECA	LMIC	6,514	6,640	31.8
Vanuatu	VUT	EAP	LMIC	3,081	3,050	0.3
Venezuela, RB	VEN	LAC	UMIC	18,281	17,700	31.6
Vietnam	VNM	EAP	LMIC	6,424	6,050	92.7
West Bank and Gaza	WBG	MENA	LMIC	2,943	3,290	4.6
Yemen, Rep.	YEM	MENA	LMIC	2,508	2,490	27.6
Zambia	ZMB	SSA	LMIC	3,922	3,790	16.6
Zimbabwe	ZWE	SSA	LIC	2,006	1,920	16.2

Source: World Development Indicators.
Note: The inventory includes the list of countries for which administrative and/or household data on social protection and labor programs are available and used in this book. GNI per capita, GDP per capita, and population values were collected from the World Development Indicators for 2016. For the cases in which data are not available, they are replaced by the most recent available data. Specifically, Djibouti 2015; Iran, Islamic Rep. 2015; Kuwait 2015; Papua New Guinea 2014; South Sudan 2015; Timor-Leste 2015; and Venezuela, RB 2013 are used to replace the missing GNI per capita cells. Djibouti 2005; Iran, Islamic Rep. 2014; Kuwait 2015; Myanmar 2015; Papua New Guinea 2014; Qatar 2015; South Sudan 2015; Timor-Leste 2015; Vanuatu 2014; and Venezuela, RB 2013 are used to replace missing GDP per capita cells. Blank cells (for example, Syria) mean no information is available. GDP per capita is in current international dollars. ASPIRE = Atlas of Social Protection: Indicators of Resilience and Equity; ECA = Europe and Central Asia; EAP = East Asia and Pacific; GNI = gross national income; HIC = high-income country; LAC = Latin America and the Caribbean; LIC = low-income country; LMIC = lower-middle-income country; MENA = Middle East and North Africa; OECD = Organisation of Economic Co-operation and Development; PPP = purchasing power parity; SSA = Sub-Saharan Africa; UMIC = upper-middle-income country; – = not available.

Glossary

Term	Definition
Adequacy of benefits	The total transfer amount received by all beneficiaries in a quintile as a share of the total welfare of beneficiaries in that quintile. Specifically, adequacy of benefits is the amount of transfers received by a quintile divided by the total income or consumption of beneficiaries in that quintile.
Average per capita transfer	For each beneficiary household, the per capita average transfer is estimated as the total amount of transfers received divided by the household size.
Beneficiary incidence	Percentage of program beneficiaries in a quintile relative to the total number of beneficiaries in the population. Specifically, the beneficiary incidence is the number of individuals in each quintile who live in a household where at least one member participates in a social protection and labor program divided by the number of individuals participating in social protection and labor programs in the population.
Benefit–cost ratio	Reduction in poverty gap obtained for each US$1 spent on social protection and labor programs. The indicator is estimated for the entire population and by program type. Specifically, the benefit–cost ratio is estimated as the poverty gap before transfer minus the poverty gap after transfer divided by the total transfer amount.
Benefit incidence	Percentage of benefits going to each group or quintile of the posttransfer (or pretransfer) welfare distribution relative to the total benefits going to the population. Specifically, benefit incidence is equal to the sum of all transfers received by all individuals in the quintile divided by the sum of all transfers received by all individuals in the population. The indicator usually includes both direct and indirect beneficiaries.
Coverage	Percentage of the population or population group participating in the social protection and labor program. Specifically, coverage of a given group or quintile is the number of benefit recipients in the group or quintile divided by the number of individuals in that quintile. The coverage includes both direct and indirect beneficiaries.
Gini inequality reduction	Simulated change (percentage) in the Gini inequality coefficient because of social protection and labor programs. Specifically, the Gini inequality reduction is computed as the inequality pretransfer minus the inequality posttransfer divided by the inequality pretransfer.
Poverty gap reduction	Simulated change (percentage) in poverty gap because of social protection and labor programs. The poverty gap index is the average percentage shortfall in the income of the poor. Specifically, the poverty gap reduction is computed as the poverty gap pretransfer minus the poverty gap posttransfer divided by the poverty gap pretransfer.
Poverty headcount reduction	Simulated change (percentage) in the poverty headcount because of social protection and labor programs. The poverty headcount ratio is the percentage of the population below the poverty line. Specifically, the poverty headcount reduction is computed as the poverty headcount pretransfer minus the poverty headcount posttransfer divided by the poverty headcount pretransfer.
Program beneficiaries, number of	Number of program beneficiaries (households or individuals) as reported in administrative data. The data indicate the original beneficiary unit (household or individual). For the household-level benefit, the data also report the respective number of individuals benefiting from the program. This information is presented in appendix C.
Program duplication and overlap	Percentage of beneficiaries who receive one or more benefits from different social protection and labor programs.
Public expenditures	Total program expenditures, including spending on benefits and administrative costs. The indicator captures both the recurrent and capital program budget and is usually based on administrative program records. Program-level expenditures are presented as a percentage of gross domestic product for the respective year, and is aggregated by harmonized social safety net program categories. Total program expenditures without health fee waivers are also presented.